URBAN DEVELOPMENT DEBATES IN THE NEW MILLENNIUM

Studies in Revisited Theories and Redefined Praxes

Volume – IV

Edited by
K.R. GUPTA

With an Introduction by
PRASENJIT MAITI

ATLANTIC®
PUBLISHERS & DISTRIBUTORS

Published by
ATLANTIC®
PUBLISHERS & DISTRIBUTORS
B-2, Vishal Enclave, Opp. Rajouri Garden,
New Delhi-110027
Phones : 25413460, 25429987, 25466842

Sales Office
7/22, Ansari Road, Darya Ganj,
New Delhi-110002
Phones : 23273880, 23275880, 23280451
Fax : 91-11-23285873
web : www.atlanticbooks.com
e-mail : info@atlanticbooks.com

ISBN 81-269-0434-8 (Vol. IV)
ISBN 81-269-0392-9 (Set)

Printed in India
at Nice Printing Press, Delhi

Preface

The multi-volume book *Urban Development Debates in the New Millennium* includes papers on urban development issues and concerns by leading academicians and practitioners from all over the world. The focus is on theories and practices for the attainment of sustainable urban development. Experiences of a large number of countries have been collected at one place and, consequently, the book covers a wide spectrum of issues relating to basic urban amenities such as water supply and sanitation services, solid waste management, sewerage and drainage, domestic electricity connections, transport and telecommunication networks, access to primary healthcare services, basic literacy resources, common property resources, law and order maintenance, markets, means of livelihood, housing facilities, gender empowerment, and street, children.

I will feel amply rewarded if these Volumes provoke fresh debates and generate new ideas about sustainable urban development with minimum social tensions.

The book would be found highly useful by town planners, municipal administrators, NGOs working in the field of urban development, and common readers interested in urban problems and policies. It will be equally valuable for policy-makers as well as students, researchers, and teachers of urban economics, urban sociology, urban geography, and public administration.

I thank all the contributors to these Volumes for their refreshingly original and insightful papers.

My sincere thanks are also due to Dr Prasenjit Maiti for helping me in editing these Volumes.

K.R. GUPTA

Contents

Urban Development Debates in the New Millennium: An Introduction

PRASENJIT MAITI
pmaiti@vsnl.com
Former Member, Resettlement Plan Implementation Working Group, Kolkata Environmental Improvement Project.

> An initial social assessment is required for every development project in order to identify the people who may be beneficially and adversely affected by the project. It should assess the stage of development of various subgroups and their needs, demands and absorptive capacity. It should also identify the institutions to be involved in the project and assess their capacities. The ISA should identify the key social dimensional aspects (such as involuntary resettlement, indigenous people, poverty reduction and women in development) that need to be addressed under the project.[1]

This collection of essays by academics and practitioners from around the world underscores issues and concerns of sustainable urban development[2] and best practices in terms of theory as well as praxes. Contributors have made an attempt to critically reconcile the hypothetical with the applied in order to arrive at innovative solutions for urban good governance in the context of steady proliferation of habitats and conurbations worldwide. Their papers more often than not transcend regional specifics to address the common agenda of urban development debates as informed by assorted modernization perspectives in the 21st century.

When this volume was planned [December 2003] in consultation with the editor/publisher it was decided that our call for papers would be flexible enough to accommodate social scientists, urban planners, development consultants, non-profit professionals as well as regulatory policymakers so that theories [old and new] and multicultural praxes might be reflected in a uniform manner in their papers based on empirical research and field-level insights. This subsequently entailed a difficult academic exercise on our part when an incipient—but problematic—rationale began to emerge from different context-bound voices and situation-specific experiences.

This was, however, anticipated because the narratives of development theory often tend to ramble along with the deterministic chaos of praxes that ordinarily precede any agenda of proposed physical work/engineering designs based on the norms of participatory development.[3] Collective choice theory plays an important role at this juncture: so does neoinstitutional theory that explores the dynamics of equations between actors [primary stakeholders/project affected persons] and their institutions.

Any agenda of urban development—whether approved or not by secondary stakeholders—is necessarily defined by the praxes of choice on the part of beneficiaries on the one hand and the regime of theoretical discourse [that is in reality an exercise in choice among options] as manoeuvred or manipulated by donor and funding agencies, NGOs, CSOs, local-level advocacy and/or activist groups and different tiers of government down to the level of the municipal administration.[4]

Such a structure of decision-making based on feedback networks decides the politics of development from above while sociability at the grass-roots—so far as the popular understanding and acceptance of the developmental philosophy and welfarist vision of urban development projects are concerned—generally emerges at a subsequent stage of the project cycle as a manufactured [following Noam Chomsky] version of consent appropriated in terms of political correctitude.

This is especially true in the developing/underdeveloped South where postcolonial LDCs are often inconvenienced by inadequate levels of regime-building and depleted stocks of social capital.[5] Major urban development projects in such a context may run the risk of disjointed planning and uneven implementation due to lack of updated theoretical knowledge, imperfect participatory monitoring and evaluation of the progress of physical work [on the part of primary as well as secondary stakeholders] and incorrect collective choice exercises that do not serve utilitarian purposes. Innovative institutional mechanisms may be designed to resolve such problems: water user groups, public-private participation, core committees/representative groups and grievance redress cells at the community-level are examples of mechanisms widely utilized by practitioners in order to tackle angularities that arise from a hiatus between theory and praxes.[6]

LDCs may be typecast by political systems where logic and rhetoric are yet to reconcile skewed issues of human development because the level playing field required for such diverse exercises [plus their implications] is not readily available. The stakeholder *versus* beneficiary debate assumes new meanings so far as the objectives of urban development debates are concerned. One such priority area of most urban good governance/best practices programmes is to downsize superfluous bureaucracy so that non-merit expenditures ["free rider costs"] are reduced and service delivery mechanisms made efficacious. Compulsions of the politics of everyday life, however, may inform radically different public policy choices. (*See* Table 1)

TABLE 1: Social Impact Assessment Variables[7]

PROJECT/POLICY STAGE				
Project/Policy Setting	Planning/Policy Development	Construction/ Implementation	Operation & Maintenance	Equity of minority groups
Project affected persons	Perceptions of risk, health and safety	Influx of temporary workers	Trust in political and social institutions	Alteration in size of local government
Distribution of power/ authority	Formation of attitudes towards the project	Change in community infrastructure	Change in income characteristics	Change in employment

This entails that human entitlements with regard to basic urban amenities such as water supply and sanitation services, solid waste management, sewerage and drainage, domestic electricity connections, transport and telecommunication networks, access to primary healthcare and basic literacy resources, common property resources, law and order maintenance, markets, sources of livelihood, housing facilities and conservation of nature—as informed by the exercise of choice—should be facilitated by urban development policies so that capacities of primary stakeholders are built in the process.[8]

Urban development strategies more often than not emerge from conflict resolution and collective choice dynamics *i.e.*, there is generally a method that underpins dislocations and conflicts that attend the inception phases of developmental projects in metropolitan cities. This is to be ordinarily expected, however, as cities generally share complex histories, cultural baggages and collective memories that are multiple and not always amenable to unilinear project interventions. Development is not extrinsic like politics imposed from the above to impact on end-users of limited resources. Actors who will interface with their own ground-level institutional arrangements/mechanisms during the project cycle/interventions should be catalyzed to facilitate social capital that coheres organic ethos of community existence.

Deriving lessons from project interventions is imperative. Urban development is often made complicated by political overtones and culture root paradigms that may not work in tandem with the project's rationale and objectives/outputs. This necessitates reassessing community-level needs and perceptions in order to minimize dislocations with regard to implementation of physical work, poverty alleviation programmes and awareness-generation activities.

It necessarily follows, therefore, that Stakeholders Consultation Process has steadily emerged as the mantra of the new millennium so far as urban development strategies are concerned. SCP is development of the community, for the community and [if practicable] by the community that involves primary stakeholders in [1] needs assessment exercises, [2] resource and benefit mapping, [3] planning for community-level needs and [4] participatory monitoring and evaluation of progress of physical work to expand networks of social capital at the community-level.[9]

SCP relates to crisis management [tactical] and sustainable development [strategic] approaches utilizing different time-frames and priorities for the purpose of resource and benefit mapping underpinned by "an authoritative allocation of values" *i.e.* who gets what, when, how, where and why.

Participation is an interactive process whereby primary stakeholders take part in the decision-making process either in a direct manner or via CBOs/NGOs. Community development events and awareness-generation campaigns are generally strategized to streamline project-related interventions and facilitate dialogues between primary and secondary stakeholders. Such programmes serve to build empathy at the community-level and facilitate dialogic rather than pedagogic terms of discourse at the project implementation, monitoring and evaluation levels. Community mobilization and participation activities are not an end but a means to secure rapport-building that may ensure acceptance of development interventions on the part of project affected persons.

Primary stakeholders may be suitably empowered to sustain developmental impacts of the project *i.e.* their entitlements should be converted into capacities [following Amartya Sen]. This will ensure that project interventions and their benefits sustain over a considerable period of time and motivate future development and further popular initiatives at the grass-roots level where communities have been made capable to make critical decisions affecting the quality of their everyday life. Axes of civic participation and/or preparedness should be identified in order to plan NGO/CBO/CSO interventions in consultation with local-level resource persons and/or key informants. Interventions should be scientifically implemented and underpinned by a definitive plan of action. This is despite the fact that development generally emerges out of flux and can seldom be planned in a rigid manner. Field-level lessons [and insights], therefore, should be utilized to coordinate between theory and praxes.

NOTES

1. "The ISA should be undertaken as early as possible in the project cycle and preferably by the time of fact-finding for a project preparation

technical assistance." <http://www.adb.org/Documents/Policies/Involuntary_Resettlement/reset400.asp>

2. "Sustainable development is defined as a pattern of social and structured economic transformations [*i.e.* development], which optimizes the economic and societal benefits available in the present, without jeopardizing the likely potential for similar benefits in the future. A primary goal of sustainable development is to achieve a reasonable and equitably distributed level of economic well-being that can be perpetuated continually for many human generations." <http://sdnp.delhi.nic.in/>
3. "Participation of the stakeholders create conditions for consensus and potential conflict resolution; people's participation not only make programmes and policies more acceptable, they make them cost-effective and enhance ownership; and the stakeholders, once brought into a participatory mode, undertake significant follow-up activities on their own accord and enhance social mobilization. These are key contributions to sustainable development." <http://www.ecouncil.ac.cr/rio/national/reports/asia/bangladesh/ban4.htm>
4. No development project can result in complete alienation of the rights, customary and legal, of people through payment of a one-time compensation or facilitated relocation. On the contrary, the process must result in the creation of new rights that will render people direct beneficiaries of the development project. <http://www.eldis.org/static/DOC7649.htm>
5. "Social capital refers to the institutions, relationships, and norms that shape the quality and quantity of a society's social interactions. Increasing evidence shows that social cohesion is critical for societies to prosper economically and for development to be sustainable. Social capital is not just the sum of the institutions, which underpin a society—it is the glue that holds them together." <http://www.worldbank.org/poverty/scapital/whatsc.htm>
6. Development tends to pose an occasional problem for LDCs—state nations that are yet to cohere [in most cases] stable political systems underpinned by norms of good governance, transparency and public accountability.
7. See Guidelines and Principles for Social Impact Assessment prepared by the Interorganizational Committee [United States Department of Commerce, National Oceanic and Atmospheric Administration & National Marine Fisheries Service] May 1994 in this regard. <http://www.nmfs.noaa.gov/sfa/social_impact_guide.htm>
8. "The contemporary view of capacity-building goes beyond the conventional perception of training. The central concerns of environmental management—to manage change, to resolve conflict, to manage institutional pluralism, to enhance coordination, to foster communication, and to ensure that data and information are shared—require a broad and holistic view of capacity development. This definition

covers both institutional and community-based capacity-building." <http://nrm.massey.ac.nz/changelinks/capacity. html>

9. See Prasenjit Maiti, "Silenced Rivers", in this connection. Trust indicates a system of values; a system of values implies social mores; and social mores are themselves an important institution. So trust can, and often does, lead to the sustenance of institutions. [This article was written in *Seminar* (2001) on the landmark grass-roots resistance movement of indigenous peoples—*Narmada Bachao Andolan* (Save the River Narmada Movement)—in Western India.] <http://www.india-seminar.com/2001/498/498%20comment.htm>

1

Urban Development in Nepal: Reality and Paradoxes (A Case Study of Lalitpur Sub-Metropolitan City)

RAGHU BIR BISTA
rbbista@wlink.com.np
Assistant Lecturer at the Department of Economics in the Patan Multiple Campus, Nepal.

ABSTRACT

Urban development in Nepal has got specifically serious attention and priority in the plan development in the recent years because of high internal and external migration towards in the cities led structural problems and its by-product environmental and social issues. The growth of cities with the growth of population, migration, basic infrastructure access and structural transformation is continuous within the certain minimum conditions and frame for cities. This trend in urbanization has raised serious debatable issue: "Is it positive or not and is it good or bad" in the mass of academician and planner after experience and observation to the cities in comparison with cities of Hongkong, Singapore, USA, India etc.

This paper covers urban development in Nepal in process, situation, and outcome on the basis of experience, observation, interview and case study methods for primary data collection and article, plan, research and discussion based secondary data. So the reality and paradoxes will be identified for good urban development in Nepal.

1. Context

Nepalese plan development over 45 years long is rural focused for rural development. It may be surprise to us. The emphasis on rural areas in resource allocation and development has raised a question, "why did Nepalese plan development imply 'big push development approach' only develop in rural areas" for 45 years.

In depth study, Nepal has basic structural reality such as:

- ❑ Demographically, 80 per cent living in rural areas
- ❑ Existence of 85 per cent land in rural areas
- ❑ Distribution of Administrative Village Development Units of 3915
- ❑ Distribution of huge natural resources

Secondly, development challenges lie rural areas. They are:

- ❑ more than 50 per cent absolute poverty and existence of vicious cycle of poverty
- ❑ mass level of unemployment in terms of seasonal unemployment and unemployment
- ❑ 76 per cent population's energy/life depending on cheap fuel wood existed as cause of high rate of deforestation
- ❑ not access to basic facilities and low living standard and low welfare
- ❑ high level of illiteracy and high level of food insecurity leading malnutrition
- ❑ no utilization of natural resources and no linkage with rural areas

Nepalese planner and academician and the politician were convinced with this reality. They believe that without rural development and poverty reduction, real development will not be accessible. Therefore, Nepalese plan development has been giving first priority on rural development until the Seventh five-year plan.

Seventh Plan (1985-1990) first time took plan development initiative in urban development introducing separate policy document of human settlements as urbanization and habitation policy.

The post plan of the *Seventh Plan* including *Eight Plan (1992-97)*, *Ninth Plan (1997-2002)* and *Tenth Plan (2002-07)* have followed the *Seventh Plan* with broad perspective in the context of unnatural and natural or plan and unplanned urban development in the main cities like *Lalitpur, Biratnagar, Bhaktapur* etc.

2. Case of Lalitpur Sub-Metropolitan City

Lalitpur Sub-Metropolitan City is one of major three cities in Kathmandu, the capital of Nepal. According to Insight Nepal (1982), the city of Patan is located on a high plateau above the course of the Bagmati River, just south of Kathmandu. Sometimes called "the town with a thousand golden roofs" or "the city of fine arts", most local people know it as Lalitpur: Lalit Patan, "the beautiful city". An essentially Buddhist City, Patan was built in concentric circles around its royal palace. Four main roads radiate from the palace to four directional stupas, earth and brick mounds said to have been erected by Emperor Ashoka himself. If true, this would make Patan the oldest Buddhist City in the world.

Whether or not this is so, Patan has been an important town since very early times. Inscriptions from the 5th Century refer to King Manadeva's palace, the Managriha or "House of Mana", which might have been located in the area now called Mangal Bazaar, adjouning Patan Durbar Square. The city's great building period took place under the Mallas, particularly from the 16th to 18th centuries. Most of today's leading monuments were built or rebuilt at that time.

With no fewer than 136 classified bahals and 55 major multi-roofed temples, Patan is really the cradle of arts and architecture of the Valley, a great centre both of the Newari Buddhist religion and of traditional arts and crafts.

The town has only recently developed beyond the limits marked by the stupas. It is at once more rural and more industrialized than Kathmandu. More than a third of its 100000 inhabitants are farmers and a substantial proportion of its population engages in small-scale home industries. The Patan Industrial Centre has attracted some of the qualified manpower, contributing to the expansion of local craftsmanship. The town also acts as a reservoir of labour, especially in the public and commercial sectors, for the ever-growing capital to the north.

Population Census (2001) of Central Bureau of Statistics shows demographic situation. (*See* Table 1)

TABLE 1

HH	Total population	Male	Female	Density population
34996	0.16 million	0.08 million	0.078 million	10758.48

SOURCE: *Population Census, 2001.*

3. Structural and Functional Analysis and Features

Structural and functional analysis on Lalitpur Sub-Metropolitan City shows that development of Lalitpur Sub-Metropolitan City is dual characters. One is cultural, historical and traditional format and value based development of city and other is established administrative centre based new development of city integrated with partial industrial pocket areas and also academic career centre.

Old Settlement

Lalitpur Sub-Metropolitan City is Old City established as Malla Kingdom in Malla Period (Medieval Period). According to Insight Nepal (1982), to protect themselves from invaders and bandits, and to preserve the limited arable land, villagers clustered together in compact settlements on upland terraces and along the man trade routes. Houses were built of brick and tile and streets were paved with bricks. In some cases, protective walls were erected around villages. The caste system ensured a tightly knit social fabric and easy domination by the rulers. Population was only Newar in Malla Kingdom, according to the present caste system. King Jaysthiti Malla introduced caste system in Newar on the basis of work for more efficiency and specialization.

After the unification of Lalitpur, population began to migrate in Lalitpur from different parts of Country because of administrative and strategic importance. Urban development process of Lalitpur Sub-Metropolitan City is continuous in terms of physical infrastructure extension and development, settlement development and migration.

Cultural, historical and traditional format and value based development of city.

Its features are:

Features of old city

- ❑ narrow road
- ❑ traditional, historical and cultural architecture in old houses
- ❑ temples, garden, drinking water tap and spaces

Modern means

- ❑ clean drinking water and sanitation
- ❑ telephone
- ❑ electricity

Change

- ❑ commercialization
- ❑ modernization

New Settlement

Established administrative centre based new development of city integrated with partial industrial pocket areas and also academic career centre. Its features are:

Features of new city

- ❑ new buildings having new western architecture
- ❑ provision to leave land for road only (but not in reality)
- ❑ no plan for land, housing, and basic infrastructure
- ❑ no so wide and black toppled road
- ❑ no plan for playing ground, entertainment, market, hospital, transport etc.

4. Indicator Analysis and Interpretation

Road Infrastructure

Clean, wide and black toppled road with street light and traffic light is a basic foundation of urban development, accelerating urbanization process. Lalitpur Sub-Metropolitan City as one of Kingdom City needs it. Its reality is very hard to be believable.

New settlement in the City has increased the length of road.

In the discussion with different categorical people (25 people) of the City (2004), almost respondents have shown not satisfaction on the current road condition and no information about new road construction. In case of maintenance and management, they thought poor performance of Lalitpur Sub-Metropolitan City. In case of traffic light and street light, they have said Lalitpur Sub-Metropolitan City should improve.

In observation, road situation is found better in the old settlement than in the new settlement in terms of black toppled and clean. Mangala Bazaar and Durbar Square is evidence. New Settlement—the outside Ring Road including Arniko side and Kusanti side has gravelled road only.

In the comparative study of outcome from discussion, interview and observation with the Base Line Survey of Lalitpur Sub-Metropolitan City, road condition is significantly bad, according to 86 percent of the Lalitpur Sub-Metropolitan City population. (*See* Table 2)

TABLE 2: Road Condition

Condition	Good (%)	Other (%)
Current road condition	14.3	85.7
Current track condition	12.7	87.3

SOURCE: *Data based on A Base Line Survey of Lalitpur. Sub-Metropolitan City with special emphasis to poverty situation, 2000.*

This is a big constraint in the course of urbanization process. In road infrastructure, Lalitpur Sub-Metropolitan City has legal confusion with Road and Transport Department, although the Lalitpur Sub-Metropolitan City is legally authorized agency, according to Local Governance Act 1992. Concerning politicians, they have not vision and programme integrating with National Plan. Besides it, the planning department of Lalitpur Sub-Metropolitan City is very weak due to a lack of specialization and also corruption. So, there is not effective plan for urbanization. So, road infrastructure is not good in Lalitpur Sub-Metropolitan City as required for maintaining Sub Metropolitan Standard facility.

Its effects are found as follows:

- ❑ Urbanization gives more choice to the people in transport. Poor road is contradiction with urbanization in the Lalitpur Sub-Metropolitan City. This reality limits to the choice option to the people. They have not decision power to improve living standard.

- It has made narrow down the potential economic activities in the Lalitpur Sub-Metropolitan City.
- It has increased cost of travel and pollution.
- Everywhere high traffic in the road, although the number of vehicle is not more. Parking system is very worse in terms of scattered and not organized, although Lalitpur Sub-Metropolitan City has charged parking.

Water Supply

Clean drinking water as a basic social infrastructure to maintain good health and clean environment of human life improves living standard of the urban people. This is also an indicator of Human development and also urban development. Economic Survey (2003) shows 65 per cent of urban people access clean drinking water. Lalitpur Sub-Metropolitan City has followed such national status.

Discussion with the urban people indicates not good water supply in almost part of Lalitpur Sub-Metropolitan City. It has irregular time, limited water supply, and polluted water in raining season. Besides it, in observation, urban people use pump set for pulling water from the main water distribution line. It has shown that urban people have to pay additional cost in purchasing pump set, its maintenance and its electricity energy as well as health problems of polluted water.

A Base Line Survey of Lalitpur Sub-Metropolitian City with special emphasis to poverty situation (2000) shows less water supply is first problem, which is followed by lack of water and dirty/polluted water. (*See* Table 3)

TABLE 3: Water Supply

Situation	Respondents	Rank
Less water supply	1131	1
Lack of water	573	2
Dirty/polluted water	395	3
Total	2099	

SOURCE: *Data based on A Base Line Survey of Lalitpur. Sub-Metropolitian City with special emphasis to poverty situation, 2000.*

This encounters to the urbanization of Lalitpur Sub-Metropolitan City. It gives a space for a question, "is it imaginable without clean drinking water for human settlement" and "what's urbanization process in Lalitpur Sub-Metropolitan City" without clean drinking water, although Lalitpur Sub-Metropolitan City has good water resource potential. In reality, I cannot. Behind it, there are issues: lack of planning and vision, no realization of responsibility and accountability, and lack of coordination and planning between the Lalitpur Sub-Metropolitan City and Clean Drinking Water Corporation. So, 30.5 per cent people have diarrhoea and other water born diseases, according to the Base Line Survey of Lalitpur Sub-Metropolitian City with Special Emphasis to Poverty Situation (2000).

It indicates "no proper planning, structural reform and legal compliance" in Lalitpur Sub-Metropolitan City. Besides it, urban development in developing countries is a big challenge of governance problem.

Drainage Facility

As well as clean drinking water, drainage is very important component of house and settlement for clean and healthy environment. It is a part of urban planning. In Lalitpur Sub-Metropolitan City, there are two kinds of drainage system. They are surface and piped drainage systems.

Surface drainage is constructed sides of the road for channeling raining water and other kitchen water. When I observed in Langenkhel, Satodobato and other places, I found that surface drainage was used not only for raining water but also toilet. Almost surface drainage system was in open and bad smelling in which the people cannot walk easily in the day of the summer. Besides it, in raining, drainage was overflowing in raining because of waste jam.

Piped line drainage system is connected almost part of the city for toilet connection. When I observed, I found that drainage system was not connected only with toilet and also other waste. In raining, it was big problem in the city.

The Lalitpur Sub-Metropolitan Corporation has directly charged drainage in the Bagmati River without filtration and purification. So, Bagmati River, a holy river has lost its natural feature has become black, dirty, bad smelling river. In the daytime of the summer, Bagmati River has polluted the city with bad smelling.

A Base Line Survey of Lalitpur Sub-Metropolitan City with special emphasis to poverty situation (2000) reflects the poor condition of drainage. (*See* Table 4)

TABLE 4: Drainage Facility

Situation	Good (%)	Other (%)
Current drainage condition	10.5	89.5
Current surface drainage	8.7	91.3

SOURCE: *Data based on A Base Line Survey of Lalitpur. Sub-Metropolitian City with special emphasis to poverty situation, 2000.*

Drainage infrastructure is also in undeveloped condition. Existed drainage system has maintained clean and healthy environment in one place of the city by destroying another part's clean and healthy environment, although the Lalitpur Sub-Metropolitan Corporation has charged money to the urban people. It is directly cleaning but indirectly polluting to the city. This unreasonable and unsustainable measure of drainage will bring new problem with new cost to the urban people and tourism industry.

Types and Connection of Toilet

Toilet is a basic physical component in the house and apartment in the civilized society for clean and healthy life. In discussion, 100 per cent (25 people) have toilet in house. According to them, modern house has flush system and old has simple toilet. In old settlement, there is public connection of toilet but in new settlement, almost have safety tank because of no public connection system.

A Base Line Survey of Lalitpur Sub-Metropolitan City with special emphasis to poverty situation (2000) shows 100 per cent people have toilet facility out of which 71.9 per cent toilet has public connection. (*See* Tables 5 & 6)

TABLE 5: Types of Toilet

Type of Toilet	No.	%
Simple	701	41.0
Flush	960	56.0
Common	43	2.5
Others	8	0.5
Total	1712	100

SOURCE: *Data based on A Base Line Survey of Lalitpur. Sub-Metropolitan City with special emphasis to poverty situation, 2000.*

TABLE 6: Connection of Toilet

Connection	No.	%
Public	1658	71.9
Safety tank	630	27.36
Others	15	0.65
Total	2303	100

SOURCE: *Data based on A Base Line Survey of Lalitpur. Sub-Metropolitan City with special emphasis to poverty situation, 2000.*

Lalitpur Sub-Metropolitan City has good awareness about toilet and its connection. The condition of insufficient and irregular water supply and drainage charging in the Bagmati River have encountered sustainability and cleanliness of toilet and its connection in aspect of environment.

Solid Waste Management and its Issues

Solid Waste management is being a multifaceted problem in Lalitpur Sub-Metropolitan City. The growth of population size and economic activities has contributed on widespreading issue in the City. According to the state of Environment Nepal (1998), waste generation lies between 0.25 to 0.45 kg/person/day. Three-fourth of the wastes is organic or biodegradable *(Lohani and Thanh, 1978; Thapa 1989; Khanal, 1993 and NESS, 1995).*

Collection of solid waste is a major part of management. When I observed in many important places of the Lalitpur

Sub-Metropolitan City, I found solid waste in different form—leaving solid waste in open space and important place of the city and in the container.

A Base Line Survey of Lalitpur Sub-Metropolitan City with special emphasis to poverty situation (2000) shows different collection methods but major one is open space and container but the most people prefer home collection. There is a big issue that solid waste container is not collected at time. (*See* Tables 7 and 8)

TABLE 7: Solid Waste Management in Lalitpur Sub-Metropolitan City

Disposal	Existing	%	Desired	%
Open Space	492	21.0	39	1.9
Container	742	31.6	656	32.1
Collected at home	813	34.7	1090	53.4
Burning	136	5.8	61	3.0
Composting	96	4.1	143	7.0
Other	66	2.8	54	2.6
Total	2345	100	2043	100

SOURCE: *Data based on A Base Line Survey of Lalitpur. Sub-Metropolitan City with special emphasis to poverty situation, 2000.*

TABLE 8: Issue in Waste Management

Issue	Response	Rank
Waste is not collected on time	834	1
Waste disposal site is not managed	775	2
Lack of needed containers	370	3
Expensive to manage waste	257	4
Containers are dirty	228	5
Lack of water to clean	164	6
Others	138	7

SOURCE: *Data based on A Base Line Survey of Lalitpur. Sub-Metropolitan City with special emphasis to poverty situation, 2000.*

Different studies indicate that bio-fertilizer is a good potential solution of solid waste management. In the name of solid waste management, the Lalitpur Sub-Metropolitan Corporation collects solid waste and transfer in the dumping site and dumps it, although it is potential for bio-fertilizer, it creates environment problem in the surrounding of dumping site and it is costlier affair. So, the Lalitpur Sub-Metropolitan Corporation has just transferred solid waste management issue, except its proper management.

5. Conclusion

In developing countries like Nepal, urbanization and urban development approach and its implementation are different with developed countries. Relatively, quality and standard of urbanization process and urban development are very poor and weak in Nepal, particularly in urban areas like Lalitpur Sub-Metropolitan City. If the existence situation of Lalitpur Sub-Metropolitan City cannot be reformed in different sides: institution, legal, planning and human resources, the growth of population led urbanization will be a big issue to the city. So, the government should give top priority on the urban planning and management for good urban development at policy level, institutional level, human resource level and legal aspect. Otherwise, Nepal should pay more for urban life.

REFERENCES

Central Bureau of Statistics (2001). *Population Census.* Kathmandu: CBS.

His Majesty's Government/Ministry of Population and Environment (1998). *State of the Environment Nepal.* Kathmandu/MOPE.

Anderson, John Gottberg (1982). *Insight Nepal.* Hon Kong: Apa Production.

Lalitpur Sub Metropolitican Corporation (2000). *A Base Line of Lalitpur Sub-Metropolitan City with reference to the urban poverty.* Kathmandu: LSMC.

Lohani, B.N. and N.C. Thanh (1978). *Problems and Practices of Solid Waste Management in Asia.* Bangkok: AIT.

National Planning Commission (2002). *Tenth Plan.* Kathmandu: NPC.

2

Land Administration and Agrarian Land Reform for Sustainable Urban Development and Poverty Reduction: The Bangladesh Agenda

MD. SHARIFUL ALAM CHOWDHURY
sharifurp97@yahoo.com
Research Assistant, Delta Planners and Builders Ltd. [Dhaka] and Student of Masters of Urban and Regional Planning (MURP), Department of Urban and Regional Planning, Bangladesh University of Engineering and Technology.

ABSTRACT

Generalized slogans on land administration with little operational grounding have been the bane of efforts to construct effective and meaningful agenda in this area (ALRD, 2001). One of the key insights gained over the last decade has been the realization that the absence of an up-to-date, systematic and universally accepted source of information on land resource availability and land rights lie at the root of much of the problems associated with land as well as with the inability to implement reform programmes (Kamal, 2002). Now-a-days, land reform is a well-discussed issue in Bangladesh, yet a solution to the problem has proved elusive. Over the last few hundred years the toiling masses have repeatedly tried to build movements to overthrow the landowners, which for lack of political ideology and organization have ended mostly in defeat (Taslim, 1999). The rare instances of success have led merely to a reconstitution of the rural tyranny. Compared to the land area, the population of Bangladesh is huge, and the vast majority live in poverty, super-exploited by the bourgeois class, itself under the direct control of imperialism (Abdullah, 1994). Throughout the 1970s and 80s the land reform agenda was almost completely missing from the political and academic arena. Since late 80s, however, in line with the international development agenda, new land reform initiatives began in Bangladesh (ALRD, 2001). Some NGOs in particular began to look for ways to mobilize the landless population and address the land rights related to religious and ethnic minorities that were ignored by government and public policy.

Key words: Land Reform, Land Administrative, Legal Reform.

Introduction

Bangladesh has a population of about 132 million of whom about 87% are Muslims, 12% Hindus, the rest are Buddhists, Christians and Indigenous People. The total Geographical area of Bangladesh is about 56,000 square miles (143,998 square kilometer). Out of which about 9 million hectares are cultivable land (ALRD, 2001). But every year the cropland is shrinking for human settlement. It is estimated that the growing population pressure will use up 50 per cent of the country's cultivable land by 2025 (Kamal, 2002). Urbanization, industrialization and acquisition of land by the government for different purposes have been causing negative impact on the life and conditions of the peasants as well as socio-economic scenario of the country. A studies conducted by UNDP & World Bank-WB calculated that due to fragmentation of 1.42 hectares into 10 holdings of 0.15 hectares each the effectiveness of net cropped area by about 1.5 per cent to a landowner. Moreover, per capita land that would support the basic needs of the population is fast decreasing. Every person working in the agriculture sector now owns only an average of 0.12 hectares of cropland. According to the classification of land, out of the total area, 63 per cent is being used for cultivation while 4.38 per cent for rural and urban housing and the rest includes forest and cultivable waste land. Bangladesh is one of the most densely populated countries of the world where 798 persons live in one square kilometer (ALRD, 2001).

The most desperate groups in the countryside are the landless peasants, or agri-labourers, robbed of their inheritance by the oligarchy, colonial planter and "green revolution" alike. Today there are over 600 million landless peasants in the semi-colonies (Abdullah, 1994). In Bangladesh, Pakistan and India, between a quarter and a half of the rural population are landless and in Central America over half is landless. In the past, agrarian movements were sparked by both academic and grass-roots movements, for example, peasant movements in the 1930s and 40s, and the *East Bengal State Acquisition and Tenancy Act* (EBSATA) after the partition of India. Since then, however, there has been no comprehensive revision of land laws, administration or management to benefit the landless poor in Bangladesh. The few changes that have taken place have in reality benefited only the rich, landed elite or government officials who already hold influence and power in society (Kamal, 2002). Since 1971 all the Governments of Bangladesh have introduced some sort of land reform programmes, at least on paper. But in most cases land turned over for this purpose has ended up in the hands of rich landowners, a result of corruption, unwieldy bureaucracy and the poverty of the landless. The failure of bourgeois land reform proves our prognosis that land reform cannot be carried out without nationalization of the land under the direct control of urban and agrarian workers. The eviction of the bourgeois forces from power is the necessary first step to carry out land nationalization (Taslim, 1999).

Reforming Land Administration: Priority Areas

There are three core components to the land administration process which are relevant to a reform programme:

- The physical form of the ownership record
- The institutional and physical method of record-keeping and
- The method of updating ownership information including updating the mouza maps and changes in use and plot size.

The key reform already under discussion is the proposed Certificate of Land Ownership (CLO) which should replace existing from of owner-based land record i.e. khatian. The policy options to consider here are:

Is privatization an option?

Should record-keeping be in hard copy or also be in electronic format?

Should electronic preservation of existing records be undertaken as a priority project?

As Land Reform is a very big subject it includes variety of issues which should be addressed. To addressed the other issues relevant to land reform a special commission may be formed to analyze the issues and find its proper solutions are:

Gender issue in land rights: changes in laws to empower women to inherit land.

Customary rights of indigenous people should be clearly spelt in land laws.

Rights to fisheries and waste bodies: Current system of lease to highest bidder should be discontinued and lease granted to those who depend on the 'mahals' for their livelihoods.

Involvement of NGOs and local governments in the identification of khas land for redistribution to the landless (Taslim, 1999).

Merger of land registration and land management under one ministry so that simultaneous updating of records taken place whenever a transaction is made by way of simultaneous updating of records take place whenever a transaction is made by way of sale/gift etc.

Special court to resolve land litigation quickly.

Ensure access to land related information by introducing GIS in upazila level.

Empower local government to resolve land related disputes locality (Taslim, 1999).

Landless in Bangladesh: Rural Poor

About 85% people, out of 132 million live in the rural areas of Bangladesh. Agriculture is their main occupation and means of livelihood. According to government report 57% people of Bangladesh are landless poor and they live below poverty level (ALRD, 2001). But Non-Government sources say that the number of landless people in Bangladesh are more than 68%. They live in perpetual poverty, hunger, disease and deprivation. The percentage of landless people over the last few decades are as follows:

1947 :	14.3%
1970 :	19.8%
1975 :	32.0%
1984 :	46.0%
2001 :	68.8%

10% absentee landowners own 50.6% of the total cultivable land of Bangladesh. According to Dr. Mahboob Hossain and Prof. Abdul Byes, 45% of the landless and poor marginalized peasants in the rural areas own only 5% of the total cultivable land of Bangladesh and receives 10% needed credit from institutional sources. They further said that 22% of the rich and middle farmers of rural areas of Bangladesh own 71% of the total land and receive 31% institutional credit (Kamal, 2002).

Land Crisis in Bangladesh: Urban Poor

Roughly about 15% of the people live in the urban areas of Bangladesh. According to the UNDP report 56% people in the urban areas are poor and live below poverty level. Some people contradict with the above statement and say that 40% people in the urban areas are poor and poverty stricken and they live in slums and shanties without any basic amenities of life. The monthly family income of the urban poor is about TK. 3000 ($60) and most of their income goes for paying house rent, food, medicine etc. and government does not shoulder responsibility for providing them with housing and other basic necessities (Kamal, 2002). A study conducted jointly by the Asian Development Bank-ADB and the Government of Bangladesh shows that if the present trend of urban population growth continues, by 2020 the number of people living in the urban areas would be about 60 million (ALRD, 2001).

Ownership of Land in the Dhaka Metropolis

About 15% of the land in Dhaka is owned by 2% of the upper class elite of this metropolis, 28% middle class families own 65% of the residential areas and 70% poor families own only 20% of the residential areas (Kamal, 2002). Most of the lands owned by the poor families are of poor quality in the outskirts and depressed areas. The slum dwelling people have no land on their own. They live on the mercy of the government, landlords, slum lords, musclemen, extortionist and terrorists. The monthly house rent they pay is much higher than what is paid by the tenants of the posh residential areas of Dhaka. They pay also much more higher amount for water, electricity, gas etc. than the people living in the posh residential areas. But the money given for house rent, water, gas, electricity etc. does not go to the government exchequer. It is eaten up by the thugs, goons, slum lords and middle men. The living condition of the slum dwellers are very poor. Unfortunately they are conditioned to live and work in most hazardous and insecure situation. Sewerage system is absent and hygiene conditions are extremely poor in the slums. Schools, hospitals and other basic services are absent in the slums. Dhaka is stated to be one of the crowded and polluted city of the world and the most victims of this pollutions are the slum dwelling poor, men, women and children (Abdullah, 1994).

Causes of Rural-Urban Migration

Unfortunately rural development policies and services pursued, practised and provided to the rural areas of Bangladesh over the last three decades both by the government and non-government organizations failed to a large extent to stop the rural-urban migration. Ruthless exploitation, deprivation, poverty and hunger, non-execution of land reform policy, centralized power and authority of the bureaucracy, corruption, nepotism and favouritism, misrule, mal-development, absence of rule of law, natural calamities, river erosion, absence of employment opportunities etc. forced the rural poor to migrate to the urban areas for food and shelter. Moreover, unplanned development policies, industrializations and urbanizations are also responsible for rural-urban migration. It is very unfortunate that although government spends 67% of the total government annual expenditure for the well-being of the people in and around Dhaka city, it does not help the slum dwellers for improvement of their living condition instead it widens the disparity between urban and rural people and between the urban rich and the urban poor (Kamal, 2002). The uprooted, destituted, internally displaced and poverty ridden people live in the slums are like refugees without state and status (Abdullah, 1994).

Issues and Objectives in Bangladesh

Agrarian reform has an enormous potential for reducing poverty in a country where the vast majority of the population earn their livelihoods from agriculture (Abdullah, 1994). Although land and agrarian reforms have already been underway in some neighbouring countries for the past few decades—for example we may contrast West Bengal with Bangladesh—we are just beginning to identify the means by which basic land reform can be implemented in this country. The objectives of this workshop, therefore, have been to assess the present situation, identify the problems, and to determine the obstacles to land reform, particularly within the present framework of land laws and administration (Taslim, 1999).

The land-related issues that require most urgent consideration in Bangladesh are:

Legal and administrative reforms

Minority land rights

Gender equity and land rights

Globalization of and sustainable agrarian reform

Legal and Administrative Reforms

After the abolition of the Zamindari (feudal landlord) system in 1950, EBSATA converted common public lands and certain categories of Zamindari land into 'khas' land. Subsequent land laws acknowledged the need of poor and landless farmers by guaranteeing them access to agricultural khas (unutilized government) land (Kamal, 2002). In reality, however, most khas land is illegally acquired and utilized by prosperous farmers and businessmen, corrupt government officials and other influential people. This illegal acquisition of land is promoted through the weaknesses in the legal and administrative framework. Two separate ministries (Ministry of Land and Ministry of Law) are responsible for the different functions of land administration, such as settlement, registration and record-keeping. Inefficiencies and systematic corruption result in different government departments under the separate ministries keeping contradictory records. Thus land disputes and false ownership claims are difficult to resolve.

Land Laws and Legal Reform

Existing laws are not appropriate or sufficient to answer the present needs of the landless. Contradictory land laws deny the landless and poor their land rights. The present body of land laws must be reviewed, revised and harmonised in order to assure these rights.

The Land Reform Act (1984) should be amended *vis a vis* sharecropping and leasing of land, *i.e.* security of tenure must be assured for tenant farmers.

The ceiling on landholdings should not be more than 15 acres (presently 20 acres).

Public access to common land should be protected—*e.g.* grazing rights, fuel collection, right of passage, etc. (Kamal, 2002).

Common property rights must be recognized by law as a concept for efficient and economic use of communal land.

The character of land should not be indiscriminately changed for ecological consideration. Specific law to this effect should be enacted.[1]

Land acquisition policy should be reviewed—for example, to enable quick payment of compensation, to stop unnecessary acquisition of land by government and to allow quick provision of resume.

Introduction of Land Bank should be implemented to avoid land disputes, illegal practice, etc.

Specific laws should be introduced to stop all kinds of fraud, forgery and malpractice related to land.

A nominal court fee for up to 0.5 acres should be introduced for disposal of land related civil matters.

Administrative Reform

The present land registration and recording system has to be made reliable, transparent and accountable.

A conclusive and independent survey of all khas land must be undertaken, recording the total amount and type of khas lands available throughout the country, whether it is under the government's control, etc. Khas land records are supposed to be available to the public.

Land administration and registration should be brought under the Land Ministry.

The land survey process in particular has to be transparent and participation of civil society and NGOs must be ensured.

The Land Reform Board has to be empowered for its proper dynamic operational role in agrarian reform, and restructured for democratic representation for example from civil society, independent land experts and NGOs.

The separation of judiciary and administration should ensure speedy disposal of land related suits—a separate land tribunal or land court should be established to settle land disputes.

There should be a policy of one family, one 'khatian' (land ownership record).

There should be decentralization of land administration and revenue.

The land administration and management system must be computerized.

Minority Land Rights

Minority land rights in Bangladesh fall into two main categories: the rights of the 'Adivasi,' or the indigenous (ethnic) minorities of the Chittagong Hill Tracts, and those of plain-lands both ethnic and religious minorities. One of the major land-related problems affecting plain-lands minorities arise mainly as a result of the Vested Property Act[2]; whereas those affecting the Adivasis arise from a number of interrelated issues (Abdullah, 1994). Therefore, the Adivasis' claims to communal land have been vulnerable against modern land laws. In the recent past this has resulted in the repeated violation of Adivasi land rights. Previous governments (dating from the Pakistan era)[3] have initiated state sponsored policies of non-Adivasi (Bengali) settlement on CHT forest and arable land. During the early 1960s the Kaptai Hydroelectricity Dam project flooded 40% of CHT arable land, displacing 100,000 people[4] (Kamal, 2002).

Recommendations

Constitutional rights, guaranteeing non-discrimination on ethnic or religious grounds and equal rights for all citizens, must be respected and enforced through legislation; statutory provisions must ensure land rights to ethnic and religious minorities.

International human rights conventions (*e.g.* UNHRC) and ILO Convention 169, to which Bangladesh is a signatory, must be implemented.

The Vested Property Act should be repealed.

All land-related laws applicable to CHT land as well as plain land minorities' land must be reviewed and revised according to the present interests of the Adivasi communities.

A separate land commission should be established (similar to that of the CHT) for minorities on plain land (Abdullah, 1994).

Land taken by non-Adivasi settlers must be returned. Article 97[5] of EBSATA must be fully enforced in order to hand back illegally settled CHT land to Adivasi communities.

In policy making decisions and implementation of policy there must be representation from minority groups or minority organizations.

Communal ownership of Adivasi land must be recognized by state law. Customary and prescriptive laws, traditional methods of documentation, recording and registration of land must be respected.

All forestry laws must ensure the conservation of oil/ natural resource rights.

The CHT Land Commission is to be properly implemented to give effect to land ownership by tribal people. The Hill District Council must be handed the rights to police their own land.[6]

Current projected plans to increase the production of hydroelectric power by further raising the water level of the Kaptai Dam reservoir must be cancelled, and those originally uprooted by the Kaptai dam must be resettled and compensated.

Gender Equity and Land Rights

As with minority groups, equal rights for women in the eyes of the law are guaranteed by the Bangladesh constitution (and the UNHCR), yet discriminatory practices against women relating to land rights and access to land are all too common. The inheritance laws prevalent throughout the country are particularly discriminatory (Kamal, 2002). Other traditional forms of work that women undertake on the land such as fuel collection and grazing of animals on common land is under threat with the increasing privatization of common property. Land-rights and agrarian reform have become somewhat marginalized within the women's development agenda due partly to the proliferation of micro credit programmes. And yet the issue of gender equity and women's development cannot be addressed without ensuring equal access to land and resources for women in an agrarian economy such as ours (Abdullah, 1994). Land reform should be the central concern for women's movements for the eradication of rural poverty and sustainable human development in Bangladesh.

Recommendations

Inheritance laws should be amended such that gender equity and social security can be ensured. A Universal Family Law, incorporating universal inheritance laws, should be enacted.

Women of minority groups must be ensured equal land rights through customary and prescriptive inheritance laws.

Women's agricultural labour must be fully recognized by ensuring their participation in the land and agrarian reform at all levels of the process-planning, design and implementation (Abdullah, 1994).

Conflicts over land can result in high levels of violence against women such as physical assault, rape and murder. Forced dowries, divorces and evictions can lead to destitution and marginalization. Agrarian and land reform should address the issue of violence against women in land conflicts.

Land and agrarian reform should be addressed together with the problems women face in a patriarchal society within the women's development agenda. Women's movements must strengthen ties and cooperate with land reform activists and *vice versa.*

Globalization and Sustainable Agrarian Reform

For sustainable agrarian reform in Bangladesh we must go beyond distributive land reform and address the long term causes of landlessness. Globalization of economy and both internal and external market forces mean that the pattern of land use has been changing in Bangladesh. Unsustainable large scale industries such as shrimp farming, commercial or industrial plantations and monoculture of cash crops not only cause landlessness in the short term[7] but such inappropriate land use results in large-scale environmental degradation which in turn leads to a long term future decline in agricultural land and resources for the poor (Taslim, 1999). However the main agents and institutions involved in international trade and economic policy—including multinational corporations, national industries, multilateral agencies and the government itself—are more interested in benefiting themselves through market forces than bringing about sustainable development (Kamal, 2002). In order to achieve sustainable agrarian reforms therefore a strongly democratic government is needed. In Bangladesh, however, institutionalized corruption has weakened the democratic structures of government (as well as the private sectors). Sustainable agrarian reform does not stop with access to land but must include the rights to all the security and resources that land rights and ownership provides providing social, economic and environmental reform can also be assured (Abdullah, 1994).

Recommendations

Indiscriminate and inefficient use of common land must be stopped. Private land management must also be monitored in order to avoid adverse ecological consequences.

The Forestry (Amendment Act of 2000) and (draft) social forestry rules of 2000 must be cancelled and replaced by laws and rules prepared through truly participatory and transparent process (Abdullah, 1994).

Poor farmers must be protected against adverse effects on the local market by large scale monoculture of cash crops.

Small farmers are forced to buy and sell grain in markets controlled by middlemen, multinational corporations and government.[8]

The average farm size is decreasing[9] because of environmental factors and adverse market forces, which leads to forced migration, urbanization and displacement. Agrarian reform must be based on land reform. But land reform alone cannot counter these effects. Agrarian reform must include social reforms (health and education), economic reforms (structural policies) and participation in democratic structures (Kamal, 2002).

Views About Development Efforts

Porf. Abul Barakat of Dhaka University says, "both the Government and the NGOs could not bring any significant change in the fate of the common people. About nine crore (90 million) people were deprived of sanitation facility, six crore (60 million) people had no access to primary health care services, five crore (50 million) adult were illiterate, about 2 crore (20 million) primary and secondary level students could not enrolled (ALRD, 2001). Since 1971, Government and NGOs received TK. one lakh 80 thousand crore ($ 31,088 million) as foreign aid but only TK. 40 thousand crore ($ 6,908 million) of the amount had been spent for the welfare of the poor people and the rest were drained out due to corrupt Government officials and NGO men" (Abdullah, 1994). The Human Development Index-HDI of the UNDP (2001) says that Human Poverty Index-HPI of Bangladesh remained stagnant as the country continued to lag behind even the South Asian average in terms of life expectancy, percentage of under nourished people, percentage of under-height children, infant and under five mortality rates, literacy rates and per capita GDP (Kamal, 2002).

According to World Health Organization-WHO report (2001) Bangladesh ranks 131st out of 191 member states in terms of overall health system. Health indicators paint a grim picture of the situation due to high rates of infant and child mortality, at 79.6 and 4.3 per thousand respectively which are unexpectedly high. Almost two-thirds of the birth do not receive any antenatal care (ALRD, 2001). Only six per cent of deliveries receive health care facilities and trained personnel assist only 22 per cent of the deliveries. Only 50 per cent of the children receive complete immunization. Malnutrition continues to be a severe health problem for both mother and children. There are only 18 doctors and five nurses for every 100,000 people (ALRD, 2001). Mr. Richard Daley (London), visited Bangladesh recently under Young Workers Exchange Project (UK). He says, "The wealth gap in Bangladesh is very conspicuous, one moment you might see crowd of women and children breaking bricks into aggregate by hands, whilst in another you'll see a Chauffeur driven, air conditioned Mercedes speeding past. The local poverty gap has been difficult to swallow" (Kamal, 2002).

Our Constitutional Commitment

It shall be a fundamental responsibility of the State to emancipate the toiling masses the peasants and workers—and backward sections of the people from all forms of exploitation (Abdullah, 1994). It shall be a fundamental responsibility of the State to attain, through planned economic growth, a constant increase of productive forces and a steady improvement in the material and cultural standard of living of the people, with a view to securing to its citizens:

(a) the provision of the basis necessities of life, including food, clothing, shelter, education and medical care;

(b) the right to work, that is the right to guaranteed employment at a reasonable wage having regard to the quantity and quality of work;

(c) the right to reasonable rest, recreation and leisure; and

(d) the right to social security, that is to say, to public assistance in cases of undeserved want arising from unemployment, illness or disablement, or suffered by widows or orphans or in old age, or in other such cases *(From the Constitution of the People's Republic of Bangladesh)*.

Global Commitment

"Within a decade, no man, woman or child will go to bed hungry" Dr. Henry Kissinger, World Food Conference, 1974 in Rome. After two and half decades of Kissinger's pronouncement we see that more than 800 million unfortunate men, women and children of this earth are going to bed hungry, malnourished and starving. The declaration of Kissinger's remained unfulfilled. There were no change in the reality (ALRD, 2001). Similarly at our national level the successive governments over the last 30 years, the professional bodies and the non-government organizations are collectively responsible for failing to translate the constitutional obligation into reality. As a result 69% of our people are landless, labourers, workers, slum dwellers and are forced to live in perpetual poverty, hunger, malnutrition and deprivation. We have over the past three decades, created two Bangladesh; one Bangladesh for the powerful minority and the other Bangladesh for the poor and powerless majority who owns nothing but create everything and keeps the wheel of the nation's economy moving for the consumption and comfort of the minority (Kamal, 2002).

What is to be done about it

Time has come for us to take all out initiatives to build and strengthen the organization of the poor and powerless people in the grass-roots both at different levels in the rural-urban areas with specific objectives of realizing their fundamental and basic rights including the right to have access to land. Some NGOs in the 70's and mid 80's fought for land reform along with the progressive forces of Bangladesh. Many researchers, academics, social scientists, politicians, professionals and NGO persons prefer to call Bangladesh as one of the poorest country of the world (ALRD, 2001). But in reality Bangladesh is not a resource poor country. Bangladesh is blessed with hard working adaptive, creative, innovative and resilient people. She is very rich in terms of her natural gifts of soil, product varieties, rivers, sea, forest, gas and mineral resources. A large number of hard working people of Bangladesh live and work in many of the countries in East Asia, Middle-East, Europe, North America, Australia, New Zealand and other countries. They also contribute enormously to our national exchequer. Moreover, per capita cultivable land is still higher than many of the Asian countries. But still without land and agrarian reform eradication of hunger, poverty, disparities and development of the poor in Bangladesh is not possible. According to the "Political Economy of Khas Land in Bangladesh" a book written by Prof. Dr. Abul Barakat and others, "identification and management of khas land (state owned land) and water bodies, distribution of the same to the landless and poor people, retention of such land and water bodies by the landless, and pertinent rules and practices within the prevailing social-political context of Bangladesh constitute prime issues of agrarian reform" (Abdullah, 1994). It may be mentioned here that there are about 3.3 million acres of khas land in Bangladesh. Out of this 3.3 million acres—0.8 million acres are agricultural land, 1.7 million acres are non-agricultural land and 0.8 million acres are water bodies. Moreover, there were no statistics of the ceiling (20 acres) surplus lands in Bangladesh (ALRD, 2001).

Prof. Abul Barakat and others say, "out of the total amount of identified khas land of 3.3 million acres, only a tiny portion has so far been distributed to the poor who faced multifaceted difficulties in both obtaining and retaining land. Most khas lands identified or un-identified are illegally occupied by the rich segments of the society who are integral part of the power structure". In order to crawl out of the abject poverty and to ensure socio-economic development of the majority of the landless and powerless poor in Bangladesh, land and agrarian reform both in rural and urban areas is a must. In order to realize this goal, people's ownership of and access to land and water bodies including those of the indigenous people and minority community should be broadened (Abdullah, 1994).

Collaborative Actions for People's Involvement in Struggle for Land

The Popular Coalition to Eradicate Hunger and Poverty/IFAD and the Association for Realization of Basic Needs—ARBAN—an NGO of Bangladesh from the middle of 2000 went for collaborative actions to ensure people's involvement in adopting and implementing land and agrarian reform in Bangladesh (Kamal, 2002). First, to bring back the land and agrarian reform issues in the actions agenda of the NGOs, peasant organizations, political parties and other progressive forces and second, to organize and mobilize the rural-urban poor for strengthening their organizational capability to exert pressure on the government machinery for adopting and implementing pro-poor land reform both in rural and urban areas of Bangladesh. Accordingly, four regional workshops were held and more than two hundred participants representing NGOs, professional bodies, peasants organizations, political parties and indigenous people attended these workshops. There were unanimous decisions that organizations of peasants and landless, slum dwellers, indigenous people and minorities in the rural and urban areas should be built and strengthened to adopt and execute pro-poor land and agrarian reform and tenurial security for eradicating hunger and poverty (ALRD, 2001). It was felt that land and agrarian reform was urgently needed for balanced development, increased production, effective use of land, forest, fisheries and water bodies, peace, justice, equality and communal harmony.

Conclusions

The struggle for land for livelihood and housing is a uphill struggle. Strong political commitment is a pre-condition to adopt and implement agrarian and land reform for those millions who are conditioned to live in slums, poverty, deprivation and destitutions. Lack and absence of commitment on the part of the people at the top, the politicians, the bureaucrats and the vested interest groups obstruct the adoption and implementation of land and agrarian reform in Bangladesh. They run the country according to their ideologies to serve their own clan interest. Therefore, if we are to progress and fulfil the constitutional obligation made to the people of the Republic of Bangladesh in 1972, fundamental changes have to be brought in the thinking process and mindset of the people in the top.

NOTES

1. In fact all land records (Tahsil office) are supposed to be available to the public for a nominal fee, but officials cause undue harassment and charge excessive fees for access to land records.
2. The Enemy Property Act, established during the Indo-Pakistan War, has never been repealed. After the war and during the post-

independence period, it has persisted upto the present-day amended only in name to the Vested Property Act.

3. The 1900 Hill Tracts Manual provided the CHT, as the homeland of the indigenous 'hill tribes,' with a degree of autonomy and self-governance as a non-regulated or excluded area. However, after the partition of India the CHT was awarded to (East) Pakistan and successive Pakistani and Bangladeshi governments gradually curtailed the autonomy and land-rights of the adibasi peoples through statutory laws.
4. One quarter of the then population of the region, the majority of whom have not been compensated or resettled by the government to this day.
5. This article states that the buying or selling of adibasi land (in the CHT) cannot be undertaken without permission from tribal chiefs.
6. The indigenous police force, first established in 1881, was disbanded in 1955 by the then Pakistani government. The state police (Bengalis) were brought in as replacements.
7. In Bangladesh cultivable land is lost through forcible acquisition of land for large scale industry (shrimp, tobacco, forestry, etc.). Land degradation occurs through such industry for example through the depletion of mangrove forest for shrimp farming and the subsequent salination of soil, or the uncontrolled use of chemical fertilizer and pesticides. The Green Revolution and the monoculture of cash crops has resulted in genetic depletion of plant resources, seeds, crop varieties, etc.
8. Government stockpiling of grain is used to artificially lower prices in order to gain urban votes at the expense of the poor rural farmer.
9. From 0.86 acres in 1983 to 0.65 acres in 1996. It has been suggested that 1-2 acres are required to sustain an average family of 5-6 members. Owning less than 0.5 acres renders a farmer 'effectively landless'.

REFERENCES

Abdin, J. and G.K. Bose, 1988. "Farm Size and Productivity Difference: A Decomposition Analysis," Bangladesh Development Studies, 25, 71-79.

Abdullah, A., 1994. "Land Reform and Agrarian Change in Bangladesh," Bangladesh Development Studies, 67-99.

Ahmed, S. and Rahman, S. (ed.), 1992. Poverty Alleviation Through Access to Land Centre on Integrated Rural Development for Asia and the Pacific, and Economic Development Institute of the World Bank, CIRDAP Study Series No. 137, Dhaka, Bangladesh.

ALRD, Bangladesh Report and Discussion Paper, 2001. "Access to Land" Innovative Agrarian Reforms for Sustainability and Poverty Reduction, *ALRD/EZE Workshop.*

Barraclough, S.L., 1995. "Agricultural Policy and Land Reform," *Journal of Political Economy*, 906-47.

Chirapanda, Suthiporn, 1988. "Access to Land—The Case of Thailand". Paper presented at the policy seminar on "Access to Land", organized by the Centre on Integrated Rural Development for Asia and the Pacific, Bali, Indonesia.

Dorner, P. 1992. *Land Reform and Economic Development.* London : Penguin Books Ltd.

Dovring, Folke, 1970. "Economic Results of Land reforms," Agency for International Development, *Spring Review of Land Reform.*

Kamal, M. Uddin, 2002. "Needs For Land and Agrarian Reform In Bangladesh" Paper presented in the Regional Workshop on Land Issues for Asia held on Phnom Penh, Cambodia.

Lipton, M., 1974. "Towards a Theory of Land Reform," in D. Lehman (ed.), *Peasants, Landlords and Governments, Agrarian Reform in the Third World.* New York: Holmes & Meier.

Raquibbuzaman, M., 1973. "Sharecropping and Economic Efficiency in Bangladesh," *The Bangladesh Economic Review*, 1, 149-72.

Rashid, Salim and M.G. Quibria, 1995. "Is Land Reform Passé? With Special Reference to Asian Agriculture," *Critical Issues in Asian Development*, ed. M.G. Quibria, Oxford University Press.

Sobhan, R., 1993. *Agrarian Reform and Social Transformation—Preconditions for Development*, Dhaka, Bangladesh: The University Press Ltd.

Sharif, M., 1991. "Landholdings, Living Standards, and Labour Supply Functions: Evidence from a Poor Agrarian Economy," *Journal of Development Studies*, 27, 256-76.

Taslim, M.A., 1999. "Redistributive Land and Tenancy Reform in Bangladesh Agriculture," *Journal of Developing Areas*, 27, 341-76.

United Nations, Food and Agriculture Organisation. Studies on Agrarian Reform and Rural Poverty Economic and Social Development Series No. 27, Rome, author, 1984.

3

Home Economics and Urban Governance: The Challenges of Globalism, Gigantism and Privatism

ANDREW KIRBY
Andrew.Kirby@asu.edu
Professor of Social Sciences, Arizona State University, Phoenix, USA.

ABSTRACT

This paper argues that changes in the contemporary American city point to the necessity of rethinking the basics of urban governance. This is occurring due to the developments that are taking place in the residential housing market, whose production is becoming increasingly globalized. The search for high rates of economic return is leading corporate builders to produce larger developments, built as privately-planned and corporately-run entities, before they are turned over to private associations that run them on the basis of legal codes rather than existing federal, state and local law. In many cities in the rapidly growing West, all new homes are constructed and managed under such terms, a development which is having large impacts on the creation and maintenance of cohesive social bonds. This new privatization is explored and its implications examined.

Key words: urban growth, homeownership, neighborhoods, enclaves.

Introduction: Home Economics

The construction industry has traditionally been one of the most rooted and place-specific. Buildings have, until relatively recently, always been constructed on site, due to the high costs of transportation. Manufactured buildings have existed for perhaps a century, but the costs of transport have also been restrictive and the design elements of limited appeal. As a result, the building industry has been locked into the economics of specific regions—as prosperity existed, so buildings were built, but once downturns came about, so the construction sector has been among the first to go into a down cycle. Historically, then, the industry has been undercapitalized and small firms have predominated, with all this implies for efficiency of operation.

In the United States, this picture began to change somewhat after 1945, as a number of factors conspired to force changes in the manner in which the home market operated. First, years of war and the prior depression ensured that there was a vast backlog of demand for new homes. Second, and for some of the same reasons, there was a demographic change taking place that also added to the demand for new homes. Third, the experience of the war had indicated ways in which construction could be undertaken at a greater pace and more importantly, at a greater scale, using prefabrication methods.

The classic example of how the industry changed was the growth of the Leavitt Company in the 1940s and '50s. Large acreages of raw land were purchased prior even to the war, and used once demobilization took place. Homes were constructed in large numbers—subdivisions were developed across hundreds of acres at a time. The nature of the homes themselves, and the roles of the women who looked after them, have been explored in numerous studies; these were social changes that transcended specific regions to eventually include most parts of the country. Familiar too is the role that the Federal government played in making this housing expansion possible, by providing cheap mortgages to returning servicemen. Less familiar perhaps is the role that the FHA played in underwriting the vast lines of credit that were needed by the large builders like Leavitt, in order for them to operate at the scales to which they became accustomed (Jackson, 1985).

So, the events of the post war era indicated that it was possible to construct homes using industrial methods and on a larger scale than had been customary. This was a trend that spread to many economies and large suburban developments became familiar around the world (Balchin *et al.*, 2000). Nonetheless, there was little evidence that individual firms operated at anything other than a national scale until the close of the 1980s. At that juncture, a series of events precipitated a second shift in the way that homes and other buildings were created.

First, the Savings and Loan collapse of the Reagan era, followed by the RTC bail out, has been described as one of the biggest transfers of assets—from public to private—ever undertaken. What the Federal government accomplished was essentially a massive re-capitalization of the property industry, although the way the property sector changed was more fundamental than that. The availability of large investment sums allowed the industry to transform itself into a component of the emerging global capital markets, via new financial instruments such as Real Estate Investment Trusts (REITs), which brought together aspects of the junk bond and the securities markets. Coupled with a secondary market in bonds, the property sector now had access to the kinds of funds never before available, and so was able to underwrite construction on a more massive scale.

Second, the emergence of information technologies in the 1990s made it possible to expand activities across national boundaries, and to facilitate the enlargement of corporations that could operate in multiple markets (Castells, 2001). This permitted real estate interests to transcend the volatile conditions that are found in an isolated property market, allowing them to invest and disinvest from regional or national markets as necessary. A third factor was then the economic and urban growth that took place in key parts of the world economy, such as some Latin American cities, post apartheid South Africa, some parts of the former Eastern bloc, and Asia prior to 1997. Although none of these growth regions were without their economic perturbations, the last decade of the century saw growth opportunities for construction and property speculation that were unrivaled. It is no coincidence that by 2003 a number of corporate entities had already accumulated the expertise to move into Iraq to claim lucrative contracts for massive infrastructural development (for a brief discussion of the way in which governments around the world depend on these corporations to construct new towns and similar developments, see also Kirby, 2003a; Swyngedouw, 2002).

All in all, the 1990s saw an integration of three processes: first, the sheer scale of growth in many urban areas implied equally massive levels of construction; second, there was for the first time an ability on the part of corporations to integrate their affairs such that they could now forecast the downturn in one region so that they could invest in more stable markets; and third, there was a steady supply of funds to make new investments continually possible. A crucial component in all of this is the manner in which the US domestic savings market has shifted so dramatically, such that there is now a continual supply of new money coming—from pension funds—into the investment markets, flowing into mutual funds and other instruments that fuel, *inter alia*, the property sector.

Links Across Scales, Across Places

So far, this narrative has indicated the way in which global opportunities and national issues intersected *vis-à-vis* the construction industry. One additional component of this story is the way that rapid metropolitan expansion in the Western states of the US has, in turn, contributed to changing the way in which some of the larger companies in this sector do business, with enormous implications for the urban and social fabric.

The growth of the Sunbelt states, due in large measure to strategic military investment, has been fully discussed and needs little re-examination (Rothman, 2003). However, much of that story has been closed since the end of the cold war and the eclipse, at that time, of many defense establishments. What has since occurred, again during the 1990s, is that urban expansion has now shifted to states such as Nevada and Arizona, where the growth of population and of jobs has been explosive. Cheap mortgages were made possible by Federal support for low interest rates that subsidized both the individual taxpayer and this sector as a whole. Through access to enormous amounts of investment funding (via REITS and CMBS, e.g. Ling and Naranjo, 1999), construction companies have moved up to a new level of operations, producing cheap suburban residential developments with 10,000, 20,000 and even 40,000 residents at a time. A single development planned for Buckeye, Arizona will eventually extend across 55 square miles (approximately 88 square kilometers).

Taken together, these trends indicate two sets of outcomes within the property sector. First, the nature of residential development has dramatically altered from small speculative developments to massive planned communities. It must be emphasized that this is planning within the private sector, distinct from planning undertaken by a municipal authority or a new town corporation. A physical infrastructure is provided by the developer and then residential rules and regulations are developed within the legal templates that have been created nationwide over recent years. Eventually, management and organization of the community is passed, in the form of a Home Owners' Association (HOA), to the residents, who must continue to abide by the same 'covenants, codes and restrictions' (CC&Rs). By definition, these neighborhoods have very different forms of governance built into them when compared to traditional neighborhoods, which raises all kinds of implications for the manner in which cities are to be run in the 21st century.

The second outcome is that although these developments are restricted in large part to cities in the Western states, they redefine the notion of profitability throughout the development industry. Already, corporations are importing the concepts developed in Arizona and Nevada back into the Midwestern United States. Nor is this only manifested in the homeowner market. The scale of development is not an economic issue restricted to owner-occupation; large-scale rental complexes have also emerged in these cities, with implications for the normative returns on investment throughout the market.

Homes and Neighborhoods

In the modern American city, the home is a crucial entity for the people who own it. Its neighborhood defines the quality of life for the residents, and is the point of entry to schools and any urban services that exist. It is, more crucially, the sole form of investment that most families possess; any equity (*i.e.* increased value) residing in the home is the only form of saving that most hold for their retirement. Analytically, we also need to see the home in a different manner as we move into the next century. Although the house contains fewer children, it is typically increasing in size. Average home construction is now in excess of 2000 square feet and may run to five or six thousand square feet in some subdivisions. The net result of this is that the home is itself becoming a fragmented social setting. Without common family spaces, the home is a series of rooms where different family members of varied generations work or pursue different interests; and do so, not with one another, but electronically; via the telephone, the television, the Internet. Significant numbers of residents now work from the home on a part-time or full-time basis.

As a result of this domestic fragmentation, the relation between the individual, the family, the neighborhood and society has changed dramatically in recent years. The neighborhood is no longer a place where everyone knows the neighbors (Putnam, 2000). Instead, for many families, it is stripped back to its more basic form as an economic entity. This is acknowledged openly in many new subdivisions that are created intact by developers and provided with an HOA that defines the terms of social interaction (see Kirby *et al.*, 2004; Low, 2003). For the most part, these are not based upon civil rights but upon communal responsibilities (these also echo the forms of covenant that were drawn up in the early parts of the 20th century to exclude and to control in order to maintain property values—see Jackson, 1985, 208).

Within these spaces, individual behavior is rigidly controlled, insofar as it can have any impact upon a neighbor, and the range of powers held by the group is enough to constitute what Garreau terms "shadow governments" (Garreau, 1991, 183-208). In such a neighborhood in Phoenix, for example, one resident has spent $75,000 in legal fees in an attempt to exert a right to fly the American flag on other than public holidays, an act that has been denied by the Homeowners' Association. It is for these kinds of reasons that the neighborhood occupies a central position within the social spaces of many residents. First, as this is the place that contains the family's primary economic investment, social mores must be policed so that nothing disturbs the appearance and thus the value of the environs (for example, good neighborly behavior becomes defined in class terms, so that unsightly pick-up trucks can be banned from parking at the curbside or even in driveways). Second, an increasing number of neighborhoods are explicitly constructed to maintain privacy and to exclude non-residents. In Phoenix, for example, a significant proportion of new subdivisions are built as gated communities; and it is estimated that perhaps as many as 42 million Americans now live in such developments (Sanchez and Lang, 2002). And third, the neighborhood becomes by default the primary location for social interaction as the family's opportunities for social intercourse are increasingly curtailed—by the sheer scale of many metropolitan areas, by fears of crime and otherness, real or imagined; and by the increase in the number of hours spent working, which leaves little time for the creation of complex social ties (Wilson-Doenges, 2000).

The most poignant example of this segregation is the example of the "neighborhood vehicle" (NV). This represents a metaphor for the new forms of residential association that are emerging across the country (see Figure 1). For example, in Florida, California and Arizona, the Del Webb Corporation is constructing new residential developments under the name of "Anthem." Anthem, Arizona consists of nearly 6000 acres and may ultimately contain 17,000 homes. Residents will eventually have exclusive access to on-site facilities and

FIGURE 1: The Neighborhood Vehicle: Source, Corporate Advertisement.

amenities such as parks, clinics, retailing outlets and a kindergarden-8th grade school that has been donated to the school district. In such large-scale developments, it is expected that residents will spend a significant proportion of their time within the neighborhood, and can thus use an electric vehicle that is not registered for use on public highways. Costing up to $15,000 fully equipped, the NV represents an inversion of the twentieth century city, a reduction of horizons to the most immediate social realities.

This reconfigured neighborhood takes on new meaning, then, both as an economic space but also as a setting for social interaction. It is a new scale of action within civil society, within which the family polices itself and its neighbors (Kirby, 2003b). Behavior is surveilled and controlled by moral suasion, legal sanction or—when necessary—by private security personnel (Staples, 2000). It is inevitable that this scale of action will take on more importance, insofar as the residents see it as a scale of political organization that is amenable to successful collective action. It does not need to be repeated here that other forms of political organization repel the individual voter—the city is seen as a growth machine that demands only that the individual participates as an investor or worker. The national political scene is a tattered compromise that is in real danger of being destroyed by neo-liberal policies coupled with reckless international adventurism.

In consequence, these closed spaces are attractive to residents who seek to maintain their property values while at the same time they can remove themselves from the responsibilities of the broader community. Anthem uses key phrases in its advertising that absolve the buyer from any responsibility for the broader social situation: the development is described in its advertising materials as "self-contained" and "paying for growth with no burden or cost to taxpayers." Clearly, the balkanization of the city, in a way that leaves residents to provide their own resources or suffer the consequences of their own poverty, is not confronted.

Much has been written about the political-economic changes that continue to define the American city, and much attention has rightly been paid to the global connections, and economic competition, between cities. City governments have cast off many of their social functions as they race to re-develop economic capacities; and ironically, this is a transformation that takes us back to the "private city" of the late nineteenth and early twentieth centuries discussed by Sam Bass Warner (1968). It is ironic, of course, insofar as this was the quintessential period of intense globalization, one barely recaptured after the construction of the political and economic fault lines that defined the cold war. While governments look outward and create partnerships to build larger office parks and larger sports stadiums, residents look inwards, and the planned community becomes a basis for human interaction. It constitutes an economic space, a site for investment, and social and political interactions become subordinated to the pursuit of stability and equity. The goal of a city on a hill has been replaced by the reality of a city behind a gate.

Urban Governance

What then do these changes imply for the social evolution of America's cities? And crucially, what do they imply for other societies, as these privatized housing enclaves metastasize around the world (Glasze and Alkhayyal, 2002; Jurgens and Gnad, 2002; Kirby *et al.*, 2004; Leisch, 2002; Salcedo and Torres, 2004). In this section, I argue that one of the key issue will be the manner in which the processes of urban governance evolve, in line with economic, social and political developments. Governance is used here to identify the widest level of political discourse, namely the "processes of regulation, co-ordination and control" (Pierre, 1999, 376). As such, the focus is much broader than studies of élites, research on growth machines, or even attempts to apply state theory to local government; it is also more general than the analysis of rules and regulations on the one hand, or collective action by citizens on the other. In the fullest sense, it invokes

> examples of governance at the local level (that) include a neighborhood co-operative formed to install and maintain a standing water pipe, a town council operating a waste recycling scheme, a multi-urban body developing an integrated transport plan together

with user groups, a stock exchange regulating itself with national government oversight, and a regional initiative of state agencies, industrial groups, and residents to control deforestation. At the global level, governance has been viewed primarily as intergovernmental relationships, but it must now be understood as also involving non-governmental organizations (NGOs), citizens' movements, multinational corporations, and the global capital market. Interacting with these are global mass media of dramatically enlarged influence (Commission on Global Governance, 1994).

To this point, a good deal of the extant literature on governance has evolved with a focus upon cities in developing nations, and has, as a consequence, several characteristics. One of the most visible is an exhortatory emphasis on empowerment that reflects the disenfranchisement of many who live in such cities: "good governance occurs when societal norms and practices empower and encourage people to take increasingly greater control over their own development in a manner that does not impinge upon the accepted rights of others" (UNDP, n.d.). In part as a result of this evolution, the governance literature has also made more use of analytical categories, such as the state, that are commonplace in much of the research on Africa and Latin America, but are less usual in North American studies: "governance includes the state, but transcends it by taking in the private sector and civil society. The state creates a conducive political and legal environment. The private sector generates jobs and income. The civil society facilitates political and social interaction—mobilizing groups to participate in economic, social and political activities. Because each has its weaknesses and strengths, a major objective of our support for good governance is to promote constructive interaction among all three" (UNDP, n.d.).

By exploring the issues that underpin the question of urban governance in this manner, we arrive relatively quickly at some important insights that accompany the analysis of the new private city [see also McKenzie, 1999]. Not least of these lies in the importance of thinking about real estate development in the spatially scaled manner indicated above, linking global, national and urban events. In the past decade, this sector has changed dramatically, in terms of the manner in which it has become fully integrated into the global investment arena (Roulac, 1998). The creation of real estate investment trusts (REITs) is only one part of the way in which the construction and real estate finance industries have reconstituted themselves, and in consequence they now assess all developments in the context of the returns available across the globe. Accordingly, the sheer pace and size of many developments is increasing, which has knock-on effects throughout the market; for instance, as the expectations of rental rates rise in the condominium market, so rents may rise in older, multi-family rentals too, with implications for housing affordability and housing density.

When we move past the economic dimension and incorporate analysis of the state, we can continue to incorporate valuable insights. For example, while it is commonly asserted that globalization is eroding the state system, there is little evidence that the nation state is likely to disappear any time soon, although the role of the state apparatus is indeed changing as we move into the new century. A global economy dictates certain preoccupations and strategies at the national scale—unsurprisingly, fiscal management is centrally important here—and complementary strategies at the local scale, including the disappearance of welfare and harsher controls of issues such as immigration. And when civil society is also introduced into the analytical equation, we are then in a position to evaluate the new forms of civic association that have been discussed already in this paper. As indicated, if association is driven more by the constraints of home ownership and the creation of home equity for the purposes of savings and retirement, then this must necessarily have important implications for the operation of, and importance of, civil society. In short, we can readily predict that the role of the resident changes, and the family becomes more focused upon its economic responsibilities than its civic obligations.

Metropolitan areas in the United States are increasingly fragmented into small cities, counties, special districts and school districts, and increasingly, these are the containers in which individuals seize opportunities to shape life in the way they choose. There is not much that they can do to influence the economic decisions of large corporations, nor can they do a great deal with respect to environmental conditions, now so frequently defined as global questions. However, they can focus upon the quality of life, defined in the broadest sense. The manner in which this ability to control the quality of life will, however, be strongly influenced by the changes in the neighborhood described above. As already noted, up to 40 million Americans live in planned neighborhoods where they control social policies via various forms of covenant and regulation. Commentators typically assume that residents have some nostalgia for the walking city (as portrayed so successfully in Disneyland, and as commodified in Celebration, Florida) or are so scared of crime that they can do nothing but wall themselves up in bunkers so as to exclude all others (Blakely and Snyder, 1999; Low, 2003). As already discussed, this myopically ignores the crucial importance of the economic dimension. However, in addition to the residents' pressing need to ensure resale values, it is also possible to detect a need to manufacture social control. Newer planned communities are being built at a scale in which residents will have direct exclusionary political control over the local high school, and the rest of the facets of everyday life. In short, what we are seeing here is a newer form of urban governance than is commonly recognized (and, moreover, given the globalization of the property sector and the standardization of design conventions, it is a phenomenon that is likely to spread to other countries very rapidly).

Unsurprisingly, this has led to a debate over the ways in which cities can be recreated as jurisdictional entities. Arguments, such as those by Young and, more recently, by Frug, argue strongly for new layers of government that reterritorialize cities, counties and suburban jurisdictions, so that inequalities of income and ethnic segregation can be diminished (Frug, 1999). Without endorsing inequality, it is important to recognize that these are dangerous arguments in that they ignore the development of new jurisdictions as social constructions and view them, consequently, as subsidiary to longer standing cities. It is also rather spurious to believe that such new developments can simply be engineered back out of existence. As already indicated, this is already an important political and economic constituency within American society.

In thinking through the return to the private city, then, we see complexity in the development of urban governance, with social and spatial fragmentation marking the interface between economy, state, and civil society. And then in turn, we must see complexity in terms of the ways in which residents are able to influence the norms of the quality of life. With highly focused partnerships between corporations, local governments and residents emphasizing quality of life concerns within planned communities, we must necessarily ask how this social fragmentation will have impacts on quality of life standards elsewhere in the city.

Conclusions

Urban management and governance are central to the next phase of urban growth that is taking place throughout the world in the new century, and which were emphasized by the United Nations as one of two global campaigns leading into the millennium. A recent Habitat document argued that "transparent and accountable urban government and the promotion of participatory decision-making processes, involving all sections of society, can go a long way in making cities more equitable, sustainable and just. The role of local authorities, and how they function, will become even more crucial in a globalized world where cities will take centre-stage in the world economy (UNCHS, 1999).

But how do these sentiments square with the massive growth of private residential communities? It seems clear that we are witnessing a situation in which the massivity of real estate corporations and the changing responsibilities of the state apparatus leave individuals scrambling to redefine civil society. As we have shown here, albeit in a preliminary manner, a significant proportion of the American city is being walled off and managed by new public-private forms (especially when we examine newer cities in the South and West). The focus of these residents is upon their own real estate investments and a relatively narrowly-defined quality of life. Does this effectively destroy the nature of civil society, removing the most affluent and therefore those most able to manipulate the political process from consideration? Or does it open up more seats at the policy table for those residents who are necessarily concerned about their own neighborhoods but also the urban fabric as a whole? At this juncture, only speculation is possible, although there is certainly plenty of it, and for some analysts, the creation of urban enclaves is but an excessively dark portent of worse to come (see extensive discussions in Blakely and Snyder, 1999; Low, 2003).

The purpose of this paper has been to emphasize the analysis of governance as an outcome of the relations between state, economy and civil society. This is a more complex insight than can be obtained by the observation solely of spatial forms, such as gated communities, edge cities or downtowns. Such studies are prone to short attention spans, an overt fondness for metaphor and a frequent nostalgia for some golden urban age. In most instances, this is nostalgia reminiscent of Las Vegas, a yearning for something that has never existed (Rothman, 2003). It is also a rediscovery of segregation and privilege within a capitalist society, which is hardly newsworthy. Nonetheless, there are important changes to be witnessed, the most crucial of which is the manner in which the real estate sector has transformed itself in the last decade of the twentieth century, a shift that is likely to rival other forms of restructuring that have occurred within the economy. This has little to do with gates as such and everything to do with ways in which neighborhoods have become primarily vehicles for investment and savings. When placed alongside the changes that have taken place within the state apparatus at all levels, then we can see that there are indeed different forms of governance ahead.

REFERENCES

Balchin, P. Isaac, D. and Chen, J., 2000. *Urban Economics, A Global Perspective.* New York: Palgrave.

Blakely, E. and Snyder, M., 1999. *Fortress America: Gated Communities in the United States.* Washington DC, Brookings Institution.

Castells, M., 2001. *The Internet Galaxy.* New York: Oxford University Press.

Commission on Global Governance (1994). Our Global Neighbourhood. available at www.cgg.ch/chap1.html.

Frug, G.E., 1999. *Citymaking: Building Communities Without Building Walls.* Princeton: Princeton University Press.

Garreau, J., 1991. *Edge City.* New York: Doubleday.

Glasze, G. and Alkhayyal, A., 2002. 'Gated Housing Estates in the Arab World: Case Studies in Lebanon and Riyadh, Saudi Arabia.' *Environment and Planning B: Planning and Design,* **29**, 321-36.

Jackson, K., 1985. *Crabgrass Frontier.* New York: Oxford.

Jurgens, U. and Gnad, M., 2002. "Gated Communities in South Africa: Experiences from Johannesburg." *Environment and Planning B: Planning and Design* **29**, 337-53.

Kirby, A., 2003a. 'When Extreme Political Ideas move into the Mainstream', 171-91 in Flint, C. ed. *The Spaces of Hate.* London: Routledge.

Kirby, A., 2003b. "How EZ is this company town?" *Cities* **20(1)**, 1-2.

Kirby, A. *et al.*, 2004. "Cities on a Hill? An examination of housing enclaves in Phoenix". Mimeo.

Leisch, H., 2002 "Gated Communities in Indonesia." *Cities* **19(5)**, 341-50.

Ling, D., & Naranjo, A., 1999. "The integration of commercial real estate markets and stock markets" *Real Estate Economics,* *27*(3), 483–515.

Low, S., 2003. *Behind the Gates: Life, Security and the Suprsuit of Happiness in Fortress America.* New York: Routledge.

McKenzie, E., 1999. 'Reflections on a new paradigm for the governance of common-interest communities,' 53-65 in Overton, B. (ed.) *Community First!* Alexandria, VA: Community Associations Institute.

Pierre, J. 1999. "Models of Urban Governance." *Urban Affairs Review* **34**, 372-96.

Putnam, R., 2000. *Bowling Alone: The Collapse and Revival of American Community.* New York: Simon and Schuster.

Rothman, H., 2003. *Neon Metropolis.* New York: Routledge.

Roulac, S.E., 1998. "Real estate investment strategies in the 21st century," *Real Estate Review Spring*, 5-9.

Sanchez, T. and Lang, R., 2002. *Security versus Status.* Census Note 02: 02. Metropolitan Institute, Virginia Polytechnic.

Salcedo, R. and Torres, A., 2004. "Gated Communities in Santiago: Wall or Frontier?" *International Journal of Urban and Regional Research* **28(1)**, 27-44.

Staples, W.G., 2000. *Everyday Surveillance: Vigilance and Visibility in Postmodern life.* Lanham: Rowman and Littlefield.

Swyngedouw, E., 2002. "Neoliberal urbanization in Europe: large scale urban development projects and the new urban policy", 195-229 in Brenner, N. and Theodore, N. (eds.) *Spaces of Neoliberalism.* Malden, MA: Blackwell.

UNCHS Press Release, Habitat (United Nations Centre for Human Settlements), March 5, 1999.

UNDP Internet Conference Forum on "Public Private Interface in Urban Environmental Management" available at www.soc.titech.ac.jp/uem/governance.html.

Warner, S.B., 1968. *The Private City*. Philadelphia: University of Pennsylvania Press.

Wilson-Doenges, G., 2000. 'An exploration of sense of community and fear of crime in gated communities.' *Environment and Behavior* **32**, 597-611.

4

The Contradictions in Enabling Private Developers of Affordable Housing: A Cautionary Case from Ahmedabad, India

VINIT MUKHIJA
vmukhija@ucla.edu
Department of Urban Planning, UCLA, School of Public Policy and Social Research, Los Angeles, USA.

SUMMARY

Through a case study of a private developer of housing in India, this paper critically examines the policy advice of enabling markets and market-based actors to provide affordable housing in developing countries. In the paradoxical case, after the public sector's enabling, the developer stopped constructing housing for low-income groups. The paper argues for a more cautious, circumspect, and varied approach because enabling strategies focused on market actors can produce highly uncertain outcomes. In addition, it emphasizes that policymakers need a better understanding of how the informal and formal sectors can overlap. Enabling informal developers can be even trickier because public support can reduce their flexibility and incentives, as well as impact the expectations and opportunities of the homebuyers.

1. Introduction

The last few decades have seen tremendous shifts in housing policies in developing countries. Previously, it was assumed that governments had to play the key role in the provision of housing, and access to better housing, particularly for the poor, was its responsibility. The traditional policy was for the governments to build public housing. Public housing projects, however, faced strong criticism. Many critics argued that the houses built by governments did not match the needs of the intended beneficiaries. Moreover, conventional public housing is an expensive strategy, and for most governments it was difficult to continue because of their fiscal limitations. In the 1970s, public housing schemes were replaced by slum upgrading, and sites and services projects. These projects were less expensive, more flexible, and allowed additional control and participation by potential beneficiaries. But by the 1980s, the very idea of government involvement in housing was under considerable attack, and the critics succeeded in seriously eroding state participation and efforts to influence the housing markets.

There were three main streams of the criticism. First, public involvement, critics argued, had been a big failure; it had been inefficient and ill conceived (Perlman, 1976; Turner, 1972; 1977). Governments were not only using too much of their resources, they were misusing the resources as public housing was poorly designed: it was poorly located, did not provide opportunities for multiple uses or expansion, nor did it allow the beneficiaries sufficient flexibility in making their payments. The corollary was that other institutional actors, such as communities and market-based entrepreneurs, were likely to be more successful in the same endeavors. Second, direct government involvement in housing production had been negligible in contrast with the housing supplied by the informal sector (Durand-Lasserve, 1987; Hamdi, 1991). Some critics suggested that the government's role in housing, therefore, was more or less limited. Others pointed out that the informal sector, unlike the public sector, also followed strict market and economic principles (Amis, 1984; Doebele, 1975; Payne, 1982). Finally, critics argued that government participation in housing markets was counterproductive. Such neoliberal criticisms emphasized the negative impacts of government involvement and argued for a cutback in its participation. They particularly attacked public regulations and the rigid bureaucracy (Linn, 1983; Malpezzi, 1990; World Bank, 1991; Zearley, 1993). For many critics, regulations—

building codes and standards, environmental policy regulations, land use and development restrictions, etc.—were the key impediment in efficient markets and housing delivery. But others also specifically disapproved of small enclave projects implemented by public agencies (Malpezzi, 1994), and the use of government subsidies (Mayo, Malpezzi and Cross, 1986). The critics also promoted the necessity, inevitability, and benefits of housing provision through the markets. Some scholars even documented empirical evidence that suggested that housing provision through private markets was the more successful strategy in improving access for the less affluent (Dowall, 1989).

The consequence of such condemnations was a deliberate attempt by policymakers to make housing policies more market friendly and encourage market agents to be further involved in housing delivery. The government's direct involvement in housing was also ardently curtailed. In contrast to being "a provider" of housing, it was redefined to be "an enabler" of housing production. Government was to enable market agents to perform well and it would support the privatization of housing delivery through market-responsive deregulation. The key document that laid out the enabling approach was a World Bank policy paper: *Housing—Enabling Markets to Work* (1993). Multilateral and bilateral aid agencies led the chorus to promote enabling (UNCHS, 1990; 1996; USAID, 1991; World Bank, 1993),[1] and similar policies to enable are being accepted and adopted by governments in many developing countries (Gilbert, 2002; Government of India, 1994; Jones and Datta, 2000).[2] The key objective of this paper is to scrutinize the soundness of the prevailing paradigm of enabling in housing policy, and to specifically examine through grounded empirical research some of the typical strategies of enabling markets and market actors. I expect this inquiry and its findings to contribute to better policymaking in the area of housing delivery, particularly from the perspective of enabling.

Enabling in the prevailing policy conception refers primarily to a focus on developing the supportive context for private entrepreneurs and other market actors. Conventional enabling does not refer to creating policy support for the housing activities of government, or para-state, agencies. Nor does it emphasize support for the activities of communities or housing cooperatives. It does however address, although inadequately, the role of non-profit organizations in developing affordable housing. (In this paper I define affordable housing as housing targeted at the low and modest income groups.) But the impacts of enabling policies on housing development are unclear, not very well researched, and questions persist about their effectiveness. Nonetheless, many critics challenge the private market bias of enabling policies (Baken and van der Linden, 1993; Jones, 1996; Jones and Ward, 1994; Sanyal, 1996). Their strongest criticism is that the private developers will not provide housing for the poor and that the most vulnerable groups will be the most adversely impacted. These scholars question the empirical evidence supporting the success of market-based policies. They emphasize the failed experience in Chile during the mid-seventies to the mid-eighties, where the evidence suggests that the deregulated private sector moved away from housing the poor (Kusnetzoff, 1987). They also highlight the less than successful deregulatory approaches to help the market actors in Bogota, Colombia—the *normas minimas* programme—(Baken and van der Linden, 1993; Mohan, 1994), and the limited success in the Philippines (Strassman, 1994). In contrast, the critics point to the innovations and targeting accomplishments of the publicly implemented Incremental Development Scheme in Pakistan (Siddiqui and Khan, 1994). According to these criticisms, support for market actors may not be the best focus for public policy, and there is a need for significant, sustained, and direct support for the poor (Baken and van der Linden, 1993; Siembieda and Moreno, 1997).

Another key set of objections that critics of enabling raise, focus on the challenges faced by planners and policymakers interested in enabling housing delivery by market actors. According to them, it is neither easy nor evident what policymakers should do. First it is unclear what the appropriate level of government involvement should be—whether the role should be "minimal" or "medium" (Pugh, 1994; 1997). Conventional wisdom seems to suggest a very hands-off role, focused on privatization, decentralization, deregulation, and demand-driven development, but research suggests the need for a more engaged government involvement in framing successful policies (Mukhija, 2001). Other critics of enabling argue that the central issue is not the level of government involvement but whether it should be responsible for housing provision or not (Marcuse, 2001).

In addition, an important issue of debate among scholars is whether the emphasis of public support for market actors should be on the formal sector, the informal sector, or on public-private partnerships. The supporters of assistance for the informal sector argue that the informal actors are the key producers of affordable housing in developing countries, and, therefore, they should be aided (Keivani and Werna, 2001a). The World Bank, however, maintains that the policies that enable the formal sector's private developers—since the emphasis is on deregulation—are also relevant for facilitating the actors of the informal sector (1993). But critics question such assertions and suggest that a more specific approach with nuances is required (Duran-Lasserve, 1999; Keivani and Werna, 2001a). Finally, there is growing agreement that enabling the markets will require institutional development and this is likely to be a long process (World Bank, 2000). However, there is little consensus on what strategies or approaches governments should follow in the interim (Keivani and Werna, 2001b). According to some scholars, public-private partnerships may be the answer to this dilemma (Ahmed, 1999; Payne, 1999; Pugh, 1994). However, it is not that clear how these partnerships should be implemented either.

I share some of these concerns, and in this paper, I critically examine the potential problems in the enabling paradigm by analyzing the case of a private developer, the Parshwanath Group, in the Indian city of Ahmedabad. I got interested in this group because it was highly regarded for its involvement in developing housing for low-income groups through formal market mechanisms. Typically in developing countries, as suggested above, only developers of the informal sector produce housing for low-income groups. But the Parshwanath Group was unusual. Although it was considered a formal sector actor, it focused on developing affordable housing, and found the practice profitable for over twenty years. Its housing, however, was not targeted at the poorest of the poor but it was developed for households with low and modest incomes. The developer's buyers included school teachers, police constables, tailors, carpenters, bus and taxi drivers, etc.

Most significantly though, the group had embedded within its practices many activities that cannot easily be classified as formal, or legal. On the contrary, the Parshwanath Group embodied an ingenious combination and overlap of formal and informal sector procedures and practices. Nonetheless in the late 1980s, the developer caught the attention of a national public agency, the Housing and Urban Development Corporation (HUDCO). HUDCO proposed to form a partnership with the developer to build the Parshwanath Township. The public agency regarded the group as a formal sector actor and seems to have ignored, or was oblivious to, the developer's informal practices. HUDCO's intention was to enable the developer to expand its housing supply and reach further down-market. The agency, in spite of its own past success at housing delivery (Bhatnagar, 1996), was also looking to reduce its direct involvement in housing production (Baken and Smets, 1999). To a large extent, the public agency's effort followed the up-and-coming policy advice to enable market actors. The partnership and the endeavor, however, were only partially successful. Paradoxically, after the enabling, and the Parshwanath Township experience, the Parshwanath Group stopped building housing for low-income groups. On the contrary, the group got involved in developing housing for affluent buyers only.

1.1 Main Arguments

Based on the evidence of the developer's experience, I caution that enabling strategies focused on market actors are treacherous and can produce highly uncertain outcomes. Private developers directly supported by public initiatives and strategies may end up developing housing for more affluent income groups than initially planned. Conventional, market-driven, enabling strategies can reduce their flexibility and incentives to provide housing for low-income groups. This criticism is particularly relevant when the enabling policies are focused on the informal sector's actors, because such policies can adversely impact and transform the informal and illegal strategies available to private developers of low-income housing. Moreover, public involvement in enabling private developers can also have unforeseen influences on the expectations of homebuyers. The research, thus, suggests a need for carefulness in uncritically embracing the enabling paradigm. It also suggests that planners and policymakers need to explore complementary and alternative courses of action. In addition, the case study illustrates how the informal and the formal sector, and their practices, can overlap, and suggests that policymakers need a better understanding of such overlaps.

Another key objective of the paper is to provide an empirical account of the production of market-based, affordable housing in developing countries. Although there are some remarkable studies of private entrepreneurs who develop housing for low-income groups through the informal sector (Blaesser, 1981; Payne, 1982), little is known about the developers that operate and prosper among the interstices between the formal and the informal sector, and are, therefore, more difficult to classify and analyze. The paper attempts to address this gap and builds on the advice of other scholars that the first step to better policy design is a grounded and robust account of the practices of the informal sector's actors (Peattie, 1987).

1.2 Methodology and Organization

The research was based on primary and secondary sources. I conducted my Ahmedabad fieldwork—semi-structured, open-ended interviews and ethnographic research—in the summers of 1996, 1997 and 1998. In addition to the residents of the Parshwanath Township and a key family member of the Parshwanath Group, I interviewed housing officials of the local government (Ahmedabad Municipal Corporation), the state government (Gujarat Housing Board), representatives of the private sector (including members of the Gujarat Institute of Housing and Estate Developers, a lobbying organization of the state's private developers), the civil society (particularly, representatives of the Self Employed Women's Association—SEWA—a leading non-governmental organization that was expected to get involved in the township project), and current and former officials of HUDCO in Ahmedabad and Delhi.

I also employed secondary sources, including previous studies, professional reports and project documents of the case. The secondary sources were particularly useful in understanding how the private developer operated in its projects prior to the public involvement (Mehta and Mehta, 1989; Wadhva, 1986; 1987; 1989), and in comprehending the nature and intentions of the public involvement and enabling (USAID, 1991). I also interviewed the authors of the secondary sources. Some of the details of the case study are incomplete because it was difficult to obtain specific data from the developer and the other stakeholders. However, I expect my narrative of the case to present a fair and representative account of the events.

Nonetheless, the paper is based on a single case and is open to criticism for drawing too many lessons from an individual case study. Definitely, it would be useful to have more case studies that analyze the impact of enabling, but I do believe that the key insights illustrated by the Parshwanath case are not unique. The principles the case illustrates—the uncertainty of affordable housing being delivered through public enabling strategies targeting private developers because of their potential adverse impact on the flexibility and incentives of the developers, and their unpredictable effect on the expectations and opportunities of homebuyers—have wider relevance for all scholars and policymakers interested in promoting housing delivery in developing countries.

The case study and the arguments are elaborated in the next few pages, and it is the heart of the paper. The case is described and analyzed in three sections. First, I explain how the Parshwanath Group operated. I describe the qualities and strategies that allowed the group to develop affordable housing and capture the attention of both researchers and policymakers. Second, I explain how a key outcome of all the attention was a public-private partnership between the developer and a public agency. The agency was interested in enabling the developer to produce more affordable housing but the project's outcome was quite different from what had been planned. Third, I elaborate on what went wrong in the Parshwanath

Township, and attempt to explain why and how. The final section of the paper recapitulates the findings, situates them in context of the literature, and suggests research and policy directions.

2. Innovations of the Private Developer

The Parshwanath Group, a private housing developer, is active in the city of Ahmedabad.[3] The Patel brothers formed the group in the early sixties. The four brothers used to be building contractors for the Gujarat Housing Board (GHB), a state housing agency (for the state of Gujarat), and constructed public housing for the board. The brothers did this for about five years and decided that there was an opportunity for them to move from being contractors to housing developers. At that time, housing finance was also available through the Gujarat Cooperative Housing Finance Corporation (GCHFC), another state agency. Since 1964, the GCHFC had been releasing credit for housing aimed at low and middle-income groups. The brothers decided that instead of competing in the relatively saturated high-income housing segment,[4] the group would leverage their construction experience in the low and lower middle-class segment, capitalize on the credit facility from the GCHFC, and develop housing for the lower-end of the market. The brothers also argue that they were guided by a social agenda (USAID, 1991). Their first project was completed in 1967.

The Parshwanath Group was quite successful in its endeavors. By the late-eighties it had developed over twenty thousand housing units (Wadhva, 1989) in almost 125 projects (USAID, 1991). Its larger developments included Ambikanagar, with 1,400 housing units, and Adinathnagar with 1,484 units. Most of its projects are in the eastern part and periphery of Ahmedabad. The majority of the city's industries are located in the east and most of the working class families live there. But its projects served a wider range of income groups, including at times, middle-income housing. The group, however, never used internal cross-subsidy as a strategy to make the housing affordable for their poorer homebuyers.

Like other private developers in the city, the Parshwanath Group was involved in a whole range of activities, from land acquisition and subdivision to the construction of housing. In addition, it also formed a housing finance company and even started manufacturing some of the construction materials. Their activities caught the attention of scholars and have been mentioned, documented and analyzed in previous studies (Adusumilli, 1999; USAID, 1991; Wadhva, 1986; 1987; 1989). According to these studies, the developer's success in delivering housing to low-income groups, through the formal sector, was based on a number of noteworthy, market innovations.

First, the Parshwanath Group succeeded in achieving tremendous economies of scale and averaged almost a thousand units of housing annually for over twenty years. This helped the developer in buying construction materials in bulk at discounted rates. The company was also able to use its labor and management resources more efficiently. Second, to further reduce its construction costs, the group started manufacturing some of the building materials—such as bricks, tiles, standardized doors and windows, and Reinforced Cement Concrete (RCC) pipes—by itself. Because of the large scale of its involvement in construction activities, it was feasible to manufacture materials and practice a strategy of vertical integration.[5] Third, the developer was innovative in design and construction. Its houses were minimal. The group used load-bearing, brick walls and rarely built a second floor but allowed for the incremental expansion of its houses. Typically, the houses did not come with fixtures, or finishes, such as kitchen counters, washbasins, cupboards, staircases, kitchen doors, plastered walls, parapet walls, etc. Homebuyers were expected to add the fittings over a period of time, based on their needs and affordability. Even some of the external amenities, such as streetlights and tarred roads, were not provided in order to lower the costs.[6] The developer's premise was that the residents' cooperatives would upgrade their settlements subsequently, and that such cost saving was necessary to make the housing affordable as well as profitable. The strategy, however, made the settlements appear like informal settlements.

Finally, the Parshwanath Group also recognized that it needed to be innovative on the demand side, and decided to help its homebuyers with housing finance. So the brothers established the Parshwanath Housing Finance Corporation (PHFC) to provide loans at competitive rates and with terms much more attractive than the prevalent lending rates in the informal sector (There were practically no opportunities for low-income groups to borrow in the formal sector). The PHFC directly extended loans to its borrowers as well as channeled funds from the state corporation, the GCHFC. The developer used the cooperative umbrella to access the public funding. In the early 1980s, however, the GCHFC stopped financing private, including cooperative, housing because of its poor record in loan-recovery (Joshi, 1995).[7] The drying up of public funds also impacted the Parshwanath Group's operations. About the same time, HUDCO became interested in the developer. HUDCO was looking for strategies to reduce its direct involvement in developing housing. It proposed to partner with the private developer, support it financially, and enable it to increase the scale of its affordable housing operations.

3. The Parshwanath Township and HUDCO's Enabling

HUDCO is the Government of India's premier techno-financing institution focused on housing and infrastructure development. It was incorporated in 1970 with the principal mandate to ameliorate housing conditions of all income groups, particularly the poor. HUDCO had primarily worked through public projects but in the mid-eighties, perhaps influenced by the new public policy faith in public-private partnerships, it was looking for a private partner. Coincidentally, the Parshwanath Group had by that time developed a reputation for being an innovative developer of affordable housing, and it was also looking for external funding.

The group had assembled a large tract of land on the eastern fringe of Ahmedabad in Naroda. Krishnanagar, the nearest bus stop, was approximately a thirty-minute bus-ride from the city center. After two years of negotiating with HUDCO, in 1988, the developer and the public agency reached an agreement. The plan was to develop almost 7,000 units of housing, for a target population of 35,000 and in three phases, with more than half the units designed as low-income housing (USAID, 1991). HUDCO also proposed to involve SEWA, the city's leading non-Governmental organization (NGO). The NGO would help ensure that the affordable housing was appropriately targeted for low-income groups. It would also help in loan-recovery.

Like the developer's prior projects, all the planned housing units were load-bearing, brick wall structures as opposed to open-lot developments. HUDCO agreed to provide the Parshwanath Group with short-term construction finance.[8] It also agreed to refinance the PHFC's mortgage loans to the homebuyers, and thus enhanced the developer's financial liquidity, as well as shared its monetary risk. In return, the group accepted HUDCO's recommendations and stipulations. It agreed to develop the township in more than three phases, and revised the project's open space and amenity provisions. The planned township was to be developed at only three-fourths the density of the group's prior projects. The Patel brothers were concerned about the impact of such concessions on their profitability but they also saw the township as an opportunity to build something more prestigious.

The first phase was completed in 1990 and the second almost two years after that. All the phases, however, were not developed. Approximately, only a third of the initially planned housing was constructed. SEWA did not get involved in the project. Most of the NGO's members could not afford the housing. The Parshwanath Group ran into litigation and financial troubles with the project and revised its scheme. It transferred the land ownership of the undeveloped land parcels to other housing development firms, including allegedly, at least, one owned by the family. But the new development firms decided to construct housing for more affluent income groups.

4. What Went Wrong and Why?

Parshwanath Township feels like a hybrid between conventional informal sector land developments that lack infrastructure, and typical formal sector housing developments that have a monotonous regularity in their appearance. The township's streets have streetlights and trees but there are neither sidewalks nor tarred roads. Many residents have used the developer's construction as a basic core and have built around it. This has created a more spontaneous appearing built fabric. However, many have not made major improvements and the regularity and commonness of the houses is also apparent. During the monsoons, it is quite usual to find small stagnant ponds of water with mosquitoes hovering around. Little piles of garbage are also not uncommon.

The residents of the township have relatively modest incomes. There were hardly any cars in the neighborhood but motorcycles, scooters and bicycles were quite normal. My anecdotal evidence indicates that most of the homes are owner-occupied. Many of the residents that I interviewed were very happy about their homes. They described the township as the "best place" and "cleanest colony" that they had ever lived in. They even mentioned that they were extremely grateful to the developer. I, however, also met some dissatisfied residents, who had stopped paying their loan instalments and had brought in litigation against the developer. (These were mostly residents of the most affordable units planned in the Township. But only a tiny proportion of the smaller units were built in the first two phases. Most were planned for the later stages.) In response, the developer initiated counter-litigation, abandoned its plans for a 35,000 resident township and sold-off the undeveloped land-pockets to other development companies.

4.1 Changes in Expectations, Opportunities, Flexibility and Incentives

But why were there such unforeseen and paradoxical outcomes in the project? A possible explanation is that the unintended outcomes at the Parshwanath Township were a result of the public enabling of the private developer. Central to the argument, however, is my observation and premise that the Parshwanath Group was not a simple, formal sector actor—and the key difference is not that it focused on the low-income market segment—but that the developer, notwithstanding its many formal market innovations discussed earlier, followed a number of informal practices. It is misleading to analyze and conceive of the group as merely a formal developer that surprisingly decided to get involved in constructing low-income housing. Indeed, as argued by many others, it is misleading to conceive of formality and informality as two separate and independent modes of practice (Peattie, 1987). On the contrary, the Parshwanath Group's operations overlapped and comprised of both formal and informal practices. Moreover, I believe that most developers in developing countries, marketing to the low and modest-income segments, are likely to incorporate such overlaps of formal and informal practices. My research suggests that market-based enabling can seriously jeopardize the performance of these entrepreneurs by impacting the behavior of both the consumers and the developers.

Some of the residents filed a lawsuit against the developer and stopped their loan repayments. They claim that the Parshwanath Group was dishonest with them. It had promised a higher quality of housing but their homes were not up to the mark. They argue that the developer's marketing was fraudulently misleading. The litigants claim that they expected fixtures and fittings in their homes but the developer provided none. The streetlights, trees, green spaces were also inadequate and less than promised. In addition, the developer had promised that the bus-service would be extended from Krishnanagar to the township (approximately, a fifteen minute walk) but this did not happen, and the residents claimed that the group was deliberately lying. Moreover, the residents also argued that the quality of construction of their homes was substandard: there were cracks in their walls and seepage in the ceilings.

My own observations, however, suggest that the quality of construction and amenities at the township were similar, or even superior, to the earlier projects of the Parshwanath Group. But why were the residents more dissatisfied? One possibility is that the homebuyers' expectations had changed. They might have, because of HUDCO's involvement and financial support, expected better quality from the group. In other words, the exaggerations in advertising and the shortcomings in quality that prior buyers of the group's housing found acceptable, almost like an informal understanding, were no longer tolerable for the buyers at the Parshwanath Township. Another possibility is that the township's homebuyers were being opportunistic. The developer claims that the homebuyers knew exactly what to expect but they were taking undue advantage of opportunities within the legal framework, including new consumer protection laws.

In the Parshwanath Group's earlier projects, the developer had a very different institutional arrangement for loan recovery. The developer would obtain post-dated checks in advance from the mortgagors, and simply cash them according to the pre-arranged, repayment schedules. Occasionally the checks would bounce because of insufficient funds in the bank accounts. In such cases, typically, the developer would give the borrower a month's notice to pay with a penalty. If that did not work, the group would use strong-arm and illegal tactics to forcibly foreclose on the property and repossess the house. Such intimidatory options, however, were not available at the Parshwanath Township, a formal project with public involvement. Formalization had adversely impacted some of the developer's flexibility.

But the magnitude of the mortgage defaults appears relatively small. Moreover, because of HUDCO's refinancing of its mortgages, the Parshwanath Group's financial exposure was limited. Yet the group abandoned its original plans to develop a mixed income township with almost 7,000 households. The group decided to sell-off almost 60% of the land. Apparently, the public involvement had negated some of its incentives to develop low-income housing. In the group's earlier developments, the developer did not obtain all the required land development permits, including the No Objection Certificates (NOCs) from the competent authority. The developer saved time and money by not applying for all the necessary permits. In particular, the process of getting the NOC is lengthy, tedious, and can be expensive (because of bribes and other unofficial charges). As a consequence, however, all its previous developments were not entirely legal, and were less attractive to middle and upper-middle class buyers, who were more concerned about legality. The more affluent buyers needed the complete paperwork to successfully access loans from some of the limited, formal sources of mortgage finance, including loans from their retirement, or provident, funds. In the Parshwanath Township, however, HUDCO insisted that the developer acquire the necessary permits. But once the group had all the required permissions, and the earlier phases of the township had established the locational value of its land, the developer abandoned the intention to develop low-income housing. Instead, the developer was opportunistic (or entrepreneurial) and, middle and higher-income housing was built on the remaining pockets of land. Even HUDCO, concerned about its cost recovery, may have condoned the intention of the Parshwanath Group to transfer its landownership for the undeveloped parcels of the township.

Nonetheless, the four brothers are still professionally active and are developing more homes but now they focus exclusively on housing for middle and higher-income groups.[9] Their experience suggests the need for caution in public support for private developers. The case study demonstrates that public enabling can have adverse and unforeseen consequences by impacting the homebuyers' expectations and opportunities, as well as the developers' operational flexibility and market incentives.

5. Conclusion

So what policy conclusions can we draw from the Parshwanath Township case? Does the enabling policy work or not? Should governments be more involved in housing delivery or is the prevailing emphasis on markets and market actors productive and positive? Are markets likely to succeed in delivering decent affordable housing to low-income groups or not? Etc. It is difficult to answer such questions with this single case, as the evidence is insufficient to assess and make a compelling argument. Nonetheless, the episode does not lend itself to optimism for the success of market-based, enabling approaches. A key objective of the paper was to throw into relief the enthusiasm for enabling markets and provide an empirical account of the potentially adverse impacts. In the case study, the public sector enabled a private developer with a track record of developing affordable housing, but soon afterwards, the developer stopped constructing housing for the low and modest-income groups. Public policy must be open to the possibility that there may be an inherent contradiction between conventional and formal market processes, and the provision of decent housing for low-income groups; even though this recognition makes the task much more difficult for policymakers, and much more challenging for urban policy researchers.

The events in the case indicate the need for a more cautious, circumspect, and varied policy approach as market-driven, enabling strategies focused on market actors can produce highly uncertain outcomes. Because of the imprecise outcomes, planners and policymakers need to be cautious. They should not rush the pace of implementing enabling policies but should rather go slow and privilege a guarded approach. Policymakers need to base evolving enabling policies on experience and evidence. A circumspect approach that involves evaluation of prior policies, pilot projects, "learning by doing," and robust research may help ensure better chances of success. Most important of all, however, is for policymakers to consider a more varied approach that also takes into account enabling and policy support for non-market actors. In addition to support for non-profits and non-governmental organizations (NGOs), there is a need for direct assistance to community groups, cooperatives, and even public agencies and enterprises. Put another way, perhaps it is necessary and beneficial to conceptualize "enabling" differently, and in place of the conventional approach of market-driven and government-assisted policies, there is an opportunity for government-driven and market-assisted approaches.

The main expositional focus of this case study, however, is not on whether to enable markets or not, but on how to enable market actors. Moreover, the focus is not on long-term institutional development for enabling but on short-term and interim strategies that can prepare the groundwork for regulatory reform and more robust policies. As I suggested in the introductory session, housing scholars propose at least two short-term and alternative avenues. First, they suggest direct enabling of market actors through public-private partnerships (Payne, 1999; Pugh, 1994; 1997), and second they recommend policy support, including public-private partnerships, for informal actors (Ahmed, 1999; Durand-Lasserve, 1999; Keivani and Werna, 2001a). In some ways, the case study is an illustration of both these approaches. But the case suggests that neither of these alternatives is easy, nor do they completely eliminate the potential of unforeseen and contradictory outcomes. Instead, the case emphasizes the possibility of such market-driven enabling strategies leading to uncertain outcomes, and that enabling can be even trickier with the informal sector.

Although the conventional wisdom suggests that regulatory barriers are the key issue in enabling the informal sector, the case suggests a richer and more complex story. Of course, enabling and public participation are likely to have an impact on the regulations in terms of higher standards because of the traditional planning and policy concerns of health, welfare and safety. Such upgrading of standards, unless offset by financial support or other benefits, may adversely impact the operations of informal developers. In this manner, public enabling may reduce the flexibility and ability of developers to produce low-cost housing. In the Parshwanath Township case the public agency made the developer reduce its density norms for the township and consequently reduced its potential profit margins. Supporters of conventional enabling predict such outcomes, and, therefore, they argue that the removal of regulatory barriers, or the acceptance of lower standards, will benefit both formal and informal developers of housing.

They, however, do not emphasize how public enabling may also adversely impact informal institutions and practices. In the case study, the developer used to collect loan repayments through pre-dated checks and the use of force. Post-enabling, such practices were illegal and untenable. I do not believe that we can excuse such heavy-handed procedures and methods, yet policymakers must acknowledge and understand that these practices were crucial features, and their elimination adversely impacts the informal developers' flexibility and opportunities of success. In addition, the conventional wisdom underplays the unpredictable impact of enabling on developers' incentives to continue producing affordable housing. It ignores the possibility of enabled informal developers, once accustomed to the more formal processes, moving up-market—as in the case of the Patel brothers—because of the larger profit margins and the greater social prestige. Furthermore, the enabling process can also have an adverse and capricious impact on the homebuyers' expectations—they may expect higher quality and standards—and their possibilities for opportunism, through enhanced access to legal and formal avenues of recourse. Thus, the case study illustrates that enabling informal sector developers can be extremely difficult and tricky because public involvement and support can reduce their flexibility and incentives, as well as impact the expectations and opportunities of the homebuyers.

Moreover, in the field of affordable housing production in developing countries, formality and informality are likely to overlap. It is prudent to expect most formal developers of low-income housing, like the Parshwanath Group in the case study, to employ some informal practices. The case study suggests a need for more sophisticated policy and robust research. Working with informal developers will require a tricky balance of regulation and deregulation. In the case study, the public agency may have achieved better success if it had deregulated its housing standards and norms—reduced the density restrictions that it imposed on the developer—and regulated the developer's ability to transfer the landownership—ensured that the group was unable to sell the land and abandon its commitment to develop affordable housing. Instead, the agency increased the density standards but failed to regulate the land transfers. To achieve success and avoid unintended outcomes, policymakers will need to get accustomed to appropriately balancing such paradoxical policy demands of regulation and deregulation.

They are likely to need the support of studies that help to reveal the nature and magnitude of the overlaps between the formal and informal sectors. Such research will help provide planners and policymakers with a more grounded knowledge of how market processes and market actors operate, and how best to support them. In addition to empirical studies, pilot projects, like the Parshwanath Township, may also be an avenue for developing our knowledge base. From a public policy perspective, the case also emphasizes Alain Durand-Lasserve's suggestion that to enable the informal sector, the best strategy may not be the direct support for informal developers, but for public agencies to accept informal and customary land tenure systems within their planning and regulatory frameworks (1999). Public agencies can also leverage the skills of informal actors, such as brokers, in publicly assisted projects. This suggestion, however, assumes that the government can be more directly involved in developing affordable housing.

Finally, and most important of all, the case is a cautionary tale for all development planners and policymaker. It emphasizes that they must be open to the possibility of things going wrong, and get better at predicting the outcomes of their projects, plans and policies. One avenue for improvement may be for development practitioners to rigorously and consistently consider the probability of self-interest oriented, even opportunistic, behavior by all stakeholders. They should expect that private developers would be interested in moving up-market because of the higher profitability, additional prestige and the perception of lesser hassles and headaches. They should also anticipate that homebuyers would protest against poor housing quality and would consider lawsuits if possible, whether they are merited or not. They should also expect that public agencies would be interested in cost-recovery in public-private partnerships, especially when faced with political pressure for better financial performance. Development planning cannot be based on naïve optimism: neither in the case of homebuyers, nor public agencies, nor, perhaps least of all, market actors.

NOTES

1. Like the World Bank, the United Nations (Habitat/UNCHS) has declared its faith in enabling strategies for private markets as the primary housing delivery mechanism. However, some scholars argue that, in contrast to the Bank, the United Nations (UNCHS, 1996) is more ready to recognize the problem of affordability, and emphasizes a role for community groups, NGOs and women as the main actors (Keivani and Werna, 2001a).
2. According to the World Bank, India's Urban Land Ceiling (and Regulation) Act of 1976 (ULCA) was a paradigmatic case of bad practice that hindered the market (1993, 29). The Indian government introduced ULCA to reduce land speculation and inequity in urban land ownership. It imposed a ceiling on the amount of vacant land that any individual could own. The excess land was to be acquired by the government and redistributed to the urban poor. Critics, however, argued that the ULCA effectively froze the urban land market as property owners locked-up their excess land in litigation. As a part of its enabling measures, the Government of India repealed the act in 1999 (*Times of India*, 1999).

Housing and real estate practitioners are still waiting to see what impact the repeal will have on the housing market (Business India, 2002).

3. The city is India's seventh largest city and has a rich history of industrial development. It is famous for its textile industry and was known as the Manchester of India. In the late 1970s and the 1980s, however, the textile industry suffered a decline. But there are still a number of active textile mills, mostly in east Ahmedabad.
4. According to one estimate, there were around three hundred private developers active in the city and almost all focused on developing housing for higher income groups (Joshi, 1995).
5. The PG recorded the transfer of building materials from their production units to their construction units as interdepartmental transfers and paid no sales tax on the transfers. However, subsequent changes in public policy brought such transfers under the sales tax net and negated some of the advantage of the vertical integration strategy.
6. Instead of tarred roads the PG used red brick powder, which was a waste material from their brick kilns, to surface the roads in their developments.
7. Developers operating under the cooperative umbrella to access finance from the GCHFC used the credit facility available through the Cooperative Societies Act, 1961, but this tradition was illegal (Wadhva, 1989). The facility was designed for members of housing cooperatives to borrow directly from. In practice, however, most of the borrowing was by private developers claiming to represent members of cooperatives. Although the GCHFC was supposed to get the loan repayments directly from the cooperatives, most of the developers would collect the money and make the repayments, and continue to borrow from the GCHFC.
8. HUDCO agreed to provide construction finance for three years at a 15 per cent per annum rate. The funding was based on a 2 : 1, debt-equity ratio, requirement (USAID, 1991).
9. The Parshwanath Group blames the litigation experience in the Parshwanath Township as its key reason for staying away from developing more affordable housing. Another reason may be the higher land costs in the city. Meera and Dinesh Mehta have argued that the introduction of the ULCA (see note 2) in Ahmedabad increased the supply of land in the short-term as many landowners sold their land to private developers (1989, 55). Consequently, many developers, like the Parshwanath Group, had access to relatively, affordable land through the late seventies and early eighties. Subsequently, however, land supply became tight.

REFERENCES

Amis, P. (1984) Squatters or Tenants: The Commercialization of Unauthorized Housing in Nairobi, *World Development*, 12, 87-96.

Adusumilli, U. (1999) Partnership approaches in India, in G. Payne (Ed.) *Making Common Ground: Public-Private Partnerships in Land for Housing*, 17-45, London: Intermediate Technology Publications.

Ahmed, N. (1999) Public/Private partnerships in Pakistan, in G. Payne (Ed.) *Making Common Ground: Public-Private Partnerships in Land for Housing*, 46-63, London: Intermediate Technology Publications.

Baken, R. and Smets, P. (1999) Better a hut on the ground than a castle in the air: formal and informal housing finance for the urban poor in India, in K. Datta and G. Jones (Eds.) *Housing and Finance in Developing Countries*, 101-18, London; New York: Routledge.

Baken, R. and van der Linden, J. (1993) Getting the Incentives Right, *Third World Planning Review*, 15, 1-22.

Bhatnagar, K. (1996) HUDCO—An innovative public sector undertaking, in K. Singh and F. Steinberg (Eds.) *Urban India in Crisis*, 49-57, New Delhi: New Age International Publishers.

Blaesser, B. (1981) *Clandestine Development in Colombia*. Report prepared for the United States Agency for International Development, Washington, DC: USAID.

Business India (2002) Real Potential, *Business India*, August 19—September 1, 42-48.

Doebele, W. (1975) *The Private Market and Low-income Urbanization in Developing Countries: The Pirate Subdivisions of Bogota*, Discussion Paper No. D75-1, Cambridge: Harvard University, Department of City and Regional Planning.

Dowall, D. (1989) Bangkok: A Profile of an Efficiently Performing Housing Market, *Urban Studies*, 26, 327-39.

Durand-Lasserve, A. (1987) Land and Housing in Third World Cities, *Cities*, 4, 325-36.

Durand-Lasserve, A. (1999) Partnerships between public sector and informal actors: Some comments on Asian and sub-Saharan African case studies, in G. Payne (Ed.) *Making Common Ground: Public-Private Partnerships in Land for Housing*, 134-52, London: Intermediate Technology Publications.

Gilbert, A. (2002) Power, Ideology and the Washington Consensus: The Development and Spread of the Chilean Housing Policy, *Housing Studies*, 17, 305-24.

Government of India (1994) *National Housing Policy*, New Delhi: Ministry of Urban Development, Government of India.

Hamdi, N. (1991) *Housing Without Houses: Participation, Flexibility, Enablement*, New York: Van Nostrand Reinhold.

Jones, G. (1996) The Difference Between Truth and Adequacy: (Re)joining Baken, van der Linden and Malpezzi, *Third World Planning Review*, 18, 243-56.

Jones, G. and Datta, K. (2000) Enabling Markets to Work? Housing Policy in the 'New' South Africa, *International Planning Studies*, 5, 393-416.

Jones, G. and Ward, P. (1995) The Blind Men and the Elephant: A Critic's Reply, *Habitat International*, 19, 61-72.

Joshi, S. (1995) *Urban Housing by Private Builders*, Postgraduate diploma in planning, dissertation, Ahmedabad: Centre for Environmental Planning and Technology.

Keivani, R. and Werna, E. (2001a) Refocusing the Housing Debate in Developing Countries from a Pluralist Perspective, *Habitat International*, 25, 191-208.

Keivani, R. and Werna, E. (2001b) Modes of Housing Provision in Developing Countries, *Progress in Planning*, 55, 65-118.

Kusnetzoff, F. (1987) Urban and Housing Policies under Chile's Military Dictatorship: 1973-1985, *Latin American Perspectives*, 14, 157-86.

Linn, J. (1983) *Cities in the Developing World*, Oxford: Oxford University Press.

Malpezzi, S. (1990) Urban Housing and Financial Markets: Some International Comparisons, *Urban Studies*, 27, 971-1022.

Malpezzi, S. (1994) Getting the Incentives Right—A Reply to Robert-Jan. Baken and Jan van der Linden, *Third World Planning Review*, 16, 451-66.

Marcuse, P. (2001) The Liberal/Conservative Divide in the History of Housing Policy in the United States, *Housing Studies*, 16, 717-36.

Mayo, S., Malpezzi, S. and Cross, D. (1986) Shelter Strategies for the Urban Poor in Developing Countries, *World Bank Research Observer*, 2, 183-203.

Mehta, M. and Mehta, D. (1989) *Metropolitan Housing Market: A Study of Ahmedabad*, New Delhi: Sage.

Mohan, R. (1994) *Understanding the Developing Metropolis: Lessons from the City Study of Bogota and Cali, Colombia*, New York: Oxford University Press.

Mukhija, V. (2001) Enabling Slum Redevelopment in Mumbai: Policy Paradox in Practice, *Housing Studies*, 16, 791-806.

Payne, G. (1982) Self-help housing: A critique of the Gecekondus of Ankara, in P. Ward (Ed.) *Self-help Housing: A Critique*, 117-40, London: Mansell Publishing Company.

Payne, G. (1999) *Making Common Ground: Public-Private Partnerships in Land for Housing*, London: Intermediate Technology Publications.

Peattie, L. (1987) An Idea in Good Currency and How It Grew: The Informal Sector, *World Development*, 15, 851-60.

Perlman, J. (1976) *The Myth of Marginality: Urban Poverty and Politics in Rio de Janeiro*, Berkeley: University of California Press.

Pugh, C. (1994) The Idea of Enablement in Housing Sector Development: The Political Economy of Housing for Developing Countries, *Cities*, 11, 357-71.

Pugh, C. (1997) International Urban and Housing Policy: A Review of the 'Cambridge Studies', 1989-95, *Environment and Planning A*, 29, 149-67.

Quigley, J. (1999) Why Should the Government Play a Role in Housing? *Housing, Theory and Society*, 16, 201-03.

Sanyal, B. (1996) Intention and Outcome: Formalization and its Consequences, *Regional Development Dialogue*, 17, 161-78.

Siddiqui, T. and Khan, M. (1994) The Incremental Development Scheme, *Third World Planning Review*, 16, 277-91.

Siembieda, W. and Moreno, E. (1997) Expanding Housing Choices for the Sector Popular: Strategies for Mexico, *Housing Policy Debate*, 8, 651-77.

Strassman, P. (1994) Oversimplification in Housing Analysis, *Cities*, 11, 377-83.

Times of India (1999) Urban Land Ceiling Act Repealed, *Times of India*, January 12.

Turner, J. (1972) Housing as a verb, in J. Turner and R. Fichter (Eds.) *Freedom to Build: Dweller Control of the Housing Process*, 148-75, New York: The Macmillan Company.

Turner, J. (1977) *Housing by People: Towards Autonomy in Building Environments*, New York: Pantheon Books.

Unchs (1990) *Global Strategy for Shelter to the Year 2000*, Nairobi: UNCHS.

Unchs (1996) *The Istanbul Declaration and Habitat II Agenda*, Istanbul: UNCHS.

Usaid (1991) *India: Private/Public Partnership in Land Development*, prepared by Lee Baker, PADCO (Planning and Development Collaborative International) for the U.S. Agency for International Development (USAID), Washington, DC: USAID.

Wadhva, K. (1986) Role of Private Sector in Urban Housing Markets: A Case Study of Ahmedabad, *Nagarlok*, 18(3), 61-83.

Wadhva, K. (1987) Housing the Urban Poor: What Can the Private Sector Do? *Urban India*, 7(2), 89-101.

Wadhva, K. (1989) *Role of Private Sector in Urban Housing: Case Study of Ahmedabad*, New Delhi: Human Settlement Management Institute (HSMI).

World Bank (1991) *Urban Policy and Economic Development: An Agenda for the 1990s*, Washington, DC: The World Bank.

World Bank (1993) *Housing: Enabling Markets to Work, A World Bank Policy Paper*, Washington, DC: The World Bank.

World Bank (2000) *Entering the 21st Century, World Development Report 1999-2000*, Washington, DC: The World Bank.

Zearley, T. (1993) Creating an Enabling Environment for Housing: Recent Reforms in Mexico, *Housing Policy Debate*, 4, 239-49.

5

Urban Governance and the Environment: An Irish Case Study

MICHAEL MURRAY
michael.j.murray@MAY.IE
National Institute for Regional and Spatial Analysis, Ireland.

G. HONOR FAGAN
honor.fagan@may.ie
National Institute for Regional and Spatial Analysis, Ireland.

EXECUTIVE SUMMARY

The new problematic of urban governance is finding dramatic manifestation in the issue of urban waste management. Popular resistance to the siting of waste incinerators in Ireland is leading to a grave legitimacy crisis for the government. The nation-state is caught in a crisis due to popular opposition to the plans and the need to meet more stringent European Union (EU) guidelines on sustainable waste management and recycling.

Key words: Ireland, Dublin, waste, incinerators, protest, globalisation.

The new problematic of urban governance finds particularly dramatic expression around environmental issues that are, in a sense, non-negotiable. This chapter explores the general comparative issues arising in relation to urban environmental governance through a particular Irish case study. The particular issue was/is the siting of a waste incinerator in a working class suburb of Dublin and the popular campaign of resistance against it that emerged. Since then the Irish government has simply abolished the local level of government in relation to urban waste management and the politics of waste has become a sharply divisive issue. What we will do here is outline first the main parameters of the 'waste crisis' in Ireland and then examine how its governance was approached in the late 1990's. We then turn to a case study of a particular local urban campaign against incineration and its subsequent generalisation as waste became the main battle-ground in the contested terrain of urban governance in Ireland. Finally, some general implications of this study are drawn out

Urban Waste Governance

The contemporary city is increasingly subject to a regime of governance (Massey *et al.*, 1999). The recent debates on governance make it clear that it is the changing forms and functions of the state that have brought to the fore new forms of governance. Neo-liberalism has, as we know, at the core of its project the need to force a state 'retreat' from its traditional social and economic functions. But the market that the neo-liberalists push in its stead cannot run cities on its own. Governance thus became a political catchword in the 1990's for a form of government without the state, at least in principle. It rested in part on the 'managerial revolution' brought about in public service delivery by the 'new public management' approach in most Western countries. Governance seeks to deal with the increasing social economic complexity of these societies in a more 'flexible' way than the traditional state. Above all we need to conceive of governance as a new process rather than an institution. As Pierre and Peter's put it "The conception of governance as 'steering' is at the heart of much of the current research in governance in different sub-fields of political science" (Pierre and Peters, 2000: 231). So what does the 'governance' of urban waste imply in practice?

In Europe the process of governance is set within the parameters of the European Union (EU) and its 'directives' on particular issues. Since the Earth Summit of Rio in 1992 and the Kyoto Agreement of 1998 there has been increased attention to environmental concerns such as the global warming, pollution and waste management. Within the EU the Environmental Commission has been strengthening its ability to regulate the environmental policies of member-states. Its aim is to achieve sustainable governance of waste and to integrate environmental priorities to all other areas. The Commission sees the amount of waste we produce and the way we dispose of it as key indicators of a country's progress towards sustainable development. Disposal of waste through landfill or incineration is not seen as desirable in Europe's heavily urbanised societies. Instead the emphasis is placed on the reduction and then recycling of waste. The stated aim of the EU is not only to achieve greater resource-efficiency in production and consumption but to create cleaner cities with a healthy lifestyle as part of a broader commitment to sustainable global governance.

The EU has built up a vast panoply of legislation around waste management and its implementation, this through 'Directives' on specific issues that member-states must implement although on how and when there is some discretion. The purpose of the Directives is to harmonise legislation and standards between nation-states and they are a good example of the regional moment of governance in the era of globalisation. Among a long list of Directives there are regulations on dangerous substances, waste oils, ground water, urban waste water, toxic waste and the disposal of animal waste. It was the 'foot and mouth' crisis in Ireland in 2001 (Tovey, 2002) that focused attention the country's waste problem as the reality of having to dispose of more than 350,000 cattle carcasses caused logistical as well as political problems. These carcasses could not be disposed of to landfill (these were full and EU regulations would not allow it), they could not be exported and Ireland did not possess the necessary incineration option facilities.

Each European nation-state has to carry out a 'translation' of EU policy into its own particular circumstances and 'marry' it to national legislation. Ireland began to comply with EU policy with the 1996 Act that incorporated the EU 'waste hierarchy' into Irish law. It set out regulatory powers for the Minister of the Environment in relation to the prevention, minimisation and recovery/recycling of waste. It also committed Ireland to creating a 'comprehensive and modern' regulatory framework to achieve higher environmental standards. While it was hoped that the 'private sector' would contribute to and benefit from waste management in practice state regulation (especially through the Environmental Protection Agency) was crucial to the development of an integrated waste management strategy. This shows clearly to what extent the 'market' cannot do certain things, contrary to neo-liberal fundamentalist beliefs. In relation to public participation in the waste management process the act called for 'a formal procedure for public consultation and input to national and local waste management plans' (Department of the Environment and Local Government, 1998: 4). Public consultation was also to be a central feature in relation to the granting of licences for running waste facilities such as incinerators.

Ireland subsequently was always lagging in terms of compliance with EU Directives and targets on waste management and recycling. The European context was a constant driver of the Irish State's environmental policies but it also provided an opportunity for environmental activists. Thus one environmental scientist we interviewed argued that:

> In the old days what drove waste management was very simply, cost. Every local authority wanted the cheapest possible solution to dump waste. That's why they bought the cheapest land in the most convenient place near the town. Then waste management began to be driven more and more by the EU. The EU demanded that we manage our landfill sites better, demanded an end to pollution.... I think that, at the moment, what's pushing waste management decisions is to some extent the EU are pushing Ireland. (Murray, 2003: 160)

There is a widespread perception that European waste management policies are more firmly based on principles of sustainability and that the Irish state has simply gone from burying waste in the ground (landfills) to the least good option incinerators that have an even worse health impact on urban dwellers.

A key element in both the EU and the Irish government's waste policy is to increase the participation of the private sector in its management by seeking to make it profitable (Fagan *et al.*, 1999). Where as once capitalist firms conceived of the environment as a cost free waste disposal facility they now have to view sustainable development as a business opportunity. The EU legislation focuses as much on 'market mechanisms' and the need for profitability as it does on sustainability. Robin Murray has gone furthest in analysing the economic potential of waste management no longer viewed as 'a cost and an economic drain on economic resources—but, rather, as 'a source of innovation' (Murray 1999: 22). In practice, however, it is not the community that is benefiting from the creative potential of recycling and innovative waste management but, rather, big business. That is because, apart from anything else, waste management infrastructure requires massive investment. With a medium-sized incinerator costing some two hundred million euros and a typical waste management contract running for over twenty years it is not surprising that multinationals like the Belgian Corporation Indaver dominate the Irish market as elsewhere.

The governance of urban waste has ultimately to deal with the location of its 'facilities', the landfills, incinerators or recycling plants. That is where the environment becomes more clearly situated in the domain of power and contestation. Invariably it is poorer or less powerful urban communities and localities that are chosen as the site for these often harmful waste apparatuses. Maher found that the location of toxic waste facilities in the US had a clear racial/class pattern:

> A part of the unwritten public policy concerning toxics seems to have been that you dump in someone else's backyard—but not anyone's backyard. Toxic waste facilities have been regularly located in areas populated by African Americans, Latinos, Native Americans, or Asian Americans. Environmental racism is a very insidious form of discrimination, sometimes destroying whole communities, other times harming people in ways that will not appear for decades (*i.e.* cancer). (Maher, 1998: 357-58)

For the governance of urban waste these are deemed 'sacrifice zones' to be doomed for the general good. In Ireland, our case study focuses on a class based 'sacrifice zone', namely the traditional working class suburb of Ringsend (Popular Resistance below). The focus on the social aspects of environmental policy and conflict is, one must say, somewhat neglected in sociology of the environment literature (Spaargarten *et al.*, 2000 and Andworth, 2003 for example) and this contribution could be seen as a useful supplement or corrective.

The Waste Crisis

In the mid-1990's the Republic of Ireland found itself in the midst of a genuine waste crisis (Fagan, 2003). It lacked the infrastructure and the policy to deal with the increasing waste created by the economic boom of the 1990's. It was not only a material crisis, but also a political crisis insofar as Ireland was simply unable to meet EU regulations in waste management within a sustainable environmental philosophy and practice. Following a belated recognition of the growing material waste problem by environmental authorities in the late 1990's (Dempsey, 1998) seven regional waste plans were developed across the Republic. The aim of the plans was to reduce the 90 per cent of waste going to landfill and to increase recycling from 8 per cent to 35 per cent over a 15-year period, so as to meet the targets set by the EU. Crucially, at the heart of the new strategy was a set of six large incinerators in Dublin, the South-East, Galway, Limerick, the Midlands and the North-East. It was this turn towards incineration as a favoured waste 'management' strategy that was to politicise the waste issue in the towns and villages near where they were to be sited.

The Irish government's policy statement on waste Changing Our Ways had called for 'constructive cooperation with local communities and neighbouring local authorities' (Dempsey, 1998: 7) in developing a 'new' approach to waste management planning. For the waste management strategy to work it was necessary to have, argued the Minister of the Environment, 'effective public consultation and participation' (Dempsey, 1998: 7). And yet even at that preparatory stage, the Minister acknowledged that new waste initiatives are usually met with 'vigorous local opposition' (Dempsey, 1998: 19). Certainly knowledge about the health impact of incinerators was widespread and ecological disasters from Sevesco to Bhopal, from Chernobyl to the Love Canal incident in the US were still fresh in the popular consciousness. So the Irish government was caught in a dilemma, with pressure from the

EU mounting for a 'practical' solution to the growing waste problem, and pressure from local urban communities to not go down the incinerator route.

To square the circle the government proposed to adopt a 'policy of transparency' in regards to waste management planning, in keeping with the language and ethos of good governance. To combat public opposition to new waste initiatives the government proposed a vigorous programme of 'public education'. Careful site selection was also advocated presumably to avoid locations where public opposition was predictable and likely to generate wider social or political support. Now 'public education' by the government on the relative safety of modern incineration methods was simply not effective compared to the information provided by environmental groups and scientists, often backed up by the international information and campaigning networks. Transparency was not something that in practice worked because public hearings generated public opposition and if this opposition was then ignored it deepened the feeling of resentment. In fact as the original feasibility study for the Dublin region waste plan acknowledges, 'public opposition is likely to develop...once a site has been identified'. The politics of place come into play and communities were galvanised into action.

Public opposition to the government's waste plans was concentrated around the issue of the regional incinerators and 'super-dumps'. There was also, particularly in the Dublin city area, growing community opposition to waste charges, through which the government sought to defray some of the costs of meeting EU targets. By the end of 2000 there were at least 15 different waste and anti-dump groups campaigning in Ireland; with over 20 co-existing in 2001 to oppose the government's Waste Management Act (see below). In Cork City a recognised 'waste disposal crisis' emerged early as local opposition to a regional 'super-dump' sharpened. The existing waste dump was already two years past its recommended lifespan and the new 250 acre site designated for its replacement was fiercely opposed by the local urban and rural communities. Increasingly it seemed that the government's waste plans would have to be postponed with the prospect of Ireland facing legal action by the EU for failure to comply with the Waste Management Directives.

Inevitably the waste issue, and controversy around it, would feed into party politics. Before the 2002 Irish general election waste was, on the whole, avoided or ignored by political parties. However, during the election campaign—mainly due to lobbying and protesting by local anti-incinerator movements—the issue of waste management came to the fore. The ruling Fianna Fáil party in its policy document Blueprint for a Cleaner Ireland had, perhaps wisely, not mentioned incinerators at all. The small conservative Progressive Democrats (part of the ruling coalition party) unashamedly backed incineration. On the other hand, Labour, the republicans in Sinn Féin and the Green Party all strenuously opposed incinerators. More surprisingly the conservative opposition party Fine Gael adopted a zero-waste policy and absolutely ruled out the use of incineration. Its spokesperson Deirdre Clune declared that: 'Public concerns regarding incineration are based on real fears relating to dioxins and particulate matter emissions' (*Irish Times*, 3-4-02). Thus waste management came to be a dividing and divisive issue in Irish party politics as well as within society at large.

While the crisis of legitimacy around the waste issue deepened as a material crisis it also needed to be resolved. In 2002 the government faced a year of court actions brought by the EU's Environment Commission around a number of environmental issues, including waste management. Increasing waste, decreasing numbers of landfill sites, inadequate recycling infrastructures and local opposition to incineration and 'super-dumps' meant that Ireland was 'on the brink of its biggest ever environmental problem' (*Sunday Tribune*, 30-01-00). The government responded to this crisis in a report by Forfás (a national policy and advisory board for enterprise, trade science, technology and innovation) that advocated setting up a National Waste Authority (Forfás, 2001: 10) to deal with the crisis. In the meantime it advocated a bland 'building of consensus' through a process of 'consultation' with communities affected by the waste management plans. Recognising that 'progress on waste management is now becoming most critical' (Forfás, 2001: iii) it argued somewhat optimistically that the primary public need was for more 'information' and called for an 'expert' information group to be set up.

The waste crisis in Ireland has generated a new urban politics that we examine in the next section. We need to understand cities such as Dublin and Cork as contested terrains of trans-national flows and struggles. They must be seen as trans-national sites as much as London or New York in the sense that they are 'a disjointed terrain of global media flows...state-centred actors that side with and oppose global actors, local and global growth machines and green movements, multi-locational entrepreneurs and multilateral political institutions, all colluding and colliding with each other *ad infinitum* (Smith, 2001: 70-71). All these intersecting and interweaving trans-national (EU), national and local flows and practices go to make up the complex waste crisis affecting Ireland's cities. The urban future is far less certain in this trans-national decentred scenario than it was in the past. What is certain is that—against any structuralist interpretation—the issue of human agency is crucial as we shall now see.

Popular Resistance

Waste is a global and national problem for sustainable development but popular resistance to government waste strategies tends to invariably be local. As Amis and Thrift put it: 'The result is a new localism that is full of policy promise.... There are new powers to be had from building local community' (Amis and Thrift, 2002: 55). It is now widely accepted that global domination produces local resistance. However, people in these local communities make sense of their world fully cognizant of the global, macro-regional and national terrain of debate. In relation to waste we found in our study that local residents were well aware of issues such as 'global warming', were completely 'tuned in' to European debates on sustainable waste management and engage fully with the national debates on a waste management strategy (Fagan *et al.,* 2001). That means we must reject a conception of place 'understood as the site of cohesive community formations existing outside the logic of globalisation' (Smith, 2001: 106). The local of our case study—Ringsend Community in Dublin—

is thus situated within complex global flows of power, information and identity formation.

There was a hidden history of popular protest against the siting of waste facilities going back to the mid-1970's (Allen and Jones, 1990). At that time there had been a number of community protests against toxic waste facilities especially in the Cork area. There had been a community campaign against a proposed toxic waste dump at Finglas in County Dublin in the late 1970's. At that time economic development held undisputed sway in the national consciousness and the protesters were easily isolated. A united front of the stare, the employers, local elites, the trade unions and even 'public opinion' served to thwart any protest on the 'downside' of intensive industrialisation. Two things were different by the late 1990's. For one a sustained economic boom had made Ireland a 'comfortable' country and the imperative of economic growth was no longer urgent. And yet by then many people—lower down in the social scale—had not received many benefits from the 'Celtic Tiger'. The other main shift in the 20 intervening years was the blossoming of the international environmental movement (Mc Cormack, 1995) and the emergence of a widespread popular and even governmental consensus that sustainable development was a *sine qua non* of human progress.

When the Irish government decided in 1999 (?) to set up its major regional incinerators at Poolbeg in the Ringsend district of Dublin to burn most of the city's commercial and domestic refuse it was clearly going to be met with local opposition. Even the planning report had acknowledged 'perceptions' of risk to health and the environment, if not the reality of this risk attendant on the construction of a large waste incinerator. There was even an admission of 'lack of trust' in the regulatory agencies to monitor and control emissions. The local community should, it was recommended, not only be 'consulted', but engaged in an interactive relationship designed to result in consensus. Presumably the intention was to isolate those who it was perceived would habitually oppose the government's waste disposal solutions such as the Green Party. Yet local reaction was scathing. As one resident declared:

> Sure the whole waste management plan is done with the minimum of everything, the minimum of costs, the minimum of standards, everything is minimum, minimum this, minimum that, that's how bad we are, everything is done to minimum standards....I mean, everything in this country is done by industry and big business and it has nothing to do with communities, it has nothing to do with governance. It has to do with who's paying the piper and who's putting what money into what party...simple as that. I mean the whole system's goddamn corrupt and I have no hesitation in saying that whatsoever.

On the basis of this generalised mistrust of the authorities opposition mounted at every step of the way, even (or even increasingly) when the government sought to engage in 'consultation' exercises. Thus in early 2003 when Dublin City Council held an 'Open Day' in Ringsend in order to outline its plans for the incinerator, the event was picketed by members of the local community. At the same time the anti-incineration group announced that it would be taking the fight to the European Union level. Dublin City Council have no intention of backing off from their plan to set up a massive incinerator at Poolbeg but, its attempts to generate 'consensus' have failed abysmally. Nor was the announced policy of 'transparency' and sharing of 'information' what the residents perceived. For them:

> ...we're classed as an underprivileged area, so I mean, who are we? Like they'll put an incinerator in...this is 'sure, they wont mind', who are we? We're just living here, we have no say whatsoever and I mean, I've said this to people who represent us, they don't bring you up to date with what's happening in your area unless you get out and do it yourself.

This view was also held by another resident, who felt that officials only imparted the information or knowledge that they judged to be appropriate:

> Anytime I've tried to acquire information, I've felt dismissed a little bit, or felt you asked a question that you're too big in your boots. And, it wouldn't be

> a personal thing, but I just felt that they would give you the information that they wanted to give you and you don't ask any questions.

Another complained about the production of unequal power relationship by officials in their interactions with them:

> ...they consistently talk down to you to the point where they can be quite insulting and degrading, even in their attitude to you. And the whole attitude is 'we know what's good for you, do what you're told'.... You're not treated as an equal, and that's from past experience, whether you're talking to an engineer from Dublin Corporation. If you question what they're doing, he'll turn around and say 'have you got a Degree in Engineering?'...if you're reading out something you'll be asked 'have you got a Degree in English?'. That's it, they're pompous...and its very 'old Ireland', it's a very dinosaur attitude....

Access to knowledge is a key element in people's mobilisation and the state's capacity to exercise power. As one resident of Ringsend pointed out:

> If you don't know what it is you're fighting, they can tell you anything because you don't have the resources and the knowledge to say 'that is bullshit'. That's why they take advantage of a huge amount of people....

This point was also made by a Member of Parliament, who compared the issues of information (or knowledge) in the context of the relationship between officials and Ringsend residents to the British civil service model employed in India:

> ...whereby knowledge was power, you kept the knowledge inside the system. You didn't give away anything to the local community because that might usurp your own powers or threaten your own position of power.

We thus see that the mobilisation against the government's plan to site an incinerator in a Dublin working-class suburb has at least reproduced if not produced by its own attempts to generate 'consensus' through 'consultation'. While government officials saw consultation as a façade, or cover for a decision already taken, a representative of a transnational environmental NGO who participated in the campaign explained that:

> ...real consultation is about empowerment, about empowering communities, about giving decisions over to the community and getting feedback...and taking that truthfully. Even if it isn't a view they need or want, it should be incorporated into the reports. This is not happening.

The reality was that Poolbeg/Ringsend was interpreted as a 'sacrifice site' (Maher 1998) where the community's socio-economic status and clustering of heavy industry in the area meant it was an 'ideal' site for an incinerator. In 1994 the community had already fought a successful campaign to have an incinerator closed down. The proposed incinerator will bring a lot more traffic into an already congested and polluted area where:

> ...if you go to the local surgeries around here, they'll tell you one in three children have asthma.... I mean, the people around here are dying regardless of whether it's an incinerator or not. There's questions asked about brain damage and brain tumours and high asthma rates.

Our relatively small-scale example of popular resistance around environmental issues forms part, of course, of a broader international environmental movement (Mc Cormick, 1995). One could even say that the global is only constituted at the local 'level' of human activity. Political activism in the deprived Ringsend community was often generated by a perceived threat to the quality of everyday life. For one resident it was something far removed from the 'ozone layer' or the 'global warming' that motivated her engagement with the anti-incineration campaign. Rather, she originally got motivated with the campaign because of 'small things, like footpaths or something that did not work' (Murray, 2003: 233). It was not 'globalisation' that was being confronted by these residents who felt dis-empowered much more by local economic, social and political power structures. And yet Dublin is a transnational city and the site, inevitably, of struggles over the future of globalisation, whether it will be geared purely to the market and private gain or be conscious of the other social interest.

Aftermath

In the aftermath of the anti-incinerator campaign by the residents of Ringsend described above the Irish government made a decisive move towards centralising decision-making in regards to urban waste management planning. An unintended consequence was a broadening of social and political opposition to government waste management strategies as we shall describe below. First we have to understand how by 2001 waste management had become one of the 'hottest' political issues following Dublin City Council's refusal to adopt a budget that would incorporate the higher waste disposal charges demanded by Central Government. The City Council in Dublin—that is to say Local Government—was prepared to face dissolution rather than implement changes that were bound to be opposed by urban residents. By the end of 2001 Dublin City Council had issued over 70,000 warnings to urban households that had not paid their waste charges. Three other local authorities—Galway, Longford and Louth were also not fulfilling their obligation to adopt a waste management plan and Central Government had to respond.

The government responded to the growing waste crisis (both material and political) by the 2001 amendment to the 1996 Waste Management Act. According to the Department of the Environment and Local Government itself the purpose of this amendment was to 'provide a legal mechanism by which the current long running waste management planning process can be brought to a satisfactory conclusion' (Department of the Environment and Local Government, 2001). Clearly what was 'satisfactory' to government would not be satisfactory to local residents acutely concerned by government plans to site waste incinerators or other such 'facilities' in their areas. But the government was quite explicit on the remedy it sought to override this opposition and effectively 'fast track' planning permission for incinerators. The Department briefing cited above went on to say that 'the making of a waste management plan will become an executive function'. Effectively from now on decision-making regarding waste management would be taken out of the hands of elected local councillors and vested with City or Council Managers responsible to the executive branch of government. The Minister stated quite unambiguously that the planning process was 'over-democratised' and that he did not believe it was 'adding anything to it by having so many layers involved' (*Irish Times*, 12-09-02).

In terms of urban governance the 2001 Amendment to the Waste Management Act was a decisive watershed. In many ways it demonstrated how fragile and politically dependent governance discourse actually is, especially when it clashes with the power requirements of the state. While earlier government statements on waste policy had waxed lyrical on the needs for popular consultation and participation in the interests of sustainable development the new tone was decidedly more 'dirigiste'. There would be no consultation, just an imposition of waste management plans. As one commentator noted at the time—'Transferring authority from councils to managers will not make the existing [waste management] strategies any more appropriate and it is likely to further infuriate an already disillusioned public' (*Sunday Business Post*, 12-08-01). The government argued that the legislation was imperative if Ireland was to meet EU regulations on sustainable waste policy. Having deepened the 'democratic deficit' with the 2001 Amendment, the government approved a new Protecting the Environment Act in 2003 whereby 'local authorities are being given explicit power to discontinue the collection of domestic waste in the event of non-payment of charges' (Department of the Environment, press release).

With their new powers in place and with Central Government now forcefully involved, urban local authorities in Dublin now began to sanction those households that would not (or could not) pay increased waste disposal charges. From mid-2003 onwards opposition to the waste disposal charged had mounted in a number of Dublin districts. This opposition was based on the widespread perception that the changes amounted to 'double taxation' insofar as this public service was already paid for in employment-based taxation. There was a further fear that the charges were a prelude to a widespread privatisation of public services. Thus one local campaign group Fingal Anti-Bin Tax Campaign argued that: 'Where the bin tax is implemented the service is generally then privatised and the charges rise to astronomical levels' (www.nobintax.info) and examples were given from across the country. A third strand generating wide social opposition was more directly political. Many local campaigners referred to the undemocratic nature of the whole process whereby, as we saw above, un-elected council members were given the power to implement waste management policy at local level, 'over the heads' of elected representatives.

The campaign against increased waste disposal charges—the Anti Bin Tax Campaign—centred around blockading the waste disposal vehicles from either leaving the local council depots or from leaving the housing estates after they had refused to empty waste disposal bins at non-tax paying households. This led to confrontations with the police and many arrests. Dublin City Council had also threatened to impose fines of up to 1,900 euros on those households that left uncollected rubbish outside their houses. Nevertheless within a few months the campaign had escalated to such a pitch that Fingal County Council—the first Dublin local council to implement the new waste charges policy—was forced to abandon collections in a number of high-profile districts. As a direct result of the protests it was also reported that three of the four Dublin local authorities were, by the end of 2003, actively considering the privatisation of waste collection and disposal services. The Dublin City Manager could claim that 'protestors are playing in to the hands of privatisation.... If bin collectors can't do their jobs it makes sense that we would look at discontinuing our service and passing it on to private operators (stated in *Sunday Business Post*).

In October 2003 the conflict between the Anti Bin Tax Campaign and the local authorities climaxed with the jailing of twelve campaigners and the City Councils launching of High Court proceedings against protestors blockading the waste disposal vehicles. Two Socialist Party politicians, a local councillor and the party leader, were jailed, thus leading to strong media interest in the dispute. While the authorities claimed that this move to 'criminalise' the waste campaign had been successful by the end of the year the media reported that there were still 50,000 households in Dublin where rubbish was not collected due to the protest. While inevitably the campaign waned the issues would not go away and the waste management issue had firmly entered the political process as a key and divisive issue.

From the Ringsend campaign against the siting of a waste incinerator through to the wider Dublin city anti-waste disposal charge campaign we see a steady politicization of the urban waste issue. The nation-state was caught between pressure from above—in the shape of European 'directives' to move to a more sustainable waste policy—and pressure from below—in the shape of popular resistance to bearing the cost of 'cleaning up' Ireland. The economic boom of the 1990's (O'Hearn, 1998) had generated a huge extra amount of waste flows. The state wished to pass on the cost to the citizen and, if that failed, to privatise the waste industry through making it profitable. Waste was a global, European, and a local issue. People within deprived communities saw waste disposal as an issue around which they could and should mobilise. In reacting against these campaigns in a heavy handed way the Irish state exposed to what extent urban waste policy was dictated by the needs of neo-liberalism and not those of sustainable urban development.

Conclusions

The contemporary city exists within a complex set of global, economic, political, social and cultural flows (Eade, 1997). However, we can only understand life in the city from a local, grounded perspective. The case study of popular resistance to the siting of a waste incinerator in Dublin provides ample evidence for this point. Global and national environmental governance comes face-to-face with a very local sense of community. These local cultural and political meanings and identities are framed within the global restructuring of space and society, and generate significant 'glocal' social movements. That means we need to refuse binary oppositions between a 'global' and a 'local' framework of analysis that privileges one or the other scale of action and meaning formation. Nor should we neglect the often-missing dimension of the 'regional' because as we have seen, it is the European waste management legislation that has provided the spur for national action on waste and a powerful legitimising force for local communities concerned with sustainability and the very 'liveability' (Evans, 2001) of their habitat.

On the problematic of urban governance the research points to a certain continuity with old state regimes rather than a radical new paradigm. The local state has certainly been restructured and the market has come to the fore as we saw with the waste issue. However, the identified shift to a 'lighter touch' governance modality does not mean that the state has gone away or even that its powers have been diminished. When popular resistance to the Irish government's waste management strategy—based on incinerators—escalated and generalised, the Irish state simply and effectively abolished local democracy. Consultation and participation, (the watchwords of the 'new governance'), was replaced by management from above. While contestation of capitalism centred in the Nineteenth century around the domain of production, in the mid Twentieth century it shifted to the realm of consumption. Will waste be a new terrain of struggle for urban residents in the Twenty-First Century?

REFERENCES

Allen, R. and Jones, T. (1990) *Guests of the Nation*. London: Earthscan.

Amin, A. and Thrift, N. (2002) *Cities*. Re-Imagining the Urban. Cambridge: Polity.

Cudsworth, E. (2003) *Environment and Society*. London: Routledge.

Dempsey, N. (1998) Waste Management: Mending our Ways. Dublin: Department of the Environment and Local Government.

Department of the Environment and Local Government (1998) 'An Overview of the Waste Management Act 1996', Dublin: Department of the Environment and Local Government.

Department of the Environment and Local Government (2001) 'Minister Dempsey Publishes Waste Management Amendment Bill', Dublin: Department of the Environment and Local Government.

Eade, J. (1997) *Living the Global City—Globalisation as Local Process*. London: Routledge.

Evans, P. (ed) (2001) *The Politics of Urban Livelihood and Sustainability*. Berkeley: University of California Press.

Fagan, G.H. (2004) 'Waste Management and its Contestation in the Republic of Ireland' in *Capitalism, Nature, Socialism*, Vol. 15, No. 1, March, 83-103.

Fagan, G.H., O'Hearn, D., McCann, G. and Murray, M. (2001) *Waste Management Strategy: A Cross Border Perspective*. Maynooth: National Institute for Regional and Spatial Analysis.

Forfás (2001) *Key Waste Management Issues in Ireland*. Dublin: Forfás.

Maher, T. (1998) 'Environmental Opposition: Who is Targeted for Toxic Exposure', *Journal of Black Studies*, Vol. 28, No. 3, 357-67.

Massey, D., Allen, J. and Pile, S. (eds) (1999) *City Worlds*. London: Demos.

Mc Cormick, J. (1995) *The Global Environmental Movement*. New York: Wiley and Sons.

Murray, M. (2003) *Waste Management in Ireland: A Case Study on the Impact of Transnationalisation on Governance*. NUI Maynooth: Ph.D. unpublished.

O'Hearn, D. (1998) *Inside the Celtic Tiger—The Irish Economy and the Asian Model*. London: Pluto Press.

Pierre, J. and Guy Peters, B. (2000) *Governance, Politics and the State*. London: Palgrave.

Smith, P.M. (2001) *Transnational Urbanism: Locating Globalization*. London: Routledge.

Spaargarten, G. Mol, A. and Buttel, F. (eds) (2000) *Environment and Global Modernity*. London: Sage.

Tovey, H. (2002) 'Risk, Morality and the Sociology of Animals—Reflections on the Foot and Mouth Outbreak in Ireland' in *Irish Journal of Sociology*. Vol. 11.1, 23-43.

6

The Politics of Urban Regeneration in Dublin

DIANE PAYNE
diane.payne@ucd.ie
Department of Sociology, University College Dublin, Ireland.

PETER STAFFORD
peter.stafford@ucd.ie
Institute for the Study of Social Change, University College Dublin, Ireland.

Key words: Metropolitan governance, urban regeneration, development, partnership, centralisation.

This paper examines innovative forms of urban co-operation and governance in periods of urban renewal and rejuvenation, during and after Irish Celtic Tiger growth. This paper highlights successes and weaknesses in the trend to participatory and inclusive forms of urban administration through regeneration projects. Our analysis explores the clash between Ireland's traditional centralised, hierarchical and clientelistic political culture and the growing call for greater participation at all levels of the political process in Ireland. The research findings point to an emergent pattern of urban regeneration projects which often results in the establishment of new one-off, institutional bodies or quangos, which report to a central government department, rather than the strengthening the existing local authority structures. The empirical analysis, suggests an emergent model of partnership around urban regeneration in Ireland, which is driven by informal, networked participation rather than rigorous democratic accountability, where the selected representation of interests is defended as being derived from shared interdependencies around the specific project, rather than the formal requirements of institutional representation. In examining specific cases of innovative forms of co-operation in urban regeneration this project will examine the weaknesses of Dublin-level government in conjunction with the changing powers of national government authorities, especially the Office of the Taoiseach. The influence of key political, economic and social actors as leaders of regeneration will be studied closely, in the context of citizen participation and urban democracy. Likewise, the expanding nature of Dublin City Council as an actor in regeneration will be highlighted. In highlighting informal and formal forms of urban governance, the role of legislation and management of change will be highlighted in real-life examples of co-operation.

1. Introduction

For most of the 1990s and into the twenty-first century, Ireland's economic recovery has been heralded as the success story of the European Union, the so-called Celtic tiger. During this period, the capital city of Dublin and its surrounding hinterland has experienced massive in-migration from other parts of the country as well as from abroad. There has been a huge expansion in the level of infrastructure, including office complexes, tourism and leisure facilities and residential areas. Moreover, some of Dublin's most derelict and crime-ridden inner-city areas have been rejuvenated and regenerated as flourishing focal points for tourism, housing and business activities. For those of us interested in the politics of urban regeneration in Ireland, there remains a curious twist to this story. This story of successful urban regeneration has apparently occurred in absence of any effective or democratic system of local metropolitan governance.

Unlike most other countries in Europe, Ireland has consistently rejected the model of decentralised decision making even in policy areas, which many observers might suggest are most sensibly located and managed by the local or regional sub-national levels of government. Ireland's system of local government is traditionally poorly organised, in receipt of very limited funding, and responsible for a very limited range of policy, which includes refuse collection, sewerage and minor local planning issues. Central government, instead of local elected officials, has traditionally managed policy initiatives tackling a range of physical and social ills in the locality or on a constituency basis. Moreover, this is coupled with a pervasive system of clientelism, supported by a political culture of "it's not what you know, but who you know". However while Irish domestic political institutions are highly centralised, Ireland's domestic governance structures have also responded to the pervasive impact of the European Union. In particular since the late 1980s, the political agenda of the European Commission has strongly supported a multi-level system of partnership based governance under the Reform of the Structural Funds and called for the effective involvement of local, regional national and European level public and private actors. Any analysis of urban renewal and policy innovation in Ireland over the last two decades is informed by the significant economic and political importance of the EU Structural Funds for Ireland and indeed for these types of local oriented policy initiatives (Payne, 1999).

In this research we are interested in examining how the political processes have facilitated the innovation of policy initiatives for urban regeneration in Dublin. Dublin's renewal has been on the political agenda in Ireland since the early 1980s. For instance, the Urban Renewal Schemes, first introduced in 1985, were designed to promote urban renewal and redevelopment by promoting investment by the private sector in the construction and reconstruction of buildings in designated inner city derelict areas. Like most European countries during the 1980s and 1990s, these schemes focused on *property-led regeneration,* whereby the incentives introduced were primarily tax-based, targeting investors in and occupiers of properties in designated areas. For most of the 1980s and 1990s in Ireland, and indeed across many European countries, these schemes operated through powerful networks of public-private co-operation. This co-operation was based on the interdependence between central and local government and private property developers, where the private sector supplied the finance and secured the economic risk in return for government unlocking land and property for development through planning, re-zoning and services provision (Atkinson, 1998, McGuirk, 2000).

However towards the later part of the 1990s, as in many European countries, this type of approach to urban renewal in Ireland came under increasing fire.[1] Increasing attention was paid to the *formal organisation* of partnership arrangements around urban renewal schemes and several writers suggest that "what is qualitatively different about the regeneration during the 1990s and the beginning of the new century is the role afforded to the community—at least in the rhetoric of regeneration" (Russell, 2001; see also Duffy and Hutchinson, 1997). In the late 1990s the Irish government introduced a series of measures that suggest a departure from the strictly property-led approach to urban renewal. A new Urban Renewal Scheme was introduced in 1999, which "looks at physical, environmental, social and economic development, and tax incentives are available only where all four elements are addressed" (see http://www.dublincity.ie/services/econ2.html). The use of Integrated Area Plans were established under the Urban Renewal Act 1998, whose preparation and implementation required consultation and partnership across a broad range of public and private interests.

In this research we examine metropolitan governance, Irish style, through the lens of urban renewal policy in the inner city of Dublin. In particular, we use case studies to examine and compare urban renewal in the *Temple Bar area* in the late 1980s with urban renewal in the *Liberties/Coombe area* of Dublin, which did not begin till the late 1990s. The regeneration of this Temple bar area has been quite successful. It is now home to many of the capital's cultural venues and contains a high density of small shops, restaurants and alternative clothes shops. On the other hand, while the regeneration of the Liberties/Coombe area is still at a relatively early stage, it is already showing very mixed results. Consultation and implementation around the Integrated Area Plan for the area has proved controversial and divisive. However, within the area, a major project known as the Digital Hub, has proceeded successfully and has established a productive management structure, with very little criticism.

In the following discussion, we begin with an examination of the institutional structures and political context within which we can set our analysis of the politics of urban regeneration projects in Ireland, and in particular Dublin. The case studies ably illustrate the curious clash between Ireland's traditional centralised, hierarchical and clientelistic political culture and the growing call for greater participation at all levels of the political process in Ireland. However, instead of strengthening the existing local authority structures, new institutional bodies or quangos are established which report to a central government department. The case studies show the continued importance of central government, and in particular the innovative role of the Department of the Taoiseach, as an incubator of these emerging frameworks of co-operation within urban regeneration. The selected representation of interests is defended as being derived from shared interdependencies around the specific project, rather than the formal requirements of institutional representation. The research suggests an emergent model of partnership around urban regeneration, which is driven by informal, networked participation rather than rigorous democratic accountability.

2. Key Institutions of Irish Political System

In 1924 Ireland adopted legislation which put in place a highly centralised system of Government policy making and which was closely modelled on the British structure of public administration "under which large sectoral departments manage complex programmes with minimal devolution to local or regional authorities" (Marshall, 2002). Key decisions affecting the type of urban regeneration projects adopted, the finance, and policy implementation are all taken at the central government level.[2] Alongside this hierarchical, centralised structure of administration Ireland's political system is characterised by a traditionally high degree of clientelism. National elected representatives (i.e. TDs) in the Dáil or parliament are generally very careful to take look after their local constituency demands, even where these are minor policy issues most appropriately dealt with at the local authority level. As a result it sometimes seems in Ireland that all politics is local, and even though local councillors are elected to office to fight for local policy demands, it is the TD at the constituency level, who will be usually be approached in the first instance.

In Ireland, the City and County Councils[3] provide the forum for local elected representatives, but these Councils have very limited capacity.[4] Executive decision-making and day-to-day management of local government is the responsibility of the city or county manager, who is directly appointed by the Minister for Environment and Local Government. Marshall has suggested that these "managers have also been responsible for liaison with national government departments on projects of local interest, thereby ensuring a sort of technocratic governance visible in rural County Kerry as well as urban Dublin" (Marshall, 2002). The issue of overhauling the system of local government had been on the political agenda. It subsequently gained momentum in the light of revised EU Structural Funds that emphasised geographically based programmes drawn up in consultation with local and regional authorities. In 1991, a new Local Government Act was passed, which subsequently saw the institution of Regional Authorities in Ireland. However, these authorities are composed of indirectly elected local councillors, a number of appointed officials, have very limited executive decision rights and very limited financial resources at their disposal (Government of Ireland, 1991).

From the 1970s onwards, most European states witnessed a strong push to decentralise to the regions responsibility for various policy areas, often including regional economic development. However Ireland's public administration, unlike most European states in the late 1970s and 1980s, showed an increasing emphasis on centralised decision-making within the public sector and a tendency towards greater central control of the activities of state sponsored bodies (NESC, 1979). The tendency in Ireland has always been to establish a single function state body that is first answerable to the central state authorities and often to a particular government department. This is instead of using a decentralised, territorial approach, as was increasingly the case in other European states during the 1980s. In the absence of functioning sub-national local and regional authorities, many semi-state bodies and public bodies had regional levels of organisation.

At this level of organisation, one finds the *ad hoc* growth of single function agencies and offices—quangos—arising mainly from decentralisation of government departments and state agencies and operating, for the most part, as autonomous actors and independent of each other. Coyle and Sinnott point to "a proliferation of regional bodies operating in differently constituted sets of regions" (1993: 79). There are numerous statutory regional bodies with responsibility for the health service, for tourism promotion and for the development and protection of inland fisheries. Marshall argues that "in no other country, save possibly the United Kingdom, do quangos and national ministries control such a wide range of programmes and services, to the detriment of devolution and local initiative" (Marshall, 2002). However more often than not, the boundaries of the territorial areas for which these different statutory bodies have responsibility, do not coincide with one another.

An understanding of the Irish political system and its distinctive governance patterns must also include an examination of the Irish partnership model. Following the 1987 General Election, a Fianna Fail Government, with Charles Haughey as Taoiseach[5], was returned to power. A consensus began to emerge at this time that an important aspect of Ireland's economic recovery was the ability of the Government and the Social Partners which included the farmers, trade unions, private business and the community/voluntary sectors, to reach and fulfil the national centralised agreements to keep public expenditure low and industrial unrest at a minimum (Payne, 1999). The 1987 Programme for National Recovery (PNR) was the first of the national centralised agreements. In 1987, the PNR agreement had already established a mechanism for communication and negotiation, called the Central Review Committee (CRC). The Department of the Taoiseach (i.e. Prime Minister) chaired this Central Review Committee (CRC). The Irish model of partnership—national level negotiations between central government and the social partners—was already underway when the Structural Funds Reform measures, including calls for multi-level partnership and subsidiarity, came into effect in 1988. Marshall points out that "whereas regional governments in other parts of Europe took the initiative in contacting and networking with trade unions, voluntary groups and business associations, the central administration was already engaging in that role in Ireland" (Marshall, 2002).

3. Facilitating Urban Regeneration

In this research we trace the development of Irish urban renewal policy and in particular, focus on urban renewal initiatives in two inner-city areas of Dublin. Urban renewal policy in the 1980s and early 1990s was distinctly oriented towards property-led development. By the mid-1990s, there appeared to be a shift in Irish urban renewal policy and accompanying legislation, apparently formalising the partnership-led approach to urban renewal and widening the focus of policy initiatives. Our selection of inner city areas in Dublin and initiatives for case study attempts to throw some light on the impact of these policy changes over time and the emergent governance patterns in the urban space.

3.1 Regeneration of the Temple Bar Area of Dublin City

The Temple Bar case study is the story of the renovation and development of a mostly derelict part of Dublin, an approximately twenty–eight acres site, which is situated in the inner city of Dublin near the river Liffey. During the 1960s and 1970s, the Temple Bar residents and small businesses were living and working in crumbling buildings owned and leased by the Irish national transport company, Córas Iompair Éireann (CIÉ). The CIÉ had plans to replace the buildings with a central transport depot. CIÉ, and not unnaturally, were unwilling to invest in the upkeep of the fabric of the buildings. The poor structure of the buildings was coupled with almost non-existent tenant rights for those on short-term leases. It was the tenants and residents of Temple Bar themselves who started the process of redevelopment in the late 1970s. Informal discussions in the café of Dublin Resource Centre amongst CIÉ tenants about the future of the area, led to an increased collective sentiment of unity against their landlord. Concern both for individual businesses and the area as a whole was increased in the 1980s when it was suspected that CIÉ plans for a transportation centre were unlikely ever to be realised. During this initial phase of redevelopment, issues for discussion amongst the tenants were negative ones: rent, the conditions of the buildings, the poor appearance of the area and the future of the businesses.

As Table 1 shows, the process of rejuvenation was one of increasing speed and momentum to develop the area away from derelict buildings towards a cultural centre of the city. There was concern among the participants that redevelopment could not be allowed to slow or stall once the initial process had begun. It relied on the enthusiasm and motivation of volunteer enthusiasts and eye-catching landmarks were deliberately created to make Temple Bar both visible amongst the general public, but also to keep up the morale of the participants themselves. Many of the original actors feared the process becoming grounded through excessive bureaucracy and meetings, and so they developed from the outset a style of management and co-operation which was *ad hoc* and informal. This quest for constant movement and speedy development has been blamed by some participants for many of the failures of the development. A lack of an effective review process in planning permission, and flaws in some architectural decisions were because of the speed of change. Likewise, despite efforts to the contrary, some actor groups notably at city level were left behind or neglected during key moments of the process. It is therefore worth spending some time examining this change and its consequences for urban governance of the area.

This research has identified three clear phases in the development of Temple Bar area. The first can be characterised by the emergence of collective solidarity through the tenants of CIÉ-owned buildings. At this point regeneration was still theoretical. Background work was being undertaken by local residents about how their area could be preserved. The second phase was when this hypothetical research crystallised into a practical opportunity to redevelop, when preliminary work such as paving and lighting was undertaken by Dublin Corporation. When provisions of legislative and financial aid to realise the redevelopment project came through, the project entered its third and most publicly visible phase. In all these three phases, informality was the most obvious characteristic of the politics of development.

TABLE 1: Chronology of Events for Temple Bar case study

Year	Key Events of the Time Period
1965	• *Transportation in Dublin* document: recommends central bus station.
1975-1976	• Skidmore, Owens and Merrill, Report for CIÉ adds impetus to former proposals by suggesting siting of central bus station in the Temple Bar area. • CIE approve this proposal and begin acquiring property in the area and leasing buildings at low rent to artists, retailers, etc.
1985-1986	• *Temple Bar—A Policy for the Future,* published by An Taisce. • Temple Bar Study Group produce report urging Dublin City Council, referred to then as Dublin Corporation,[6] to rethink their support for bus station.
1988-1990	• Temple Bar Development Council, make submission to Dublin City Council Planning Department on Draft City Development Plan. • In anticipation of 1991 European City of Culture, Dublin City Council prepares an Area Action Plan for Temple Bar. • Department of the Taoiseach in partnership with the Temple Bar Development Council prepare a proposal for submission to the EU for funding of Urban Pilot Projects under Article 10 of the ERDF. This proposal is successful and awarded IR3.6m pounds by the European Commission. • The Minister for Transport and Tourism directs CIE to abandon its plans for a transportation centre in the area.
1991	• The Dublin City Council's Temple Bar Area Action Plan is included in the Dublin City Development Plan, 1991.

TABLE 1 (*Contd.*)

Year	Key Events of the Time Period
	• The Finance Act, 1991 sets out the tax provisions that would be available in the Temple Bar area until 1996. • The Temple Bar Area Renewal and Development Act, 1991 establishes the financial and statutory powers of the two new companies set up to deal with the development of Temple Bar. • October—Urban Design competition initiated by TBP, to provide an architectural and urban design framework for the project. Competition won by Group 91 (comprising 8 architectural practices).
1992	• March—Temple Bar Properties publish a Development Programme for Temple Bar, which has six component sub-programmes.
1994	• EU Structural Funds Operational Programme for Local Urban and Rural Development—Sub Programme 3, Measure 5 outlines ERDF and Exchequer funding for continued development of Cultural Programme.
1996	• November—Planning application lodged by Temple Bar Properties for redevelopment of west end of Temple Bar—mixed use residential and retail.
2000	• Development of Cultural Centres completed with the opening of the Project. The development of the West End of Temple Bar is also complete.

Working without funding, residents of the Temple Bar area, and in particular tenants of the local shops in the area, decided to establish a Temple Bar Development Council, which relied on the efforts of personal contacts and friends. As they had no public funding or public visibility, tenants were unworried about claims of cronyism or corruption. It was felt that when—or indeed if—the project gathered any momentum a more formal and accountable organisational structure would be needed. Until such a point, the early development of Temple Bar was characterised by amateur enthusiasts using their limited circle of friends and own resources to unite in order to preserve their businesses.

In 1988, there was the first significant turning point in the development of the Temple Bar area. Informal discussions had led to the creation of the Temple Bar Development Council (TBDC) whose first main task was examine the possibility opposing the transportation centre through a submission to Dublin City Council's Draft Dublin City Development Plan. At a public meeting of residents and interested bodies, a slim submission was produced containing seven general aims for the area. Each of the seven proposals was deliberately pitched to bodies ranging from national to city level. It was felt that pitching initiatives at national level would put downward pressure from national government onto the City Council. The 1988 Submission reveals a great deal about the general aims of the emerging Temple Bar organisation. Its aims were suitably modest for a body whose realistic expectations were fairly low. The most ambitious was the proposal regarding tax incentives to raise revenue for building refurbishment. The suggestion that the Department of Finance be approached came from within Dublin City Council who were unable to make financial provisions of that level and to raise the public profile of the whole proposal.

The submission needed to strike a balance between being innovative enough to be eye-catching at national level but modest enough to be feasible. Internally, Temple Bar Development Council felt it crucial to prevent their progress from being undermined by splits within the ranks of Temple Bar businesses. Much of the initial work undertaken by members of the Council was to survey and inform their potential supporters. As one senior figure noted, cultural organisations and groups (which were the employers of many of the Council) are not good networkers. They were often rivals for limited public funds and the culture of collaboration was not easily created. Nevertheless it was also recognised early on that coherence amongst groups within Temple Bar could only increase the bargaining power of the Temple Bar Development Council and their submission.

TABLE 2: 1988 Temple Bar Development Council Submission Proposal

Proposal	Body to which Proposal was Aimed
• To disallow any proposal for a CIE transportation centre from being included in the Development Plan.	CIE (National)
• To draw up a local area action plan which would facilitate the rejuvenation of the Temple Bar area.	Dublin City Council Planning Department (Local)
• To upgrade the streets with paving, pedestrianisation, landscaping, lighting, etc.	Dublin City Council Paving Department (Local)
• To offer tax incentives specifically directed to encourage the refurbishment of existing buildings and the suitable development of infill sites.	Department of Finance (National)
• To act upon An Taisce recommendations regarding the listing of buildings in the Temple Bar area.	Dublin City Council Planning Department (Local)
• To assist in creating a central, attractive business and residential area providing on going employment and residences for Dublin people.	Department of Trade and Tourism/Board Fáilte (National)
• To establish Temple Bar as the cultural centre of the city and as a major tourist attraction.	Department of the Taoiseach (Arts and Culture) (National)

Parallel to this progress, Ireland's first EU Community Support Framework (CSF) under the Structural Funds Reform Framework was being negotiated and agreed between central government and the European Commission. A key principle of the Reform of the Structural Funds legislation was the call for multilevel partnerships involving the public and private actors, at the relevant local, regional and central levels of administration within the member state. Given the hierarchical and vertical nature of Irish government and its administration, coupled with the weakness of local authority structures, this resulted in rather varied and ineffective participation of sub-national public and private interests in the policy negotiation, and subsequent implementation, of the Structural Funds in Ireland (Payne, 1999, 2000). In relation to the impact of the Structural Funds supported projects impacting in the Greater Dublin Area (GDA). Marshall argues that "the lack of an overarching urban policy framework for the GDA, along with the area's balkanised local authority structure, ensured that the first CSF did not bring about local authority-led partnerships or positive changes in metropolitan governance (2002). Structural funded urban projects were planned and managed directly by sectoral government departments, rather than at the territorial level thus fostering horizontal networks across relevant local and regional actors. Marshall is strident in his critique suggesting that "central government was able to control the pace and structure of urban renewal in Dublin, to the consternation of the Dublin City Council and the county councils in the surrounding suburban jurisdictions" (2002). In many instances, the central government sectoral department established a separate body, effectively a quango, to manage the structural funded urban projects, rather than go through the existing local authority structures and the elected base of local representatives. Returning to our case study of the regeneration of the Temple Bar area, this will prove a useful illustration of this emergent urban governance pattern in Ireland.

In the later part of 1988, there was informal contact between the Temple Bar Development Council and Paddy Teahon, the dynamic and influential General Secretary of the Department of the *then*-Taoiseach, Charles Haughey. His access to the Taoiseach allowed the Temple Bar residents to by-pass the normal formal and time consuming political ladder and instead have access to the heart of government. The Taoiseach was in a position to pluck "pet projects" from the pool of schemes for his own attention. One architect involved in the plans believed that Charles Haughey, the Taoiseach, saw Temple Bar as a visible cultural initiative in which he could promote himself as a statesman in the dying days of his premiership (interview material). Haughey saw the Temple bar area "as the new 'cultural quarter' for Dublin to serve as a showpiece for the capital, which had recently been designated the 1991 European City of Culture" (Marshall, 2002). Temple Bar was an eye-catching project at the heart of the capital city, and activists were delighted when Haughey publicly confirmed the importance of the area:

> *Temple Bar is one of the most important, traditional, attractive and noteworthy parts of the city, and it has to be refurbished and kept and I won't let CIÉ near it.* Haughey, 1985

Article 10 of the European Regional Development Fund was established by the European Commission to fund innovatory projects, which included during the period 1989-1991 a total of 32 Urban Pilot Projects. The Department of the Taoiseach facilitated a partnership with the grass-roots Temple Bar Development Council, who then developed an application for ERDF designation as an Article 10 of Urban Pilot Project. In November 1990 an application was made under Article 10 of Regulation No. 4254/88 for ERDF grant aid for an Urban co-operation with local development groups notably the Temple Bar Development Council. The Urban Pilot Project submission was the first time that the cultural quarter's role had been officially defined. In the event, the application was successful, and IR£3.6m was granted for planning, infrastructure, and the construction of the Irish Film Centre in Eustace Street (Marshall, 2002).

Moreover, soon after the announcement of the ERDF award, the Department of the Taoiseach requested a speedy creation of legislation to establish new institutional structures to manage the development of the Temple Bar area.[7] The relevant legislation included the 1991 Finance Act and the 1991 Temple Bar Renewal and Development Act. Temple Bar Renewal Ltd. was set up with the remit to approve development proposals to enable them to avail of the incentives provided for in Chapter VII of the Finance Act, 1991. Temple Bar Properties Ltd. is the Development Company for the Temple Bar Area so designated under the Temple Bar Area Renewal and Development Act, 1991.[8] Funding under the auspices of the EU Urban Pilot Project together with the package of tax incentives outlined in the Finance Act 1991, provided the financial mechanisms to underpin urban renewal in the area. The establishment of two new companies Temple Bar Properties Ltd. and Temple Bar Renewal, provided the organisational and management framework to give form and focus to the renewal process. Central Government commitment to the project in the form of the support of the Department of the Taoiseach was also vital to ensure that the project would succeed.

The story of the regeneration of Dublin's Temple Bar area is a story about centralised government, combining with the personal interest of the *then*-Taoiseach, Charles Haughey and tireless work by grass-roots activists, who together bypassed the largely powerless local government structures in the form of Dublin City Council. Temple Bar Properties (TBP) was set up to enable governmental control of regeneration as well as to undertake of community consultation. It was a new layer of government to facilitate partnership with local business people, artists, and residents and ensured that "the agencies in Temple Bar have deliberately adopted a strategic management approach to the area" (Montgomery 1995: 137). It is also useful to note that some of the key individuals involved in the original Temple Bar Development Council also subsequently took management responsibilities within Temple Bar Properties. Over the course of the first (1989-1993) and second (1994-1999) CSFs, Temple Bar attracted some IR£40.6 million in EU and State funding, of which IR£22.1 million came directly from the European Regional Development Fund. Despite the European Commission's strong desire for subsidiarity—policy-making and implementation at the lowest possible level—the Temple Bar project was managed in a way wholly consistent with the centralised Irish approach to governance (Marshall, 2002). The sponsoring department, in this case that of the *Taoiseac*h, implemented partnership and subsidiarity on its own terms, creating a brand-new State agency to serve as an implementing authority with the participation of local-level actors and the social partners.

For some commentators, the new institutional structures created such as Temple Bar Properties (TBP) are seen in a negative light. Marshall argues that "the creation of a special regime for Temple Bar further eroded the power of existing local authorities" (Marshall, 2002). For others, such as Montgomery (1995), "the government was careful and very sure to keep Dublin City Council at arm's length from the whole initiative...the effect has been to free the area from the dead hand of bureaucracy", thereby ensuring efficient implementation and progress (Marshall, 2002). Russell suggests that "local authorities acted as a facilitators and enablers of private sector development, rather than as the key drivers or implementing agencies of urban renewal" (Russell, 2001; see also KPMG *et al.*, 1996; Prunty, 1995 and Society of Chartered Surveyors, 1993). Certainly these contrasting critiques go to the heart of the debate about the principle of local democratic participation and representation in this emergent Irish urban governance model. Moreover, this issue becomes more relevant when it is noted that the Temple Bar governance structure was later replicated throughout the Dublin area as additional European funds were directed to urban initiatives.

Certainly the European Commission was unhappy with the heavily centralised manner in which the Irish Government was implementing the Structural Funds and called for greater subsidiarity (Payne, 1999). In the run up to the second round of the Structural Funds, the Irish Government established sub-national Regional Authorities[9] and claimed to endorse a more central role for local government. However the reality of the implementation of the Structural Funds on the ground was very different (Payne, 2000). During the second round of the Structural funds, the model of "lead government department" was retained and strengthened (Payne, 1999). The development of Temple Bar remained a project under the auspices of the Department of the Taoiseach up until 1993, when there was a general re-organisation of government departments. Responsibility for the Temple Bar Project was then shifted to the Department of the Environment, a body better suited to overseeing the formal development of a project, following its incubation period in the Department of the

Taoiseach. The partnership between the local community in Temple Bar and central and sectoral oriented government departments remained strong as did the exclusion of the relevant sub-national authorities, namely Dublin City Council, from key executive decisions affecting the Temple Bar Project. Despite this, the success of this flagship project, Temple Bar, "is striking: from the initial ERDF block grant in 1991, TBP was able to leverage an additional IR£37 million in cultural funding from the EU and the Exchequer over the course of the 1989-93 and 1994-99 CSFs" (Marshall, 2002). Moreover the Temple bar area has been transformed into a cultural, economic and social arena for the city and surpassed all expectations as a project in urban regeneration.

In this research we explored the Temple Bar case study in some more detail to see if we could shed some more light on this issue of local authority participation and its relevance to the Temple Bar project. At about the time of preparing the initial ERDF Urban Pilot Project proposal, and indeed during the subsequent drafting of legislation, the Planning Department of the Dublin City Council was split between the more conservative-minded planners, who viewed Temple Bar as an opportunity for traditional heritage design to attract modest tourism, and those younger planners, within Dublin City Council, who were enthusiastic for change and whose efforts thus far had been limited by finance. Certainly, the Urban Pilot Project (UPP) submission was built on Dublin City Council's initial aspirations to create internal permeability in the area via an east-west central pedestrian route. Dublin City Council envisaged that this route would link the existing lively retail area centred on Crown Alley, with the cultural uses of the Olympia Theatre and the Project Arts Centre and, provide associated new public urban spaces. However, the final UPP submission for ERDF funds envisaged the creation of a cultural hub, which went far beyond the more conservative plans called for by Dublin City Council's mainly senior planners at the time. In making a case for the European applicability of the Urban Pilot Project and in stressing its innovative elements, a case was made for integrating urban design with cultural provision. The application for the Urban Pilot Project stated:

It is also innovative in seeking to link cultural provision, youth recreational consumer demand and tourism revenue potential by the provision of exhibition/performance spaces along a new pedestrian walkway. (Urban Pilot Project Application, 1990)

At the outset of the regeneration programme, many within Temple Bar believed that the Dublin City Council's passive stance on their proposals was based on a suspicion that it would never see fruition. At the same time, the Temple Bar Development Council had little faith in the capacity of the Dublin City Council to deliver.[10] Projects that could be undertaken by the Dublin City Council were limited by tight financial control. It had no cohesive over-arching development plan for Dublin, nor did it have the finances to undertake one even if the desire had existed. There seemed little hope that the changes, demanded by the local business interests and residents, could be undertaken by the local authority.

Whatever way we judge the Temple Bar project, the impact of the legislation introduced in 1991 is clear: it gave a new dynamic to the regeneration project and created new working patterns amongst the key partners to the process. At one level within Dublin City Council there is a deep sense of grievance that it has been effectively sidelined in terms of the executive decision-making regarding the development of the Temple Bar area. Marshall has pointed out that "Dublin Corporation was included on both of Temple Bar's management committees, but as day-to-day executive decisions remained the province of TBP, the city's elected government played a comparatively minor role in the formulation of redevelopment policy. The Corporation's only leverage over the Temple Bar project was in planning approvals; unlike the Docklands, Temple Bar was not designated an independent planning area" (2002).

However our research work also suggests that planners and architects within Dublin City Council, while recognising their limited role, have also successfully worked together with Temple Bar Properties in the intervening period. Together, they oversee the implementation of architectural framework for the Temple Bar area, which is led by a private group of architects called Group 91.[11] The working model is that each area of development within the Temple Bar area had its own individual style based on the plans of the constituent architectural company within Group '91, but agreed within the general parameters set in collaboration with the Dublin City Council planners, the architects and the Temple Bar Properties. This arrangement has been hailed as the most successful aspect of the redevelopment and there was a view within the Dublin City Council that this approach—pulling together as many disparate groups as possible—was an effective framework for future Dublin re-developments (interview material). Moreover, our research suggests that a new generation of planners was emerging within Dublin City Council, who are more ambitious and confident about the potential role for the City Council in large scale regeneration projects.

3.2 Community Partnership and Local Government Reform in the 1990s

From the late 1980s onwards, the Irish government came under increasing pressure from the European Commission to institute appropriate sub-national governance structures to facilitate participation in the preparation and co-ordination of the Structural funds process. As the discussion of urban regeneration process in the Temple Bar area of Dublin suggested, the favoured response of the Irish government departments was to establish a separate statutory body—a quango—to manage the policy process. This often involved either bypassing entirely or relegating to a minor role the participation of the appointed and elected officials from the relevant local government offices, as was the case for the Temple Bar project.

At the micro level of local development policy and social renewal, a similar tactic of bypassing local government was adopted. In early 1990s, the Irish government established a number of Area Based Partnerships[12] in disadvantaged areas and subsequently, a range of other types of local development groups, such as EU LEADER groups, which "were playing a pioneering role in social renewal of their respective areas" (Russell, 2001, see also Parkinson, 1998; Walsh *et al.*, 1998). Nevertheless, over time there were increasing demands from the local government sector, particularly by elected representatives, that they should have a much more central role in these local development initiatives, reflecting their democratic mandate at the local level. It was usually the case that local community activists in these groups did not seek or welcome the involvement of the local authority, fearing that the local development process would become bogged down in political cronyism or local bureaucracy. Local government officials, along with other statutory agencies representatives, did participate as senior board members in these local partnerships but they tended to be very defensive of their role as service providers. As Russell suggests "this feeling of defensiveness was exacerbated for local authorities, who unlike many of the other statutory agencies, saw themselves as having a local development remit, the appropriate administrative structures and comprehensive geographical spread, for playing the role allocated to the partnerships" (2001). At the same time, local authorities, as key providers of public housing, were blamed for the growth in social problems associated with the spatial concentration of poverty, such as those which are generated in some of Dublin's housing estates and flat complexes (Fahey, 1999; Fahey and Williams, 2000). In defense of the local authorities, they had neither the financial resources nor statutory role to be able to tackle these wider social issues. Indeed Russell suggests that "the establishment of ABPs, just as with the establishment of single focus regeneration agencies can be viewed as an element of a centralising government and an effort to bypass ineffective local government" (2001). Rather than initiate a difficult and complex reform, local government in Ireland was, once again, sidelined in the policy process. Moreover serious questions about the accountability and democratic representation of partnership-led policy initiatives for local development continued to arise.

By the mid-1990s, we see further reforms being introduced, which was particularly relevant for urban renewal policy. As pointed out earlier, there was increasing criticism raised about the property-led focus of the Urban Renewal Schemes used in Ireland since the late 1980s. A major report of urban policy was published at this time, wherein "a consortium of consultants headed up by KPMG in Ireland clearly outlined this failure" (KPMG *et al.*, 1996 in Russell, 2001). Also in 1996, a document was published by the Irish Government entitled "Better Local Government—A Programme for Change" which set out a programme for the future development of local authority services in Ireland. In 1998, there followed the Report of the Task Force on the Integration of Local Government and Local Development Systems which called for the establishment of County/City Development Boards (CDBs) to bring about an integrated approach to the delivery of both State and local development services at local level.[13] In 1999, this was followed up by an initiative entitled "A New Deal for Local Government" which, for example, increased by about a third the funds of local government for discretionary day-to-day expenditure (see http://www.environ.ie/DOEI/DOEIPol.nsf/wvNavView/Overview). At the same time local authorities were asked to establish Strategic Policy Committees (SPCs), whose remit is to prepare the groundwork for policies to be decided on by the county/city councils. Alongside elected councillors, a minimum of one third of the membership of each SPC is drawn from sectoral representatives, giving sectoral interests and communities an opportunity for input to local government policymaking. Such committees were also used in the preparation and monitoring of implementation the Integrated Area Plans (IAPs) for certain areas designated for urban renewal.[14] These latter policy initiatives, particularly the more formalised approach to partnership-led local development combined with targeted policy approaches to designated areas promise a more balanced approach to urban renewal. Our second case study of the urban regeneration in the Liberties/Coombe area provides a useful opportunity to test this.

3.3 Regenerating the Liberties/Coombe Area of Dublin City

The Liberties/Coombe area has a rich history of market trading as well as production of goods. Traditionally the area also served as a main focus for meeting and selling of agricultural and farming produce. Although still associated with open market trading, most of the small firms or family businesses associated with the traditional manufacturing and trading of goods have not survived. For much of the twentieth century the area became associated with poverty, unemployment and the variety of social ills that emerge in these conditions.

This case study describes two interwoven policy processes for urban renewal in the Liberties/Coombe area and the chronology of main events for this case study is given in Table 3. Legislative and policy changes in the second half of the 1990s prompted the Dublin City Council, to begin the process of developing Integrated Area Plans for Dublin city, including one for the Liberties/Coombe area. The Liberties/Coombe Integrated Area Plan (IAP) was completed in March 1998 and was submitted by Dublin City Council to the Minister for the Environment for endorsement.[15] The Liberties/Coombe is one of five areas in the inner city targeted by Dublin City Council for redevelopment under an Integrated Area Plan (IAP). The objective of developing an Integrated Area Plan is to bring about sustainable urban regeneration by encouraging a framework of intervention that achieves a balance between social, physical and economic renewal.[16]

In order to ensure this balanced approach to planning and implementation of the Integrated Area Plan, a Monitoring Committee was established to oversee the IAP progress. The Monitoring Committee comprised of local authority elected representatives, community representatives, and a number of representatives from the private business sector and trade unions. Initially there was a reasonable level of enthusiasm for this new type of initiative in urban renewal policy, and in particular, the community representatives welcomed the invitation to be consulted on forthcoming plans to develop their area. However, it seems that early on in the work of this Committee, serious difficulties arose for the community representatives. The three local elected representatives from Dublin City Council insisted that the chair of the Monitoring Committee should be rotated between themselves, the elected representatives, despite the objection from the community representatives that this was not a requirement specified in the terms of reference of the Committee.

Subsequent to this and through the Monitoring Committee, the community representatives made a number of proposals for changes to the implementation of certain aspects of the IAP. These proposals reflected local concerns about the need for adequate parking facilities and pedestrian walkways. The vast majority of these proposals were rejected by Dublin City.

TABLE 3: Chronology of Liberties/Coombe IAP and the Digital Hub Project

Year	Key Events of the Time Period
1997-98	• Preparation and completion of Liberties/Coombe Integrated Area Plan (IAP). • Establishment of IAP Monitoring Committee.
1999	• Enterprise Ireland report recommends development of digital media in Ireland. • Government announces plan to support establishment of Media Lab Europe (MLE) in Dublin associated "media village".
2000	• Digital Media Development Limited established by a Government decision under the aegis of the Department of the Taoiseach.
2001	• "Digital Hub" discussion document published outlining vision for development of the area. • Dublin City Council approved a variation to the City Development Plan (includes Liberties/Coombe IAP) to provide for a core development of the Digital Hub. • Responsibility for Digital Hub transferred to the Department of Public Enterprise. • IAP Monitoring Committtee fail to endorse their Annual Report.
2002	• Digital Hub Development Agency bill published. • Private sector partners in place. • Urban Design Framework Plan (with reference to IAP) agreed. • IAP Monitoring Committee fail to endorse their Annual Report. • Two Community representatives resign from IAP Monitoring Committee.
2003	• Digital Hub Development Agency Act 2003 signed into law. • First Phase of Digital Hub Implementation completed.

Council, which resulted in claims from the community representatives that the work of the Monitoring Committee was no more than a cosmetic exercise, and that property developers' demands were more important than the needs of the local community (Interview material). Indeed following the ongoing objections of the community representatives, the Monitoring Committee failed to reach a unanimous agreement and could not endorse either the 2000-2001 or 2001-2002 Annual Reports of the Liberties/Coombe IAP Monitoring Committee. As stated, "following the non-approval of the Annual Report 2000-2001 by the Monitoring Committee, a Minority Report outlining a number of serious and unresolved concerns on the part of the Community Representatives was prepared and submitted to the Minister for the Environment and Local Government" (Liberties/Coombe IAP Annual Report 2001-2002). By November 2002, the Minister's office had issued a response and following this, two of the four community representatives resigned from the Monitoring Committee. Following this breakdown in communications, the IAP Monitoring Committee has met infrequently and the work of the Committee has remained, to some extent, hampered by these unresolved issues.

Despite these difficulties within the Liberties/Coombe IAP Monitoring Committee, there is also another story of public/ private and community partnership around an urban renewal initiative within the Liberties/Coombe area, which has been very successful. This is the story of the Digital Hub project, which we will now outline below.

The Digital Hub project is located on a nine-acre renovated site, which formed part of the famous St. James Gate Guinness Brewery complex situated in the Liberties/Coombe area of inner city Dublin. The aims of the Digital Hub project is to create a type of cyberspace village by clustering together Irish and international digital media start-up companies and research facilities in one area through the provision of state-of-the-art infrastructure. The broader aim is to encourage the growth of research, enterprise and investment in the digital media industry in Ireland.[17] In 1999, a number of coincidental events occurred which led to the establishment of the Digital Hub project. First a government commissioned report[18] became available in 1999, which, stressed the increased importance of digital media as a growth industry and recommended that the Irish government formulate a policy to embrace this developing technology.[19] Other reports by Forfás, the State's policy and advisory board for enterprise and technology, suggested that a defined area of the city be set aside for media development. At about this time also, the Massachusetts Institute of Technology (MIT) was seeking locations in Europe for their Media-Lab Europe (MLE). MIT's proposal for a Media Lab Europe would build on its already pioneering partnership of corporate financing and academic research, which characterised the MIT Media Lab in Cambridge, Massachusetts in the USA. Part of the MIT proposal included also the opportunity for companies investing in Media Lab Europe to avail of the technology insights developed at the MIT Media Lab in Cambridge. In terms of location and property suitable to house the proposed Media Lab, an opportunity arose through the Guinness Brewery company,[20] which was seeking to sell a lot of its now derelict property in the Liberties/Coombe area. This property formed part of the St. James's Gate Guinness Brewery which itself covers a total area of about 64 acres.[21] The coincidental timing of these developments meant that preliminary enquiries into the possible foundation of the Digital Hub could begin immediately.

For the purposes of this research, we can separate the political process of establishing the Digital Hub into two phases: the initial planning phase 1999-2001 and subsequent first phase of implementation up to 2003. During the initial planning phase, the Department of the Taoiseach played a central role in setting the pace of development. The Irish Government, led by Department of the Taoiseach, reacted rapidly to the opportunity presented by the MIT proposal. By late 1999, the Taoiseach's Department had already reached a provisional agreement with MIT that would see the location of the Media-Lab Europe in the Liberties/Coombe area and in a restored warehouse originally used by the Guinness company. To secure the deal, the Irish Government would later purchase the Guinness properties on behalf of Media Lab Europe, as well as provide substantial seed capital for them to attract start-up companies to locate their business there. Between 1999 and 2001, a broader strategy was rolled out which would lead to the decision to develop the area as a Digital Hub (Digital Media District), with the Media-Lab Europe as the anchor tenant. Alongside this, the Irish Government established the Technology Foresight Fund, which aims to bring world-class researchers to Dublin's universities.

The Department of the Taoiseach facilitated the preparation of a strategy for the phased development of the Digital Hub project and also selected partner organisations to work together with the Taoiseach's department to plan for the Digital Hub project. At the outset, there were probably five different government departments that could have made a legitimate claim on the sponsorship of the project. Instead officials from these departments were seconded to the Department of the Taoiseach where the project had the full attention of the Secretary General, the most senior civil servant in the department. This was also a very public way of confirming that the project had the full support of the Taoiseach. Alongside these interests, senior representatives of the statutory agencies Enterprise Ireland and IDA Ireland, both with various responsibilities for industrial development, were also asked to become involved in this planning phase. The most striking aspect of the Digital Hub development is the speed of progress made and the key role played by the most central government actor, the Department of the Taoiseach, at least in the initial start up phase. The flexible and influential nature of the Department of the Taoiseach means that projects with no natural government departmental home can be "incubated" by the Taoiseach's Department until developed enough to be given a more permanent home in one of the government departments.[22] Our research suggests that it is questionable whether the Digital Hub would have ever taken off at this point had it not had the visible support of the government (interview material). Others have said that the individual patronage from the Taoiseach, Bertie Ahern, also lifted the project out of the possibility of it becoming mired in inter-departmental politics.

In 2000, a separate body or quango called Digital Media Development Ltd. (DMDL) was established to manage the implementation of the Digital Hub project. This agency (DMDL) has responsibility for the delivery of the proposed mix of digital media, enterprise, learning, retail and residential development in targeted Digital Hub area. DMDL also has responsibility to work along the public sector to develop the Public Private Partnership (PPP) financial model, which will fund the Digital Hub project over time. So far the Irish Government has committed an estimated 130 million Euro, and it is planned to expand this budget to 250 million Euro through these public/private partnerships with key business and research interests. Over the longer term (by 2010) it is envisaged that the Digital Hub project, currently located on a nine acres site will expand to cover about forty acres of land in the wider Liberties/Coombe area.

This almost immediate establishment of the agency, DMDL, to manage the policy and implementation process reminds us that that there is still a very strong tendency to resort to this kind of model of governance, as opposed to enhancing the role and management capacity of existing sub-national government structures. At the time of the announcement of the government's investment in the MIT-branded media lab, there was some criticism of the government decision from opposition parties and backbenchers, as well as from the academic community. Questions were raised as to why public money was being used to fund what was seen as a private enterprise. Irish academics criticised the government for funding "a research facility with an American university's brand name rather than an Irish one" (http:// www.darwinmag.com /read/ 070101/eire.html). The setting up, at arm's length, of an agency or quango like DMDL, like the earlier establishment of Temple Bar Properties, is a useful tactic to be able to ensure reasonably smooth implementation of a major multifaceted project such as Digital Hub. For example, this type of institutional structure provides some distance for the central government, and particularly the Department of the Taoiseach, from the day-to-day political issues and controversies that will inevitably arise. It also easily facilitates the contracting in full-time executive management services from the private sector and offers a pool of individuals skilled in business and project management, as well public relations.[23] Moreover, many of the public and private sector representatives, involved in the

Temple Bar redevelopment project, were also participants in the later Digital Hub development.[24] The relevant government departments and semi-state agencies continued to be represented on the management committee of DMDL and in the public/private partnerships being formed to develop the Digital Hub over time. Indeed during the start up period of DMDL, the Secretary General of the Department of the Taoiseach took up the position of executive chairman of the agency.

From its inception, the Digital Hub project was clearly defined by the Department of the Taoiseach as a policy initiative to be driven from the national level. However the project is in fact clearly linked to the development of a particular defined area within inner city Dublin and addresses the multifaceted aims for urban renewal in that area, as identified in the Liberties/Coombe IAP. When the Digital Hub was first mooted in Government circles, the Dublin City Council was keen to be one of the main actors in the development process. The Digital Hub was a perfect opportunity for Dublin City Council, particularly for the planning and economic development sections, to demonstrate how much had changed in terms of its organisational capacity. While the lead remained at level of national government, the Dublin City Council was asked to come on board the planning process with a view to it co-ordinating the necessary planning and development of infrastructure in the area to facilitate the Digital Hub project. Unlike the Temple Bar project, there was no attempt to sideline the Dublin City Council. Instead it seems that DMDL recognised that a collaborative partnership approach with Dublin City Council would be much more beneficial and early on, Dublin City Council was asked to participate in the DMDL management committee.

Another rationale for involving the Dublin City Council from an early stage was the need to change the original Integrated Area Plan for the Liberties/Coombe area (*i.e.* part of the Dublin City Development Plan) to accommodate the Digital Hub proposal. While this change went through with reasonable speed and relatively limited controversy in late 2001, early on in the Digital Hub process it seemed very likely that this might not be so. Our earlier discussion of the work of the Integrated Area Plan Monitoring Committee suggests that the relationships between Dublin City Council and the community representatives were becoming increasingly strained over this period of time and there was a chance that this controversy would spill over into the Digital Hub project. The DMDL quickly realised that given the proposed location of the Digital Hub in a very traditional community, it was important that local residents and businesses support and feel they can gain from the redevelopment of their area. The DMDL looked across the river Liffey to the Irish Financial Services Centre (IFSC), developed after Temple Bar and before the Digital Hub, which has been plagued with local disquiet and vandalism from its excluded local community. Worried that negative stories in newspapers may frighten potential clients for the Digital Hub, it was deemed more efficient and practical to bring the community into the project. It was better for DMDL to consult with the community—however tokenistic this may be—than to have the community on the outside without any forum to register their views, except for the media or resorting to vandalism (interview material).

The response from DMDL to this problem is very informative and in particular shows the skill of the DMDL (contracted in) executive services team, and others within to DMDL, to manage and effectively defuse a potentially difficult situation. DMDL sought to involve neighbourhood residents, sending questionnaires to residents and business owners asking what they thought of the plans, which buildings in their area they wanted to see renovated, the kinds of jobs they wanted to see created and what kind of training they wanted. The DMDL also directly met with and asked more than 140 different area community groups to help draw up a mission statement that will reflect as many local perspectives as possible. Local groups were quick to organise themselves into committees when meeting representatives of the Digital Hub.[25] Some within DMDL believe that the consultation was primarily a face-saving exercise which may be able to effect minor issues, but which can have no major effect on what is a purely commercial venture. It is difficult to estimate what outcome this community participation has had on the Digital Hub project, but it is certain that local dissatisfaction about the re-development has generated less media interest than that in Temple Bar.

Moreover, many in the community worry that with all the new money pouring into the area, housing prices will rise to the point where they and their children will be priced out of the market (http://www.darwinmag.com/read/070101/eire.html). In response to these concerns, the creation of affordable, new housing has been identified as one of the objectives of the urban renewal associated with the Digital Hub project over its medium term development. To conclude this section, the Digital Hub Development Agency Act was signed into law in 2003 and this put the DMDL on a statutory basis as the lead agency for managing the Digital Hub project. The Digital Hub Development Act modified the organisation of the Board and specifically listed its powers, making separate the roles for overall project management Board and day-to-day executive powers. Moreover, the Act specifically establishes the role and participation of local community representatives in the Digital Hub Management Board, as part of a three way partnership model between public/private and community interests.

4. Patterns of Governance for Urban Renewal in Ireland

Our empirical research has spanned a critical time period in the urban regeneration of Dublin's inner city. From the case studies presented, it is clear that the institutions of Ireland's centralised government remain deeply rooted and powerful. Partnership based governance, Irish style, increasingly involves central government departments initiating or directly engaging with micro level community actors and social partners in the initial stages of a local development initiative. Moreover over the 1990s there was a significant increase in the capacity of central government departments to effectively engage directly with local level actors and social partners more generally, often for the purposes of managing EU funds (Payne, 1999). This increase in capacity refers to changes in the internal organisation of the government departments, such as the provision of extra personnel and other resources, in separate dedicated sections within the overall department structure.

Following the Reform of the Structural Funds, the European Commission sought to persuade and coerce Ireland's political elite to enhance and strengthen the country's sub-national government structures for regional and local representation.

For the most part, the response of central government in Ireland was to sideline the traditional forms of local and regional government. In order to be able to bypass local government and yet establish a credible mechanism or process for partnership, the Irish central government has consistently resorted to the model of a stand-alone agency or quango. This agency has responsibility for effectively managing these partnerships "between central government 'lead' departments, these arm's length agencies, the social partners and micro-level groups at the community level, thereby satisfying the Commission's demand for broad participation and consultation" (Marshall, 2001). Indeed, at this stage there are numerous statutory or non-statutory based agencies or quangos, like Temple Bar Properties or the DMDL, with responsibility for particular types of policy implementation. Some commentators are highly critical of this approach and argue that "the Dublin area now has one of the most convoluted structures of governance in the entire EU, a status which may ultimately threaten to undo its newfound success" (Marshall, 2001).

5. The Future: Contested Governance and Urban Renewal

Our research findings suggest that there is emerging and contested pattern of governance for urban renewal in the Dublin city. The story of evolving governance patterns in Dublin is also one of growing and persistent calls for greater representation in the policy process. While this call has been echoed across the Irish political system, in particular, we have observed that public and private actors at sub-national level have become more aware and confident in their own potential contribution to the policy process. Perhaps this is not too surprising given Ireland's long tradition of clientelistic politics, which has always encouraged individuals and local community groups to take their political grievances directly to the top, to their national elected representatives in the Dáil. Moreover the impact of the various EU financed initiatives directly targeting local communities has allowed new actors to enter a political process, which has traditionally been centralist and hierarchical. Despite the limited effectiveness that these new actors actually enjoy there, there is little evidence, at the local level at least, that the enthusiasm for the partnership approach to policy-making is on the wane

(Payne *et al.*, 2001). Marshall suggests that "grass-roots actors, accustomed to a place at the table following a decade of EU-mandated partnership arrangements, show no intention of withdrawing from the urban policy process despite the progressive wind-down of EU funding for Dublin city-region" (2001).

This research suggests that the *ad hoc* approach to partnership governance in Ireland has led to a kind of confusion and irreverence about the distinction between participative and representative democracy. Often this has resulted in the pursuit of partnership led governance for its own sake, with little attention paid to who is representing who, on what basis and with what capacity to do so. Our research points to the general lack of trust, which characterises local level relationships between the local public elected representatives and the local private sector and community interests. Local urban development initiatives are seen to be successful often in spite of local government, which has usually felt threatened and sidelined by these activities.

The introduction of the various local government reforms from the mid-1990s onwards promises a stronger co-ordinating role for democratically elected local government in Ireland. Moreover, these reforms also attempt to incorporate into their model of local government the widespread demand and popularity of participatory form of local governance. However the research findings presented here suggest that, by themselves, these reforms seem unable to facilitate city and county councils to engage constructively with local partners and establish a clear advisory role or voice for the local community and social partners in local government policy. The findings second of the area-based case studies, particularly the discussion of the IAP in this research point to these failings. While this move towards a more formalised approach to partnership at the local level and within local government is welcomed by many of those involved, the really difficult and thorny issues of enhancing the resources, management capacity and policy remit of democratically elected local government in Ireland remains essentially untouched. In the absence of real progress on this front, Ireland's favourite response, innovative but *ad hoc*, effective but of dubious democratic credentials, the ubiquitous quango seems likely to remain the only game in town.

NOTES

1. For instance in the Irish case, the role of the appointed officials such as planners in Dublin City Council was usually sidelined as were the views of the local community interests, who often failed to benefit from the property-led approach to urban renewal in the city (McGuirk, 2000). Russell has pointed out that "major reviews of urban policy such as that carried out by...a consortium of consultants headed up by KPMG in Ireland clearly outlined this failure" (KPMG *et al.*, 1996 in Russell, 2001).
2. Under the Structural Funds, these central government departments became the "lead departments" directly managing the implementation of the Operational Programmes.
3. Local government in Ireland consists of a number of local and regional authorities at three levels. These are: at county/city level: thirty-four local authorities are the mainline providers of local government services—twenty-nine county councils and five cities; at sub-county level: eighty town authorities carry out a representational role for the town with a varying range of local government functions; at regional level: eight regional authorities co-ordinate some of the county/city and sub-county activities; they play a monitoring role in relation to the use of EU structural funds; two regional authorities, known as Regional Assemblies: were established in July 1999 under new structures for regionalisation.
4. Local councillors have "reserve powers" which implies that under some exceptions they may act to amend the county or city development plan.
5. The Taoiseach is the equivalent of Prime Minister in the UK Parliamentary system.
6. Under the Local Government Act 2001, the county boroughs of Dublin, Cork, Waterford, Galway and Limerick had their title changed from "Corporation" to City Council.
7. This legislation was introduced it on the last day of the sitting of Dáil Éireann, when fewer TDs were in attendance, instead of waiting until the start of the autumn sitting.
8. Temple Bar Properties was founded to oversee the development of Temple Bar as a bustling residential, cultural and small business precinct of the city. This mission statement was formalised through provisions of the Temple Bar Area Renewal and Development Act, 1991. As well as ability to compulsorily acquire property in the Temple Bar Area and to acquire and manage the lands, buildings and leases, Temple Bar Properties were given control over the manner in which their tenants in the area sub-let, shared or sub-leased their buildings. The Act also

allowed the Minister for Finance to guarantee borrowings by Temple Bar Properties up to an amount of IR£25 million.

9. Eight new Regional Authorities (RA) were created under the second CSF to provide a new regional focus for the implementation of Structural Funds programmes made up of unelected bodies composed of town and city councillors, who "never enjoyed a high profile in central government, political or parliamentary circles" (Knox and Haslam 1999: 27) the RA's were demanded by the European Commission which had been adamant that a regional tier be established for the administration of ERDF and ESF programmes. They were granted only a token consultative and oversight role over the course of the CSF. The Dublin Regional Authority and its sister organisations exist predominantly to satisfy the formal European requirements of partnership and subsidiarity, and have almost no resources or credibility amongst national political actors. Ireland's central government once again played the key role in programme design, implementation, and partnership in the second round of Structural funds.

10 "Outwith the Dublin Corporation, there are presently three County Councils, responsible for local authority functions: Fingal County Council, Dun Laoghaire—Rathdown County Council and the South Dublin County Council. These bodies were created in 1991, when old Dublin County Council was disbanded. This local government reform, in turn, caused serious disruption of the metropole, as new institutions had to be created (or often duplicated)" (Marshall, 2002; see also Fitzgerald, 1992).

11. In October 1991, several teams of Dublin-based architects were asked to submit proposals for a framework plan for Temple Bar, to spark discussion on the visible aspects of the area. The competition was won by Group '91 a loose team of eight separate practices which formed itself into a company in order to submit a collective proposal. This informal grouping became responsible for much of the visual aspect of the area, reflecting similar informal patterns elsewhere in the project.

12. "Under the national social partnership agreement, the Programme for Economic and Social Progress (PESP) in 1991, twelve Partnership companies (legally constituted under the Companies Act and limited by guarantee) were set up to pilot an area based response to long term unemployment over the period 1991-1993. In 1992 a EU Global Grant for local development—provided funding for the 12 Partnership companies and for an additional 28 local development groups. The Global grant placed greater emphasis then the PESP on community development and on building capacity in local organisation so that they could participate in an effective manner in the local development process. In 1995 under the Operational Programme for Local Urban and Rural Development a further 26 Partnership Companies were created" (Russell, 2001).

13. CDBs are representative of local government, local development bodies (*e.g.* Area Partnerships, LEADER Groups etc.), the State agencies or

quangos and social partners (*i.e.* business, trade unions and farmers interests) operating locally.

14. Following this initiative, the Local Government Act, 2001 (No. 37 of 2001) was enacted. The stated aims of the Act are to enhance the role of the elected member; to support community involvement with local authorities in a more participative local democracy; and to modernise local government legislation, and provide the framework for new financial management systems and other procedures to promote efficiency and effectiveness.
15. A large section of the south-west inner city is included in the plan, from the Liffey quays in the north to the Grand Canal in the south and from Patrick Street and Clanbrassil Street in the east to St. James's Hospital and Rialto in the west.
16. This type of approach to planning was also supported by the changes in government policy regarding the focus of the 1999 Urban Renewal Scheme for tax designated areas.
17. "The digital hub, as it is commonly called, will house companies that specialize in everything from special effects and digital TV to electronic music and technology R&D—all within a deeply traditional neighbourhood of about 20,000 people" (http://www.darwinmag.com/read/070101/eire.html).
18. Irish Council for Science, Technology & Innovation (ICSTI) led this report. The Irish Government set up the ICSTI in 1997 with the aim of building a strategic science, technology and innovation policy for the country.
19. The report argued that while the Irish government's low corporate tax rates of the late 1980s and early 1990s succeeded in luring technology leaders such as EMC, Dell and Microsoft to Ireland, most of the jobs created were in support sectors—such as manufacturing or call centers—which do not generate much intellectual capital. Moreover, these jobs were also dependent on labour costs staying low and as the wages of Irish workers continued to rise, so the incentive to stay would soon disappear. For Ireland's economic prosperity to continue, its leaders needed to build a framework to support homegrown innovation (http://www.darwinmag.com/read/070101/eire.html).
20. The Guinness company is owned by the multinational foods and drinks conglomerate Diageo and Guinness is now brewed in many different locations outside of Dublin and outside of Ireland.
21. The Guinness Brewery has been located in the area since nineteenth century and at its height employed up to 4000 people. In the later part of the twentieth century, this figure had dwindled to about 400 and much of the Guinness site became redundant and derelict.
22. By 2001, the Department of Public Enterprise had taken the role of "lead department" on the Digital Hub project. By 2003, this responsibility was to move to the Department Communications, Marine and Natural Resources.

23. "The Board of DMDL commissioned an executive services team, comprising a consortium of companies to implement the first phase of The Digital Hub project with public sector, private sector and community partners up to December 2003. The consortium, which provides executive services to The Digital Hub is led by Magahy & Company and includes Price Waterhouse Coopers, Murray O'Laoire Architects, BDO Simpson Xavier and Judo Design" (DMD, 2001).

24. One of the most noticeable aspects of Irish political life is the relatively small pool of people from which political actors are taken. A small population has given Ireland a small and readily accessible political elite. However, this may also have a downside. More recently, another high-profile urban redevelopment project in Dublin has collapsed in part because of negative rumours surrounding the personal friendship of its major partners. Such has been the narrow band of people involved in urban redevelopment projects that the Dáil Public Accounts Committee questioned whether tenders were awarded on the basis of friendships or on merit. A number of state-sponsored tribunals have been founded in Ireland to examine corruption in planning and other issues, partially resulting from informal practices in un-regulated areas of the economy. Collins and O'Shea's study into corruption in Irish politics has noted the overlapping of public duties and private interests in many political projects and the often informal nature of decision-making processes, especially "golden circles" or "cronyism" in matters of urban planning (Collins and O'Shea, 2000, 71).

25. In July 2001 the Liberties/Coombe Integrated Area Plan Monitoring Committee established an Advisory Group, under the chairmanship of Clive Brownlee, Assistant Managing Director of Diageo Ireland to examine the potential benefit for the community from The Digital Hub. The Advisory Group has produced a report which helped to shape this development strategy particularly in the areas of potential long-term benefit for the community (DMD, 2001).

REFERENCES

Primary Sources

An Taisce (1993) *Temple Bar in the Balance* (Dublin: An Taisce).

An Taisce (1996) *Ireland's Designated Areas: Lessons from Temple Bar* (An Taisce Discussion Paper).

Dublin Corporation (1990) *The Temple Bar Area Action Plan 1990* (Dublin: Dublin Corporation).

Government of Ireland (1989) *National Development Plan 1989-1993*. Dublin: Government Publications Stationary Office.

Government of Ireland (1991) *Local Government Reorganisation and Reform* Dublin: Government Publications Stationary Office.

Government of Ireland (1991a) *Programme for Economic and Social Progress* Dublin: Government Publications Stationary Office.

KPMG (1996) *Study of the Urban Renewal Schemes* (Dublin: The Stationary Office).

Temple Bar Development Council (1988) *Submission to Dublin Corporation Planning Department on the Draft Dublin Development Plan* (Dublin: TBDC).

Temple Bar Properties (1995) *Final Report on the Urban Pilot Project: A Report to the European Commission on the Operation of the Pilot Programme of Urban Regeneration in Temple Bar, Undertaken under Article 10 of Council Regulations* (EEC) no. 4254/88 (Dublin: Temple Bar Properties).

Temple Bar Properties (1991) *Temple Bar Lives! Winning Architectural Framework Plan* (Dublin: Temple Bar Properties).

Temple Bar Properties (1992) *Development Programme for Temple Bar* (Dublin: Temple Bar Properties).

Secondary Sources

Adair, A., Berry, J., McGreal, S. (1994) 'Investment and Private Sector Residential Development in Inner-city Dublin' *Journal of Property Valuation and Investment*, vol. 12, no. 1, 47-56(10).

Adair, A.S., Berry, J.N., McGreal, W.S. (1994) 'Taxation Allowances and Profiles: Commercial Property Development in Dublin' *Journal of Property Finance*, vol. 5, no. 1, 9-13(5) .

Bannon, M.J. (1999) 'Dublin town planning competition: Ashbee and Chettle's "New Dublin-A Study in Civic Planning"' *Perspectives*, vol. 14, no. 2, 145-62(18).

Bennett, R. and D. Payne (2003) 'Re-negotiating Regional economic Development in England—who has "Joined-up?" in: A. Deffner, D. Konstadakopulos and Y. Psycharis (eds.) *Culture and Regional Economic Development: Cultural, Political and Social Perspectives*, University of Thessaly Press, Volos, Greece.

Chubb, B. (1993). *The Government and Politics of Ireland.* (London: Longman).

Conway, M. and Konvitz, J. (2000) 'Meeting the Challenge of Distressed Urban Areas' *Urban Studies*, vol. 37, no. 4, 749-74(26).

Coyle, C. and Sinnott, R. (1992) *Europe and the Regions in Ireland: A View from Below.* Dublin: CEEPA Working Papers.

Hardiman, N. (1988) *Pay, Politics and Economic Performance in Ireland, 1970-1987* (Oxford University Press).

Hart, J. (1985) 'The European Regional Development Fund and the Republic of Ireland'. In Keating, M. and Jones, B. (ed.) *Regions in the European Community* Oxford: Clarendon Press.

Healey, P., Cameron, S., Davoudi, S. and Mandani, A. (eds.) (1995) *Managing Cities: The New Urban Context* (Chichester: John Wiley and Sons).

Laffan, B. (1996) 'Ireland: A Region without Regions—The Odd Man Out?' In Hooghe, L. *Cohesion Policy and European Integration: Building Multilevel Governance.* (Oxford: Clarendon Press).

McGreal, S., Berry, J., Lloyd, G. and McCarthy, J. (2002) 'Tax-based Mechanisms in Urban Regeneration: Dublin and Chicago Models' *Urban Studies*, vol. 39, no. 10, 1819-31.

McGuirk, P.M. and MacLaran, A. "Changing Approaches to Urban Planning in an 'Entrepreneurial City": The Case of Dublin' (2001) *European Planning Studies*, vol. 9, no. 4, 437-57(21).

McGuirk, P.M. (2000) 'Power and Policy Networks in Urban Governance: Local Government and Property-led Regeneration' in *Dublin Urban Studies*, vol. 37, no. 4, 651-72.

Moore, N.M. (2002) 'From indigenous industry to foreign finance: The changing face of Dublin Docklands' *Land Use Policy*, vol. 19, no. 4, 325-37.

National Economic and Social Council (1979). *Urbanisation and Regional Development in Ireland*. No. 45, Dublin: NESC.

Payne, D. (1999) *Policy Making in the European Union. An analysis of the impact of the Reform of the Structural Funds in Ireland*. Amsterdam: Thela Thesis.

Payne, D., R.J. Mokken and F.N. Stokman (2000) "European Union Power and Regional Involvement—A case study of the political implications of the Reform of the Structural Funds for Ireland" in P. Moser, G. Schneider and G. Kirchgassner (eds.) *Decision Rules in the European Union. A Rational Choice Perspective*. London: Macmillan.

Payne, D. (2001) "Regional Economic Development in England—The role of multilevel partnerships in the new Regional Development Agencies" at European Consortium of Political Research (ECPR) University of Kent, Canterbury, September 2001.

Payne, D. (2002) "Analysing Borders and Networks in Ireland. A model-guided approach" at Recycling the State. The Politics of Adoption in Contemporary Ireland, Conference in Association with the Institute for the Study of Social Change and the Department of Politics, University College, Dublin, 20 April 2002.

Pickard, R. (1994) 'Urban Conservation in the Republic of Ireland: The Dublin Example—Part 1' *Structural Survey*, vol. 12, no. 4, 24-30(7)

Pickard, R. (1994) Urban Conservation in the Republic of Ireland: The Dublin Example—Part 2 *Structural Survey*, vol. 12, no. 5, 23-30(8)

Prichard, D. 'On the Edge: Regenerating a Dublin suburb' (2000) *City: Analysis of urban trends, culture, theory, policy, action*, 1 April 2000, vol. 4, no. 1, 65-80.

Quinn, P. (ed.) (1996) *Temple Bar: The Power of an Idea* (Kinsale: Temple Bar Properties).

Russell, P. (2001) 'Integrated Urban Renewal in Ireland: Constraints to achieving integration in the H.A.R.P. Project Dublin.' Paper presented at the European Urban Research Association Conference Area-based Initiatives in Contemporary Urban Policy-innovations in City Governance, Copenhagen, 17–19 May 2001.

7

Urban Development Debates: Challenges of Greening Urban Environment in Nigeria

LABODE POPOOLA
labopopoola@skannet.com
Department of Forest Resources Management, University of Ibadan, Nigeria.

Urbanization

Urbanization is a normal feature of the development process. Most urban areas were hitherto small, native and rural settlements, which gradually evolved into peri-urban areas and eventually into cosmopolitan and in some cases megalopolitan centres. They have evolved according to Lefcoe (1979) in situations when neighbourhood interests will have to yield totally to other forces, when the need is overwhelming for a highway, a park, or a massive re-development project, and no amount of care in design or implementation can preserve the area largely as it had been.

In the Nigerian situation as it is with most developing countries, these expansions have not been due totally to the exigencies of development as dictated by authorities governing such areas, but due in the main, to job seekers drifting from the drudgery of farming in rural areas in search of "less tasking" and "better paying" jobs in urban centres. Such massive movements have resulted in creation of sub-standard satellite settlements at the fringes of urban areas such as Nyanya, Gwagwalada, Kubuwa, Zuba, Karu, etc. in Federal Capital Territory (FCT), Abuja and Agbado, Maroko, Magodo Mile 2, Egbe, Ikotun, Isheri, Ketu Alapere, etc. in Lagos among several other cities such as Ibadan, Onitsha, Enugu, Kaduna,

Maiduguri, etc. With time, these slums are taken over by exigencies of urban expansion and the drift continues. According to Oguntala (1993), urban environment in many parts of Nigeria is in a deplorable state with most open spaces or green areas being taken up for the development of concrete situations. The problems are compounded by uncontrolled rural to urban migration of people which further stresses the already inadequate housing, drainage and recreational facilities in such urban areas.

According to Lefcoe (1979), cities and individuals mature in similar ways. They reach an age and status where certain crucial choices have to be made, choices concerning what they are about. For an individual, this involves settling into a vocation, becoming comfortable, living with a mate or alone, and adjusting to wants and means. A city selects its vocation when it decides whether to be primarily a city of commerce, giving its hearts to banks, office space, and employment generally or a habitat city for residents.... Most cities of any size are part habitat and part cities of commerce; the problem is striking the balance. Striking the balance however, requires well-thought out plans, designs and implementation. Unfortunately, this is the bane of urban development in Nigeria. The major cities *i.e.* Abuja, Lagos, Ibadan, Port Harcourt, Kano, Kaduna, Enugu, Calabar, Jos, Maiduguri among several others have masterplans which in most cases have not been adhered to. It is not uncommon to find a factory with its emission of pollutants sited right in a residential area. The vogue now is the siting of fuel stations in residential areas not minding the inherent dangers to adjacent residents. In Abuja, the new Federal Capital Territory, structures were erected on pipelines and places designated as green areas. Gladly, most of these properties have come under the heavy weight of bulldozers since the last quarter of year 2003.

Environmental Concerns

The total land area of Nigeria is 923,678 km^2 with an estimated population of over 120 million people. The country's forest area has however been on a continuous decline. In 1900 the area under forest was 971 km^2 or 0.01% by 1970 there was a remarkable increase: 9342 km^2 or 10%. However this has now dropped to 46,542.14 km^2, a mere 5.04%. Several reasons have been adduced for this situation (FORMECU, 1999), which include the rapid creation of states from 12 in 1967 to 37 in 1996 (including Abuja, the Federal Capital Territory) with several new state capitals some of which were actually semi-urban settlements before their new status as state capitals. Apart from the heavy demands of wood for construction and other purposes some previously constituted forests actually gave way to development of some of these cities. Other factors according to Popoola (2004) is the non-forest policies particularly, energy policies, which have continually, posed a grievous threat to the forestry sub-sector. Budget allocations to forestry have dropped to a mere 2% of total annual allocation of public funds, while states still embark on aggressive revenue generation through unplanned and uncontrolled logging. Nigeria being the third poorest country (UNDP, 2002) in the world with GNP per capita of less than US$ 800.00 and with high level of adult illiteracy makes its more than 80% urban and rural poor heavily dependent on forest products for sustenance. Most of the highly valued indigenous species such as *Milicia excelsa* (iroko), *Cordia millenii* (omo), *Afzelia africana* (apa), *Entandrophragma utile* (ijebo), *Khaya ivorensis* (oganwo), *Khaya grandifoliola* (gedu), *Lophira alata* (eki) *Terminalia* spp (afara) among several others which were common some four decades ago in the forest reserves have now become rare. Ironically, relics of these species can be found only in some urban enclaves. For example, the University of Ibadan, which was founded in 1948 on the outskirts of Ibadan, is now right in the city centre and still harbours the relics of several of these species and also one of the most mature and contiguous stands of *Tectona grandis* (Teak) in the country. This has further strengthened the argument that urban forests have a great potential in the conservation of rare or threatened forest species.

Popoola and Ajewole (2002) have observed that the nature of urban environment and the diverse needs of man, place heavy responsibilities on trees and forests as important components of a conducive living urban environment. This makes the role of urban forestry in environmental conservation and rehabilitation crucially important. Ironically, urbanization has figured as one of the principal causes of forest destruction

(Popoola and Ajewole, 2001). For instance, FAO (1997) projected that the world population will reach 8500 million by the year 2025, and an expected 17 million hectares of forest will need to be destroyed annually to meet the various infrastructural needs of this burgeoning population. According to Oguntala (1993) increase in urban population in Nigerian cities has led to decrease in recreational facilities with its detrimental consequences on the mental and physical health of the people. Indeed, more and more mentally retarded people are now common features in our cities. The choking of the cities is also indicated by the lack of spaces for dumping urban wastes, which now accumulate on the streets, causing health and environmental hazards. Between 1960 and the present time, for example, there has been massive deforestation in Ibadan and environs for 'developmental purposes'. Some of these are highlighted in Table 1.

TABLE 1: Trends in Forest Destruction and Consequences in Ibadan Metropolis

Location of Forests Destroyed	Development Project Substituted	Environmental Impacts
Sapati* Hill Fuelwood (Ogunpa dam) Plantations (1960s)	Premier Hotel	Large scale erosion and flooding of Ogunpa river
Bodija Wetlands (1960s and 1970s)	Housing estate	Destruction of the source of Ogunpa river
Sapati* Hill Fuelwood (Ogunpa dam) Plantations (1970s and 1980s)	Cultural Centre	Destruction of Agodi Gardens and fish ponds, continued massive flooding resulting in over 300 deaths
Jericho (Alalubosa) Forest Reserve, including FRIN Forest Gene Pool (1980s and 1990s)	Alesinloye market and housing estates	Siltation and pollution of Alalubosa Lake
University of Ibadan Teak Plantation (Early 1980s)	Proposed 5 Star hotel	Massive erosion
Eleyele Fuelwood Plantation (1970s)	Dual carriageway (road development)	Siltation and flooding of Eleyele Lake—source of Water to parts of Ibadan
Scout Camp Fuelwood Plantations (1990s) Area of Ibadan	Proposed Shopping Complex	Massive erosion and flooding in challenge

SOURCE: Popoola and Ajewole (2001) as modified from Oguntala (1993).
*Corrupted pronunciation of 'Shepherd Hills'.

In Enugu, Southeastern Nigeria, the famous Apaka forest reserve has been partially dereserved to make way for a Government Reservation Area, ostensibly for residential purposes. Communal clashes in Kaduna State have resulted in massive displacement of people who now find forest estates in peri-urban areas such as the Afaka forest reserve and Mando Forest for cemetery in Kaduna city as alternative settlements, thereby inflicting heavy vegetation losses. The uncontrolled logging of *Tectona grandis* (Teak) for export between 1990 and 1998 also resulted in serious vegetation losses in urban and per-urban areas, which had plantations of that species. Worse still is the increasing price of domestic energy, which has compelled, an adjustment to the use of fuelwood and charcoal. The implication of this on deforestation is better imagined. Popoola (1992) has chronicled the upward trend in the prices of domestic energy and concluded that it portends dangers to sustainable development in the country.

The Need for Greening Urban Areas

The quality of life in an urban area is greatly influenced by the amount and quality of its green spaces including forests; hence the need for urban renewal through re-introduction of trees and increasing the green areas becomes pertinent and urgent. The largest source of carbon dioxide is the use of fossil fuel, followed by deforestation. Emission control strategies should therefore typically focus on reductions in the rate of fossil fuel consumption and/or deforestation (Adeleke, 1992). The industrialized world consumes the greatest percentage of the world's fossil fuels. They do not however seem willing to dramatically reduce this level, as suggested by the Intergovernmental Panel on Climate Change (IPCC), in order to stabilize the concentration of carbon in the atmosphere (Adeleke, 1992). Since trees, like all green plants, absorb carbon dioxide during photosynthesis, restoration is often suggested as a means of countering the increase in greenhouse gases in the atmosphere (Schroeder, 1991). This has resulted in shifting attention to reforestation/afforestation as a way of containing the carbon dioxide build-up in the atmosphere.

The areas of forests plantation required to have a significant impact on the amount of carbon dioxide in the atmosphere are colossal (FAO, 1993). For example, one study (Sedjo and Solomon, 1989) indicates that the current net annual increase in atmospheric carbon (approximately 3000 million tonnes) could be sequestered in approximately 465 million hectares of plantation forests for about 30 years, or as long as they remained alive. To this end, several research workers have estimated the amount of carbon stored by standing forest. A hectare of most tropical primary forest in Brazil can hold over 300 tonnes of carbon, while a hectare of mature Douglas fir forest in Canada can retain over 600 tonnes (French, 2000). The contribution of urban trees and others outside forests to the total requirement can therefore not be overestimated.

FAO (2001) has defined trees outside forests (TOF) as including among others those in urban environment (human settlements) and infrastructure environment such as parks and gardens, trees around buildings and in lines along streets, roads, railways, rivers streams and canals. It states further that such trees are sources of a wide range of non-wood products (Table 2). These huge potential benefits are yet fully untapped because of undefined institutional arrangements regarding tree and land tenure in Nigeria. Unfortunately

TABLE 2: Trees Outside the Forest: Source of a Wide Range of Non-wood Products

Tree parts	Some products	Production systems	Some uses
Fruit and seeds	Fresh and dried fruits, seeds (coffee, shea-nut).	Fruit orchards, home gardens parklands.	Food, cosmetic and pharmaceutical products.
Foliage	Animal fodder, leaves for human consumption.	Agrosilvipastoral systems.	Feeds, food and medicinal uses.
Stems and bark	Latex, gum arabic, resin, tannin, fibres.	Plantations, hone gardens, parklands.	Food, tires and treads, hides and textiles, agrofood and pharmaceutical industries, cosmetics.
	Cork, bark products, essential oils.	Agrosilvipastoral systems.	Corks, wall coverings, insulation, pharmaceutical derivatives.
Flowers	Honey, essential oils.	Agrosilvipastoral systems.	Food, pharmaceutical industries.
Sap	Alcoholic drinks, beverages.	Agrosilvipastoral systems.	Alcoholic drinks.

SOURCE: FAO (2001).

however, the government that holds the forest "in trust" by statute for society has inadvertently become the "protagonist" of urban deforestation, by unwittingly giving higher priorities to other land uses over forestry, Popoola and Ajewole (2001). Challenges faced by society will therefore include how well it can harness its resources in such a way as to be able to restore the declining urban environment through concerted and focused efforts.

Prospects for the Greening of Urban Environment

It is very well established that by virtue of their anatomical structures and physiological functions trees (forests) serve as natural purifiers of the environment. Also because of their size, shape, colour and seasonal variations, forests become the most visible natural living element that engenders serenity and harmony within the urban environment. Forests can equally be used as excellent indications of the quality of urban environment since they integrate both positive and negative factors to present a defined urban physiognomy. Many more of these attributes of urban forests are well documented (Ogigirigi, 1986; Olembo and de Rham, 1987; Mbakwe, 1992; Oguntala, 1993; Osemeobo, 1993; Laverne and Lewis, 1996; Freer-Smith, 1996; McPherson *et al.*, 1997; Xie *et al.*, 1998 among several others).

It is also a fact that trees (and forests) were indeed a common feature in many ancient cities in Nigeria. For example avenue plantings with *Azacdiracta indica, Khaya spp, Prosopis africana* and *Delonix regia* were commonplace in such cities as Kano, Maiduguri, Ibadan, Kaduna, Yola. The appropriateness of some of these species, particularly *Delonix regia* has however been a subject of debate as it is believed, and it appears true that the heavy lateral rooting system of the species creates cracks on avenues while the crown, if unmanaged creates debris and sanitation problems on the highways.

The level of awareness of urban dwellers of the importance of urban forests is not in doubt in Nigeria. Results of a survey of 120 randomly selected respondents in six major cities within the six geopolitical zones of Nigeria (Table 3) gives a clear indication of this.

TABLE 3: Awareness of the importance of urban forests among urban dwellers in Nigeria

	Geopolitical Zone	City	Level of awareness %
1.	North Central	Kano	95
2.	North East	Maiduguri	97
3.	North West	Sokoto	93
4.	South East	Enugu	85
5.	South South	Port Harcourt	78
6.	South West	Lagos	81
	Mean		88.2

SOURCE: Popoola (2002).

The result of the survey compares favourably with the findings of Popoola and Ajewole (2002) in Ibadan, Nigeria, wherein 77.3 per cent of the respondents indicated their willingness to even pay or, in other words make financial contributions to a proposed Ibadan reforestation project. In a similar study in Nigeria Popoola (2002) reports that 69.71 per cent of the surveyed respondents expressed their willingness to pay certain amounts, ranging from ₦ 100 ₦ 5000 per annum, for reforestation within their locality (Figure 1).

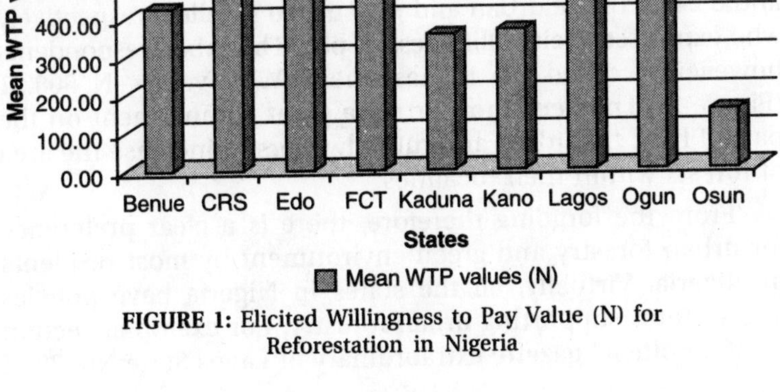

FIGURE 1: Elicited Willingness to Pay Value (N) for Reforestation in Nigeria

The respondents however varied in their perceptions of the purposes of such forests. While most respondents in the semi-arid to arid zones of northern Nigeria perceived forests as being basically for amelioration of the harsh environment those in the moist southern zone perceived them as being for recreational purposes and when the need arises for consumptive uses. These perceptions tend to follow *a priori* expectation arising for environmental circumstances of the various zones. Similarly, almost all the respondents (94 per cent) expressed their wish for the continued preservation of urban forests where they exist. Again, this agrees with the findings of Popoola and Ajewole (2001) in Ibadan, Nigeria (Table 4).

TABLE 4: Percentage distribution of respondents' reasons for supporting continued preservation of urban forests in Ibadan

		Provision of Physical Needs	Environmental Protection	Recreation	Total
Neighbourhood	Number	68	67	40	175
	%	38.9	38.3	22.9	100
Non-Neighbourhood	Number	65	74	56	195
	%	33.3	37.9	28.7	100
Pooled	Number	133	141	96	370
	%	35.9	38.1	25.9	100

SOURCE: Popoola and Ajewole, 2001.

Popoola (2002) also considered location factors in his study on Willingness To Pay for reforestation in Nigeria and found out that 83.17% of respondents from the rural areas were willing to pay for reforestation, compared with the 64.93% and 63.48% of the urban and peri-urban dwellers respectively who expressed their willingness to pay. The urban respondents however recorded the highest mean WTP value—N 508.21 (Figure 2). This tends to portray a great commitment on the part of both the urban and rural dwellers to increase the area of forests within their localities.

From the forgoing therefore, there is a clear preference for urban forestry and green environment by most residents in Nigeria. Virtually, all the states in Nigeria have policies and statutes supporting urban forestry. For example, Section 16 of an official gazette extraordinary of Lagos State No. 29 of

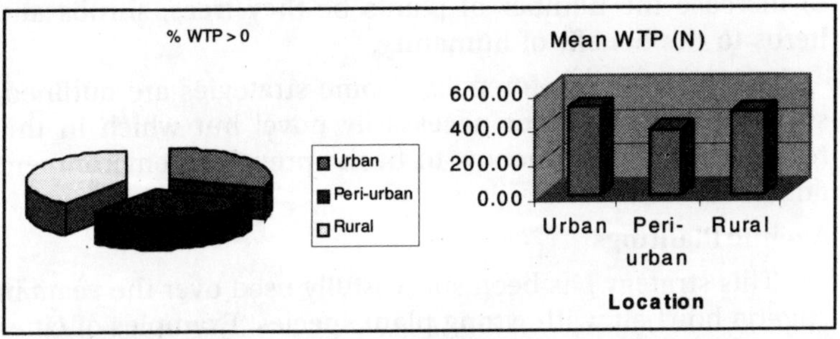

FIGURE 2: Effect of location factor on the proportion of people willing to pay for Reforestation and mean WTP values (₦)

27th July, 1996-Part A entitled "Forestry development (Private Participation) and Forestry Trust Fund edict, 1996 recognizes *inter alia* recreation (Botanical and Zoological Gardens, City Parks, Amenity Plantings and Leisure) and social (urban forestry, avenue plantings, community forestry) as important forestry based projects desirable for sustainable economic development. The critical issues are however the implementation of this ideal and the enabling environment to make such activities succeed.

Strategies for Greening the Urban Environment

The need to return the earth to its natural form, by engaging in planting activities to bring back lost plants in order to mitigate adverse environmental problems created by man is being gradually realized. However, there are still some limiting factors, though somewhat surmountable. The inadequacy of terrestrial space is staring humanity in the face. This has arisen because of geometrically increasing human population and the concomitant need for food and fibre to sustain it. Land being a limited natural resource has to be fully exploited for food production and plants, which have little or no nutritive values, are bearing the brunt of the exploitation of land for food production. Under the influence of civilization and with technological advancement, natural landscapes have been changed through mining and crude oil and solid mineral exploration and exploitation. Man: land ratio has therefore continually shrunk. This is indeed a challenge to urban foresters to maximize the use of the limited spaces in crowded areas to increase the number of plants be they trees, shrubs and herbs to the benefit of humanity.

Arising from the foregoing, some strategies are outlined, some of which are not necessarily novel but which in this text are modified somehow to fit the prevailing environment and circumstances.

Avenue Plantings

This strategy has been successfully used over the years in Nigeria howbeit, with wrong plant species. Examples of cities where these can be found are Kano, Zaria, Sokoto, Kaduna, Maiduguri, Damaturu, Dutse, Katsina, Birnin Kebbi and Yola in the Semi-arid north; Makurdi, Lokoja, Jos, Jalingo in the wetter middle belt zones. The common species used include *Khaya* and *Azadirachta indica* (neem). It has also been practised in the premises of corporate organizations with large expanses of land such as universities, research institutions. The limitation here, particularly with neem is the usually unmanaged crown and the profuse fruiting of the species, which creates huge debris on the highways. In the more humid southern cities of Lagos, Ibadan, Enugu, Calabar, Ilesa, Port Harcourt and Benin City the most commonly used species had been *Khaya spp* and *Delonix regia*. The latter suffers the same weakness as neem. The main problem with *Khaya spp* and neem have been the incessant debarking for medicinal purposes, which tends to create openings for fungal attack and making it prone to other opportunistic pests and diseases. Additionally, the debarking is usually done in such a way that reduces the aesthetics of the tree and the scenery.

However, some other species have been introduced lately. These include *Gmelina arborea, Poliandra politricum* (locally called police or masquerade tree) and *Cassuarina* (Christmas tree). A good example is the about 40 km dual carriage way from the Nnamdi Azikiwe International Airport, Abuja which is planted with *Gmelina arborea* and *Poliandra politricum.* The former can also be found on the dual carriage airport road leading to and from the Murtala Mohammed International Airport in Lagos. This species has indeed become the toast of avenue planting and also within premises in Nigeria. Other species which can provide multiple benefits without being damaged should be tried. In this regard such candidate species include *Irvingia spp, Prosopis africana, citrus, sena spp, Terminalia spp, Cassuarina, Eucalyptus, Syzigium mallacensis, Gmelina arborea.* In addition, planting and maintenance should be planned and not done on *ad hoc* bases as it is currently the case. Professionals should also be engaged to handle necessary operations while all stakeholders within localities that are planted should be part of decision-making process (from conceptualization to implementation). Of course, this can only be better achieved by evaluating public perceptions of the project. Periodic impact assessment would also be desirable.

Open Spaces/Recreation Areas

Recreation areas are normal features in urban design and planning. However some adverse socio-economic factors have tended to relegate this to the background in Nigeria. For example, Ibadan City in the Southwestern Nigeria with a total land area of 130 km^2 has one of the lowest percentages of open spaces (1.38 per cent) among Nigerian cities (World Bank, 1992). This does not imply that other cities are indeed spectacularly better. As had been mentioned earlier, most open spaces meant for recreation have been converted to concrete structures, and as such very few recreation centres exist in our cities. But for the intervention of the Forestry Association of Nigeria in 2002 and the sound judgment of the immediate past Governor of Oyo State, Alhaji Lam Adesina, the Agodi Gardens in Ibadan was already earmarked for allocation to residential development. There is, therefore, the need to revisit city masterplans to restore the scenic beauty of the cities. The Ministry of the Federal Capital Territory, Abuja, is effectively pursuing this and it has led to the demolition of several illegal structures. The reclaimed areas are also being rehabilitated. Relevant enabling laws however appear obsolete and in some cases weak to deal decisively with breaches. A review of such laws should be carried out while relevant agencies and Non-Governmental Organizations with interest in rehabilitation and conservation of green areas in cities should be empowered to perform their duties.

Homegardens/Orchards

Homegardens are quite common in residential areas in the rural and peri-urban setting of Nigeria, particularly in the southeastern part of Nigeria. They are often made up of indigenous fruit trees and shrubs occupying different strata within the garden. In a typical homegarden can be found such species as *Chrysophyllum albidum, Dacryodes edulis, Irvingia gabonensis, Kola nitida, Garcina kola, Dialum guinese, Spondias mombin, Jatropha gossypifolia, J. curcas, Denettia tripetala* among several others. They serve the multiple purpose of provision of food, medicine, fodder, shade, soil stabilization as well as mitigating adverse environmental effects around the residential areas. This method can also be practised in urban settings, particularly where space is not a limiting factor. Even where this is so, few stands of some of these multipurpose trees and shrubs may be planted in the residential terrain. On the aggregate, they do contribute to the greening of the cities.

Woodlots

The basic objective of woodlots is to provide individuals, communities and institutions poles for roofing and fencing or for fuelwood and other wood products. Woodlots are usually planted on small parcels of the farmlands of individuals or communities. Apart from the major objective of woodlots, they also stabilize and improve the soils, as well as, provide fodder for animals.

Between 1988 and 1996, the International Bank for Reconstruction and Development (IBRD) funded a massive afforestation programme in nine semi-arid states of Adamawa, Bauchi, Kebbi, Borno, Jigawa, Kano, Katsina, Plateau and Sokoto. Five types of woodlots were established *viz.*, demonstration woodlots, community woodlots, institutional woodlots, private woodlots and marginal land planting. Choice of species was then determined by the Project Coordinating Units that raised the seedlings for the available species, which were in most cases *Azadiracta indica, Eucalyptus and Moringa oleofera.* These woodlots were mostly in the rural areas and made tremendous impact on the livelihoods of benefiting farmers until funding ceased in 1996. Bada *et al.* (1996) observe that private woodlots showed high degree of success in all the communities they visited. Of 38 farmers visited 26 (68%) owned woodlots ranging from 0.1 ha to 4 ha of various species. These achievements appear to have experienced decline as a result of waning funding.

Woodlots can also be introduced on marginal and unused lands and waste dumping sites, which abound in many of our cities, particularly Ibadan, Kano, Abeokuta and Yola among others. They have an advantage of not requiring extensive use of land. Their potential contribution to the greening of urban environment is substantial and this is in addition to the provision of needed products for the use of urban dwellers.

Landscaping

The word landscape was coined from two Dutch words: "land" meaning land and "schap" meaning state or condition. The first recorded use of the word was in 1598 when it was used as a painter's term. The Dutch word "landschap" had earlier meant simply "region/tract of land" but it acquired the artistic sense, which is brought over into English of "a picture depicting scenery of land". Ayeni (2004) has noted that, over the years, various authors have defined landscape differently. Some of the definitions include:

- Scenery of fields and forest, mountains and streams. (Wiens, 1995)
- An expanse of land that can be seen in a single view. (Thesaurus, 2000)
- All the natural features (*i.e.* water, hills fields, forests, etc.) that distinguish one part of the earth from another. (Gregorich *et al.*, 2001).

From the definitions stated above, one thing is clear and that is the fact that a landscape is a natural scenery (*i.e.* the general appearance of a place and its natural features from a picturesque view) irrespective of its size, shape and pattern. The physical landscape described is not what it used to be previously, as a result of the change in interaction pattern between man and the other components of the environment. Since the industrial revolution the landscape of nature literally gave way to harbours, roads, rail lines, factories, markets, airports, dams, etc. Deforestation held sway leading to incalculable loss of biodiversity and global warming. People tend to be taking up the challenge of re-introducing nature into their immediate environment and different people around the globe now give a new kind of reverence to plants along the view of landscaping. According to Moughton (1999) respect for natural landscape is deep rooted in the British psyche and among the country's greatest achievements are the landscape gardens of the 18th Century. For most Americans, the love of plants and gardens, now, seems to be inherent and this can be seen in their rural, sub-urban and urban settings (Simmonds, 1983). Also according to Buddha (1989), plants have always been part of the Indian Culture since the Vedic times and this has not changed even till date.

There are two major types of landscaping viz. hard landscaping (rock gardening and water gardening) and phyto landscaping. The latter is of greater interest and relevance in this discourse. It is all about the beautification of the environment by the planting and the maintenance of ornamental trees, shrubs, grasses and creepers primarily for their aesthetic values and for other purposes as well. Ornamental plants are thus termed because of their bright colours, beautiful leaves and flowers, nice scent, systematic branching, bloom and possession of special or unique structural features.

Nigeria is yet to attain the desirable levels of development in landscaping. Ayeni (2004) has reported that in Ibadan 153 out of 186 respondents perceived landscaping as nice, good, beautiful, pleasant and cool practice, which is breathtaking and adorable to hold. To them, landscaping ensures the beautification of the immediate environment by planting of flowers, trees and grasses; and blending and bonding human with nature, a worthy concept with an environment and utility value and the achievement of an aesthetic good. Consequently, a large percentage of people under this category are people who have formal education, travel experience and fore knowledge of landscaping. They are also those that have access to reasonably sizable areas of residential land in reservation areas. This category constitutes less than 10 per cent of the Nigerian population of over 120 million people! In the same study four respondents perceived landscaping as a waste of valuable land, which can be diverted to other uses. Twenty-nine respondents had nothing to say about landscaping, perhaps due to the fact they lack awareness on landscaping, are landless and most probably uneducated and resource-poor. The last two categories of respondents represent better, the possible perception of the larger Nigerian society. Herein lies the challenge.

It becomes pertinent therefore to create awareness about the importance of plants to the environment, and on the benefits of having them around living areas. Government's role should include engaging the services of landscaping of roadsides and public areas, while giving incentives to owners of well-designed landscape structures. Municipal Town Planning Units could make landscaping an integral part of the requirements for the approval of building plans.

In situ Conservation of Indigenous and Other Plant Species

Recent experiences have shown that several valuable indigenous plant species that are now endangered and rare as a result of irrational logging in forest reserves and unprotected free areas can still be found within some urban protected enclaves. Cases in point are the campuses of the University of Ibadan, Ibadan, Obafemi Awolowo University, Ile-Ife, the Polytechnic, Ibadan, Forestry Research Institute of Nigeria (FRIN), Ibadan, International Institute of Tropical Agriculture (IITA), Ibadan, Cocoa Research Institute of Nigeria (CRIN), Ibadan, Rubber Research Institute of Nigeria (RRIN), Benin City. These institutions have the advantage of being of the first generation and therefore had the pioneering advantage of large tracts of land for their development on the outskirts of the cities. With urbanization, some of them are now right within the cities. The advantage is that the trees are better protected from loggers, except where they are selectively logged when they constitute dangers to residents. Indeed, the Council of the University of Ibadan has since 1997 instituted a Campus Tree Management Committee with responsibility to manage all trees on the campus. Today, such rare species as *Milicia excelsa, Khaya sp, Terminalia,* etc. are found dotting the landscape of the University. There is also a sizable hectare of mature stand of *Tectona grandis,* which has so far escaped the chain saws of loggers as a result of its protected location within the University enclave. Ola-Adams and Soaga (2003) confirm the importance of such campuses as repository of flora when they listed over 100 plant species in several families which they stated was by no means exhaustive within the campus of the University of Agriculture, Abeokuta, Ogun State.

Other places in this category are government houses of some first and second-generation states such as Kaduna, Kano, Oyo and Ogun, some of which were the residences of Colonial District Officers (DOs). The residences which were usually located in the hilly areas of town with vegetation of various indigenous species interspersed with some exotics were then called *'Oke DO' in Yoruba* (the DO's Hill). It therefore becomes pertinent that such institutions and monuments be treated as conservation areas and be given incentives to further protect these valuable species. More areas can also be brought into conservation, particularly within university and other institutional campuses where effective use of infrastructual holdings is presently low.

Creation of Enabling Institutions

FAO (2003) identified various factors that impact forests and forestry as being global, regional, national and local. These driving forces can be grouped as:

- Policy and institutional;
- demographic;
- economic and social;
- technological.

By far the most fundamental of these factors in Nigeria is policy and institutional. The FAO (2003) has rightly observed declining capacity of the public sector institutions, presenting most African countries with major problems. Institutions however remain a veritable driving force in achieving sustainable development, particularly for forestry in urban areas where residents are an aggregation of individuals and groups from various socio-economic, cultural, political, tribal and even ethnic backgrounds. The need then arises for the strengthening of existing institutions while creating others that are essential. In the Nigerian context there is an urgent need to:

- **Create Urban Forestry Units at the national, state and local government levels.** Johnston (2000) reports that in August 1995, the Department of Environment (DoE) in Britain announced the formation of the National Urban Forestry Unit (NUFU)...with an initial grant of £ 700,000 over a three-year period. This created positive impact on urban forestry and urban greening in the country. This can be adopted in Nigeria. Such a unit should however involve all stakeholders in its activities to ensure success. Part of the unit's assignment should include environmental education (EE). This should be result oriented and should therefore be as much as possible isolated from the bureaucracy of the mainstream civil service. To be effective and acceptable, its activities must be participatory and should give an optimistic, local outlook; involve people in positive acts that enhance their environment; and do things to develop sustainable environment. According to Muthoka and Rimbui (1993) for this to be possible, EE must be characterized by **correctness**: should deal with real issues (in urban forestry and greening of the environment) that currently affect the lives of the educators and the learners in their own environment; and **conceptualization:** educators need to concentrate on meaningful concepts (in urban forestry and greening of the environment) that help learners to understand the significance of the holistic approach and relate such concept to their daily lives. In other words, EE will create awareness, concern, commitment and individual and collective actions that will lead to a better environment at both the micro and macro levels in the urban settings. The Urban Forestry Units should be encouraged to collaborate with such outfits as the National Tree Nursery Development Programme (**NTNDP**) which was instituted by the Federal Government in the year 2000 as a component of the National Food Security Programme to backstop stakeholders in massive high quality seedling production based on local species preferences and effective distribution to reclaim the degraded biophysical environment and enhance food security and poverty reduction. An alliance with the outfit will create a steady supply of required planting materials for urban plantings and more.

- **Institution of enabling laws:** Existing forestry laws in the country are generally obsolete and too weak to protect our trees, whether in reserved areas or outside the forest. There is the need for a complete overhauling of these laws to conform to changing trends and realities. Such laws should encourage the opening up of the forestry sub-sector to sincere private participation, transparency and good governance. Enforcement of instituted laws is also germane to success hence the enforcement agencies should undergo re-orientation that will ensure harmonious working relationship among all stakeholders as against the cat and mouse relationship hitherto existing.

The adoption and implementation of the outlined strategies have the potential to create a win-win situation which is summarized and depicted in Figure 3.

Conclusion

Urbanization is an inevitable process in national development. In most developing countries however, it is associated with several negative tendencies, paramount amongst these being deforestation, creation of urban slums and other environmental problems. Rehabilitation of the urban environment is therefore a challenge to policy makers, planners, managers, land users and all other stakeholders concerned with urban development. Urban forestry remains one the ways to resolve some of the problems associated with urbanization. From time immemorial trees have been known to be an integral part of urban environment, though with varying applications in different cities as a result of several differential factors associated with the growth process. The importance of the trees in the landscape are very well known and documented. Where they have been destroyed

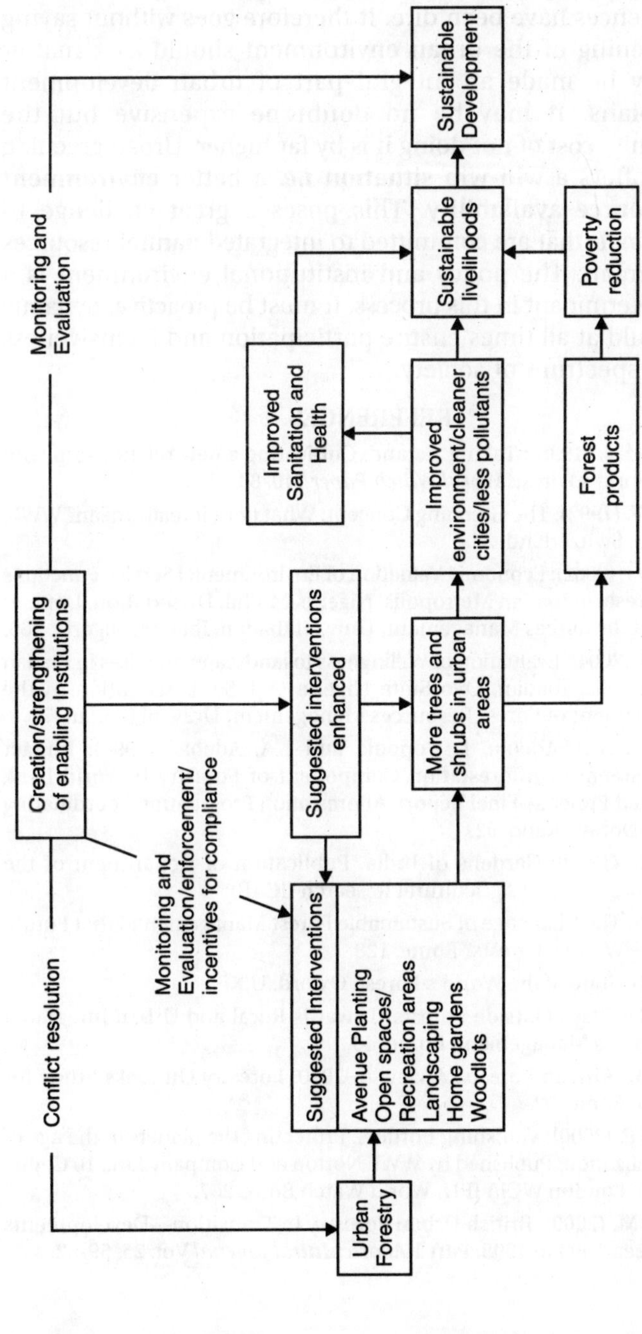

FIGURE 3: Schematic representation of expected output suggested interventions urban forestry

due to the 'exigencies of other development initiatives' the consequences have been dire. It therefore goes without saying that greening of the urban environment should as a matter of policy be made an integral part of urban development masterplans. It may be no doubt be expensive but the opportunity cost of not doing it is by far higher. Urban greening indeed offers a **win-win situation *i.e.* a better environment and resource availability.** This poses a great challenge to professionals that are committed to integrated natural resources management. The policy and institutional environment is a major determinant in this process. It must be proactive, dynamic and should at all times ensure participation and inclusiveness a broad spectrum of society.

REFERENCES

Abramovitz, J. (1998): Taking a stand: Cultivating a new relationship with the World's Forest. *World Watch Paper* 140, 88.

Adeleke, W. (1992): The Greening Concept: What does it really mean? WWF, Gland, Switzerland. 28.

Ajewole, O.I. (2002): Economic Valuation of Environmental Service Functions of Forests in Ibadan Metropolis, Nigeria. M.Phil. Dissertation, Dept. of Forest Resources Management, Univ. of Ibadan, Ibadan, Nigeria. 165.

Ayeni, B.O. (2004): Evaluation of Willingness to landscape premises in Ibadan Metropolis, Ibadan, Oyo State Nigeria. A B.Sc. Dissertation in the Department of Forest Resources Management, Univ. of Ibadan. 71.

Bada, S.O., A.O. Adeola, L. Popoola and L.A. Adebisi (1996): Impact Assessment of Afforestation Component of Forestry II World Bank Assisted Project—Final Report. Afforestation Programme Coordinating Unit, Dorayi, Kano. 92.

Buddha, L. (1989): Gardens of India. Publication of Department of the Indian Council of Agricultural Research (ICAR).

FAO (1993): The Challenge of Sustainable Forest Management: What Future for the World's Forests? Rome, 128.

FAO (1997): State of the World's Forest. Oxford, U.K.

FAO (2001): Trees Outside Forests: Towards Rural and Urban Integrated Resources Management, Rome. 40.

FAO (2003): African Forests: A view to 2020. Forestry Outlooks Study for Africa, Rome. 92.

French, H.F. (2000): Vanishing Borders: Protecting the planets in the age of Globalization. Published by WWF Norton and Company Ltd., 10 Coptic Street, London WCIA IPU, World Watch Book. 257.

Johnston, M. (2000): British Urban Forestry in Transition—Developments between 1993 to 1998, Part 1 *Aboricultural Journal* Vol. 25. 59-92.

Lefcoe, G. (1979): Land development in crowded places. Lessons from abroad. The Conservation Foundation Washington, D.C. 151.

Mbakwe, R. (1992): Prospects of Recreational Forest in Nigeria. In Akinsanmi, Proceeding of the Annual Conference of the Forestry Association of Nigeria. 36-39, Ibadan, Nigeria.

McPherson, E.G., Nowak, D. Heirsler, S., Grimmond, C., Souch, C., Grant, R. and Rowntree, R. (1997). Quantifying Urban forest structure functions and value: The Chicago urban climate project. *Urban Ecosystems*, I (1), 49-61.

Moughton, C. (1996): Urban Design: Green Dimensions. Reeds Educational and Professional Publishing Limited. 127-28.

Muthoka, M.G. and Z.K. Rimbui (1993): Concepts, Definition and New Dimensions in Environmental Education. 21-31.

Ogigirigi, M.A. (1986): Deforestation: Its impact on the Environment in Oguntala (ed.) *Proceedings of the 16th Annual Conference of the Forestry Association of Nigeria*. 49-57.

Oguntala, A.B. (1993): Forestry for Urban and Rural Development in Nigeria, with particular reference to urban environment. (In ed.) E.A. Oduwaiye: Proceedings of the 23rd Annual Conference of the Forestry Association of Nigeria. 1-10.

Ola-Adams B.O. and J.A. Soaga (2003): Preliminary checklist of plants at UNAAB Permanent site, Alabata, Abeokuta. University of Agriculture, Abeokuta Herbarium (UNAAB Herbarium) Bulletin No. 1, 18.

Olembo, R.J. and P. De Rham (1987): In two different worlds. *Unasylavia*, 155 (39:1), 26-35.

Popoola, L. (1992): An Assessment of the Effect of Structural Adjustment.

Programme on Fuelwood Consumption in Nigeria. *Journal of Tropical Forest Resources*. Vols. 7 & 8, 30-38.

Popoola, L. (2002): Participatory Forest Finance in Nigeria: Problems and Prospects. Paper presented at the Workshop on Lessons Learnt on Sustainable Forest Management in Africa, 09-13 February, 2004, Nairobi, Kenya. 20.

Popoola, L. and O. Ajewole (2001): Public Perceptions of Urban Forests in Ibadan, Nigeria: Implications for environmental Conservation. *Aboricultural Journal* Vol. 25. 1-22. A.B. Academy Publishers, Great Britain.

Popoola, L. and O. Ajewole (2002): Willingness to pay for rehabilitation of Ibadan Urban environment through reforestation projects. *Int. J. Sustainable Dev. and World Ecology*. Vol. 9, 256-68.

Schroeder, P. (1991): Carbon Storage Potential of Short Rotation Tropical Tree Plantations. United States Environmental Protection Agency, Washington, DC.

Sedjo, R. and A. Solomon (1989): Climate and forests. Paper prepared for Workshop on Controlling and Adapting to Greenhouse Forcing,

14-15 July 1988, Washington DC, USA. United States Environmental Protection Agency, National Academy of Sciences.

Simmonds, O.J. (1983): Landscape Architecture, 2nd edition. McGraw Hill Book Company. 66-67.

The Canadian Society of Soil Science (2001): Soil and Environmental Science Dictionary; Gregorich, E.G., Turchenek, L.W., Carter, M.R. and Angers, M.A. (eds.) Published by the CRC Press. 204.

Thesaurus (2000): The American Heritage Dictionary of the English Language, 4th Edition. Published by Houghton Mifflin Company.

Wiens, J.A. (1995): Landscape Mosaics and Ecological Theory. Chapman and Hall, London.

World Bank (1992): *Forestry Sector Review*, Washington DC. 7-30.

Xie, W., Du, H., Wang, Z., Li, C.H. and Yan, M.S. (1998): Research on integrated environmental efficiency from urban circulating forest in Fushun City. *Journal of Plant Resources and Environment*, 7 (2), 42-47.

8

Stochastic Energy Source Access Management in Urban Centers

KAI STRUNZ AND KIA LASHGARI
Department of Electrical Engineering, University of Washington, Seattle, USA.

ABSTRACT

The increasing scarcity of fossil resources and the detrimental environmental impacts of fossil fuel based electric power generation call for the creation of sustainable energy systems based on renewable resources. A solution for sustainable energy systems in urban centers is proposed in this work. In particular, rooftops of buildings are identified as suitable sites for wind and solar energy conversion. Through the concept of Stochastic Energy Source Access Management (SESAM), the renewable energy sources with intermittent output are combined with storage modules of complementary characteristics such that electric power output can be controlled in accordance with load demand. Hydrogen is selected as carrier for the storage of large quantities of energy. This hydrogen can be used to generate electricity in fuel cells. It can also be made available as a fuel via a hydrogen infrastructure. The second type of storage is aimed at providing electric power within response times that are shorter than the ones fuel cells can achieve. A good overall power quality is so attained. The complementary long-term and short-term access storage modules can be integrated within buildings.

Key words: Distributed energy resources, fuel cells, hydrogen, power electronics, renewable energy, solar energy, sustainable energy systems, urban planning, wind energy.

I. Introduction

Today's energy system of centrally located generation, transmission networks and distribution networks is expected to evolve into an infrastructure where small-scale distributed energy resources and loads are common. Technologies for distributed generation include diesel and gas engines, microturbines, fuel cells, wind and solar energy converters. Installing distributed energy resources close to the loads can improve the overall efficiency of the power system as transmission losses can be reduced. Distributed energy resources can also lower the burden on the existing grid infrastructure and enhance the quality and reliability of the power delivery. Most importantly, when based on renewable energy, the use of distributed energy resources reduces the dependence on fossil fuels and adverse environmental impacts. Fossil fuel based power generation is associated with the problems of global warming and acid rain.

While environmentally friendly, the intermittent availability of wind and solar energy is a barrier to their large-scale development. The concept of Stochastic Energy Source Access Management (SESAM)[1, 2] is a solution to this problem, since it combines the stochastic source with multi-level access storage such that the power output can be controlled. Hydrogen is made available as a fuel generated from renewable sources. In this work, the use of SESAM in the context of an urban environment is discussed. In section II, selected renewable energy sources are discussed. In section III, energy storage technologies are reviewed. The concept of SESAM is introduced in section IV. The application of SESAM in urban centers is proposed in section V. Finally, conclusions are drawn in section VI.

II. Renewable Energy

Renewable energy is obtained from resources that are constantly replenished. Examples include bio energy, geothermal energy, hydro energy, ocean energy, solar energy, and wind energy. The use of renewable energy resources for the purpose of electricity generation is essential to the development of sustainable energy systems. In what follows, selected issues of solar and wind energy conversion are considered in more detail.

II.1 *Solar Energy*

The sun is the primary source of energy for the earth, and this energy can be utilized by a variety of technologies. Through passive solar heating, cooling, and daylighting, buildings can be made more energy efficient. Part of such concepts can for example be the design of large south-facing windows and the use of appropriate materials. In solar hot water and space heaters, the energy coming from the sun heats water or a heat-transfer fluid in collectors. Hot water or heat can so be made available to industrial facilities, businesses or homes. If the sun's energy is concentrated using mirrors, then the temperatures can be made high enough so that steam can be produced and electricity generated.

A very different way of generating electricity is given through photovoltaics technology. Photovoltaic solar cells are made of semiconducting materials and directly convert sunlight into electricity. Such technology is widely known to provide power to calculators. On a larger scale, many solar cells can be connected to form panels of significant size. As shown in Figure 1, the panels can be installed on rooftops of buildings or any place with satisfactory solar radiation to harvest sun's energy.

FIGURE 1: Solar panel

Over the past years, the cost of electricity generation using photovoltaics technology has dropped significantly. This trend is illustrated in Figure 2.[3] The cost of generating 1 kilowatt-hour (kWh) of electric energy is given in levelized U.S. cents. Levelized costing accounts for the buying power as of today and comprises all capital, operating and maintenance costs associated with the generation of the electricity over the presented time frame. The development and growing popularity of the solar technologies has contributed to these overall cost reductions. However, photovoltaics technology is still expensive.

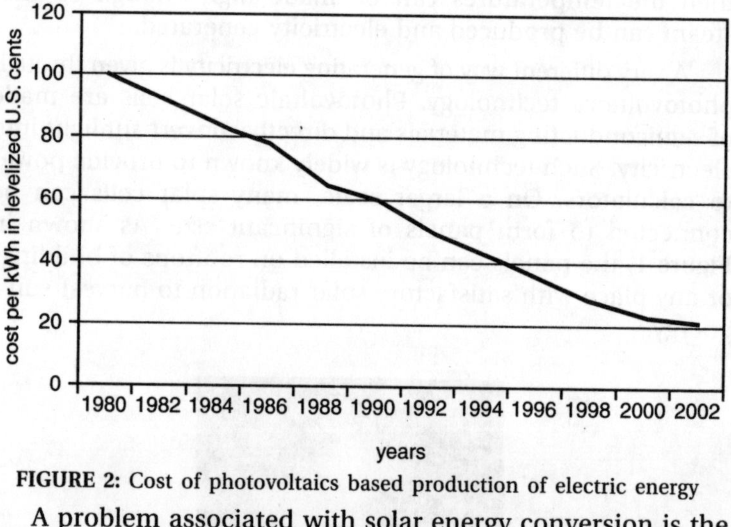

FIGURE 2: Cost of photovoltaics based production of electric energy

A problem associated with solar energy conversion is the intermittent availability of this resource. Weather conditions change stochastically, and there is no sunlight during nights. The solar radiation expressed in watt-hours per square meter (Wh/m^2) over the period of one month is shown in Figure 3. The stochastic character of the solar radiation is clearly visible.

II.2 *Wind Energy*

Wind energy has been used by man for centuries for applications ranging from the pumping of water for farms to generating electricity. A modern wind turbine, as the one shown in Figure 4, harvests the energy from the wind, and a generator converts the kinetic energy into electricity. The largest

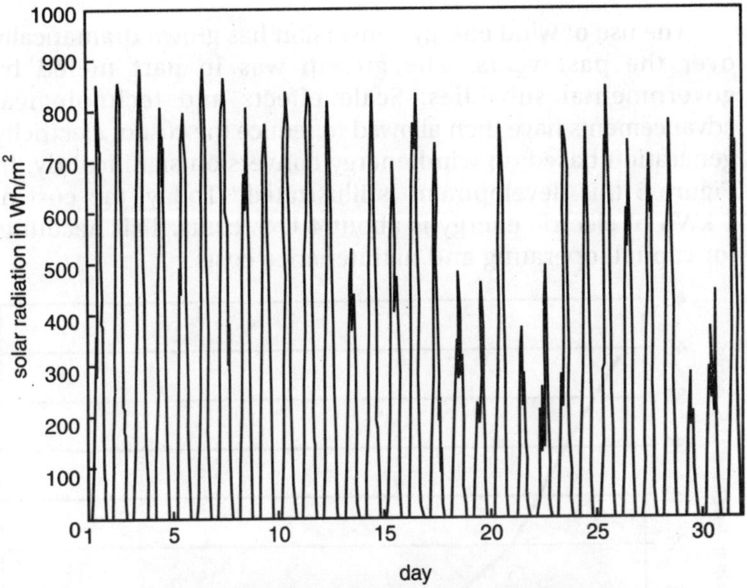

FIGURE 3: Example of solar radiation measurements over one month

FIGURE 4: Wind turbine

wind turbines available today have power ratings of several megawatts.

The use of wind energy conversion has grown dramatically over the past years. The growth was in part fueled by governmental subsidies. Scale effects and technological advancements have then allowed to reduce the cost of electricity generation based on wind energy conversion significantly. In Figure 5 this development is illustrated.[4] Today, the cost of 1 kWh of electric energy is about 4 U.S. cents. This accounts for capital, operating and maintenance costs.

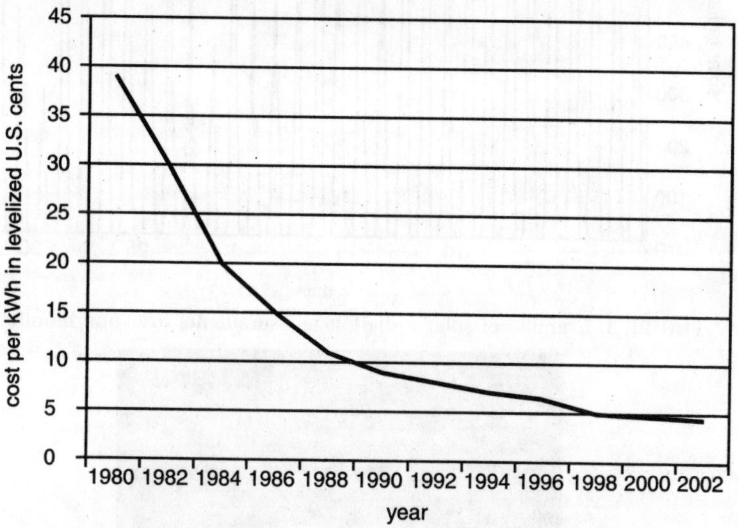

FIGURE 5: Cost of wind based production of electric energy

The electric power produced by wind turbines depends on the cube of the wind speed. In Figure 6, measurements of the wind speed are depicted in the form of a time series over one month. Given the changing wind speeds, it is obvious that the stochastic form of power output poses problems for the loads. Customers expect electric power to be available at their convenience rather than being a function of the wind speed. This constitutes a barrier for large-scale network integration.

III. Storage

A wide spectrum of technologies for energy storage is available.[5] In pumped hydro storage systems, a body of water in a reservoir at a relatively high elevation is used to store

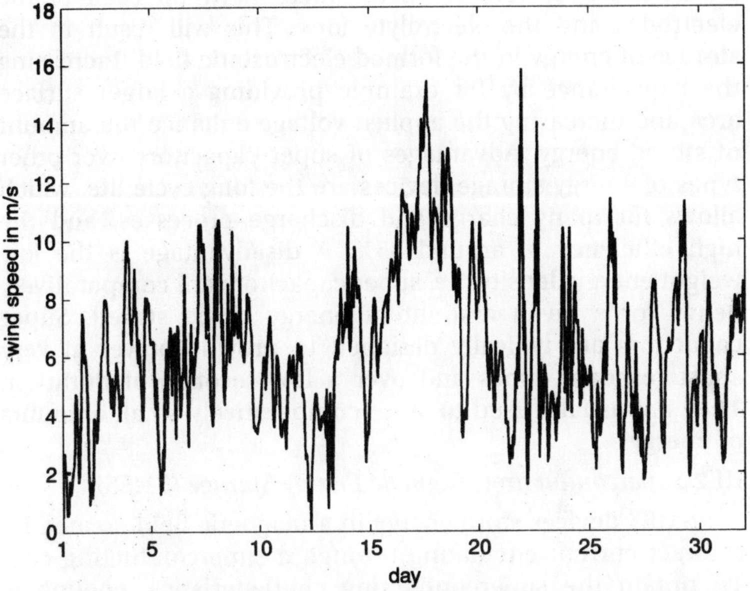

FIGURE 6: Example of wind speed measurements over one month

potential energy. For compressed air energy storage systems, caverns are popular reservoirs. Such storage schemes can provide significant capacity of energy storage when the appropriate geology is given.[6] In general, this cannot be expected to be the case within an urban center. In the following, selected energy storage systems that can be conveniently scaled for use in the urban environment are considered: super capacitors, superconducting magnetic energy storage (SMES), flywheels, batteries, and hydrogen storage. The relative merits of the associated technologies are reviewed. The outcome has important implications regarding the design of the SESAM concept.

III.1 *Super Capacitors*

Capacitors allow for the storage of energy in an electrostatic field, which is due to the separation of electric charges. The highest level of performance is obtained with electrochemical capacitors, also referred to as super capacitors. A direct voltage is applied between the electrodes that are separated by an electrolyte. A polarized layer is formed to provide charge separation over very small distances between each of the electrodes and the electrolyte ions. This will result in the storage of energy in the formed electrostatic field. Increasing the capacitance by for example providing a larger surface area and increasing the applied voltage enhance the amount of stored energy. Advantages of super capacitors over other types of energy storage devices are the long cycle life, which allows for many charge and discharge processes, and the high efficiency of around 95%. A disadvantage is the low weight energy density, *i.e.* super capacitors are comparatively heavy for a given amount of energy to be stored. Super capacitors are typically designed to provide power at very short response times and over a few seconds of duration. They are usually used to store comparatively small amounts of energy.

III.2 *Superconducting Magnetic Energy Storage (SMES)*

SMES devices store energy in a magnetic field created by a direct current circulating through a superconducting coil. To obtain the superconducting characteristics, cooling is required. Liquid helium or nitrogen can be used for this purpose. Increasing the inductance and increasing the direct current enhance the energy storage of the SMES. An advantage is that the lifetime of the SMES does not depend on the number of charge and discharge operations. The efficiency of the order of 90% is good. A disadvantage is the low weight energy density. SMES systems are particularly interesting for high power applications in the megawatt range. They can provide such high power in a very short response time and up to seconds. However, the stored amounts of energy are relatively low.

III.3 *Flywheels*

Flywheels store kinetic energy within a rapidly spinning wheel-like rotor or disk. High-velocity flywheels are operated in vacuum vessels to reduce friction. Increasing the moment of inertia and increasing the rotational velocity of the flywheel enhance the energy storage of the flywheel. A long cycle life and a high efficiency of the order of 90% are among the advantages. The very low weight energy density is a disadvantage. Flywheels can provide power at short response times, and certain designs are able to deliver rated power for minutes. Among those storage devices that can provide power rapidly, the capital cost associated with flywheels is comparatively low. Efforts are underway to increase the capability of flywheels to provide rated power over periods of several hours.

III.4 *Batteries*

Battery technology provides one of the oldest means of storing energy. Applying a voltage between the electrodes causes an internal chemical reaction inside the battery, and energy can be stored. When this process is reversed, the stored energy can be accessed. In recent years, interest has shifted to so-called flow batteries. Principal elements are two electrolyte tanks and a cell stack that is composed of individual cells. Rather than being stored at the electrodes, energy is stored by chemical changes to the electrolytes. During charging and discharging, ions are exchanged between the two electrolytes through membranes in the cells. An advantage is that energy and power ratings can be specified independently. The amount of energy that can be stored depends on the size of the electrolyte tanks, while the amount of available power depends on the size of the cell stack. Efficiencies are of the order of 80%. Weight energy densities are low. Flow batteries are typically designed to store relatively large amounts of energy and good response times have been reported. A concern is the use of the chemical solutions involved. They can have harmful effects on the environment.

III.5 *Hydrogen Storage*

With strong interest in the development of the hydrogen economy, hydrogen is widely seen as the key energy carrier of the future. While hydrogen is widely available, it is so in the form of compounds. For the purpose of generating electricity in fuel cells, however, hydrogen must be made available in pure form. This is for example possible through electrolysis where water is split into its component parts of hydrogen and oxygen. In order to run the electrolysis, electric power is necessary. In sustainable energy systems, the latter would come from renewable energy sources. An advantage is the high weight energy density of hydrogen storage. The amount of energy that is stored depends on the size of the hydrogen tanks. The amount of power that can be provided depends on the size of the fuel cell stacks. Hydrogen storage systems are fully scalable. Hydrogen is environmentally friendly and can be stored economically. Response times depend on the fuel cell types, but are not considered as very short. Strong research programs are underway to improve the efficiency of fuel cell and electrolyser systems so that storage efficiencies of the order of 70% can be reached within the next years.

IV. Concept of Stochastic Energy Source Access Management

A model plant for the generation of electric power would comprise the following desirable specifications:

(a) renewable energy based,

(b) environmentally benign,

(c) capable of deterministic generation of electric power,

(d) rapidly controllable,

(e) cost and maintenance efficient,

(f) compatible with hydrogen economy.

Through items (a) and (b), the use of fossil fuels and harmful pollution are avoided. Items (c) and (d) are crucial to satisfy the load demand, and they also enable proper participation in electricity markets and contribution to power quality. Item (e) is important for economic considerations. Item (f) is desirable regarding the future. The concept of SESAM meets these specifications.

IV.1 *Plant Overview*

A schematic overview of the proposed plant is shown in Figure 7. It consists of four major modules interconnected through a Direct Current (DC) bus. All modules comprise power electronic converters. Using power electronic switches, the latter allow to control the flow of electric power between the modules and to bring voltages and currents in the format needed for the operation of the respective modules. Variables *k*, *m* and *n* indicate the number of connections made. The stochastic source module provides power P_{ss}, whereas P_{lt} and P_{st} are associated with the larger long-term access and smaller short-term access storage modules, respectively. The values of P_{lt} and P_{st} can be either positive or negative depending on whether the storage is charged or discharged. The real power output to the electricity infrastructure, P_g, is adjusted through the grid interface module. Given that the efficiency of the grid interface module is designated through η_g, then the input power of the grid interface is $P_{ds} = P_g/\eta_g$. For a lossless DC bus network, P_{ds} is obtained as follows:

$$P_{ds} = P_{ss} + P_{lt} + P_{st}$$

While P_{ss} comes from a stochastic source, P_{lt} and P_{st} are adjusted such that P_{ds} appears to come from a deterministic source.

The control system is structured hierarchically. Each module is associated with a local controller. The operation of the local controllers is coordinated by a global control system. The controls make sure that the voltage across the capacitor of the DC bus is maintained at the desired value and that the desired power output is obtained.

The major contribution of the design in Figure 7 is that all the conditions of a model plant as set out above are met. The stochastic source module comprises an environmentally benign renewable source. The long-term and short-term access storage modules provide storage capability at multiple levels. While the long-term access storage is designed to store large amounts of energy, the short-term access storage module has much less storage capability but offers very fast controllability. The grid interface module allows, in addition to the transfer of real power, the generation of reactive power. The decomposition of the overall design into modules with well-defined interfaces promotes cost and maintenance efficiency.

IV.2 *Grid Interface Module*

The grid interface module comprises a transformer and a power electronic converter. The transformer provides galvanic decoupling and changes voltage levels between the two terminals on the electricity infrastructure and power electronic converter sides, respectively. The power electronic converter transforms DC to Alternating Current (AC) and is therefore of the AC-DC type.

The amount of real power P_g that is exchanged between the DC bus and the electricity infrastructure is adjusted by

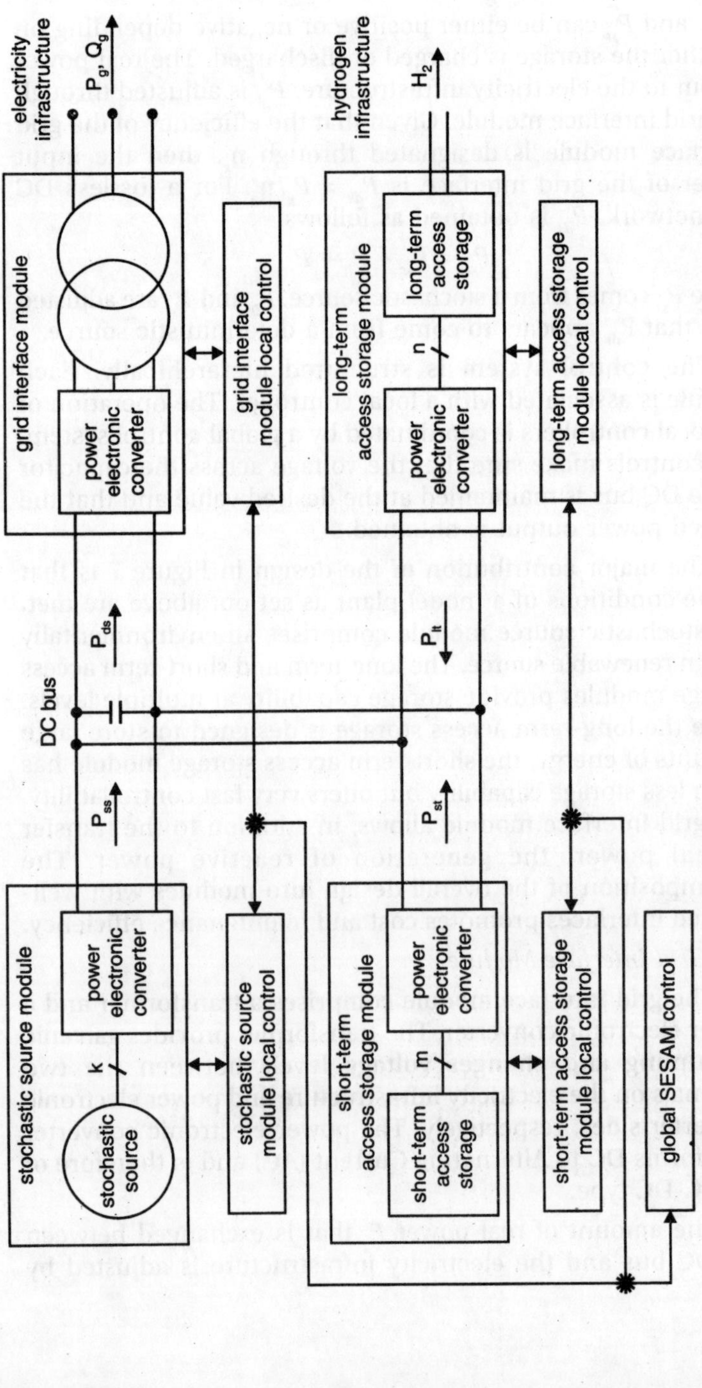

FIGURE 7: Modular concept of Stochastic Energy Source Access Management

modifying the phase shift between the fundamental frequency component of the AC voltage generated by the power electronic converter and the AC voltage on the side of the electricity infrastructure. In addition to P_g, the so-called reactive power Q_g is controlled. The purpose of this control is to provide satisfactory power quality, for example by keeping the AC voltage magnitudes at the electricity infrastructure side within a desired range.

IV.3 *Stochastic Source Module*

The stochastic source module comprises the renewable energy sources with stochastic output. Typically, it would be based on wind or solar energy conversion or a combination of both. Through the management and control unit, a maximum power tracker is realized such as to obtain the maximum power P_{ss}. Since this maximum power obviously depends on the variation of quantities such as the wind speed and solar radiation, the stochastic nature of the source results.

IV.4 *Long-Term Access Storage Module*

From the solar radiation and wind speed measurements shown in Figure 3 and Figure 6, it can be recognized that the power output of solar and wind energy converters can change quite erratically over time. It is the role of the large-size long-term access storage module, shown in Figure 8, to provide storage so that the power output P_g to the AC grid can be

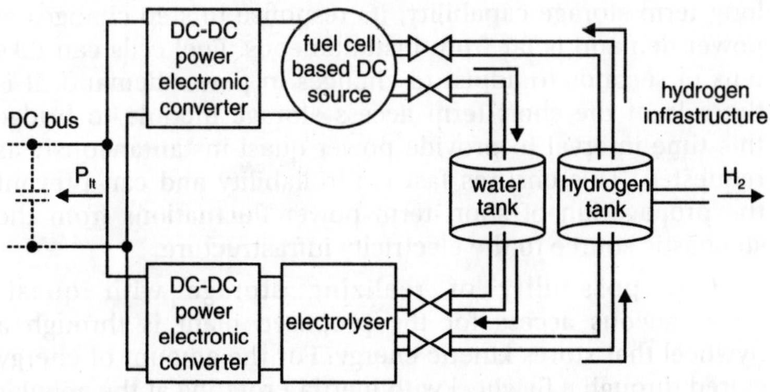

FIGURE 8: Long-term access storage module in form of hydrogen production, storage and conversion unit

provided in accordance with commitments and customer demand. The storage needs to be sufficiently large so that the requested power can be supplied in a time frame ranging from several minutes to several months.

Principle elements are the electrolyser unit, the fuel cell based DC source, the hydrogen tank, and the water tank. Instead of separating fuel cell and electrolyser physically, a reversible fuel cell can be used, too. For simplicity, compressors are not shown but will be needed to obtain the desired level of pressure in the hydrogen tank. The module is interfaced to the DC bus through DC-DC power electronic converters. From the hydrogen tank, a connection to the hydrogen infrastructure can be established.

When the power P_{ss} of the stochastic source exceeds the power P_{ds} to be transferred to the grid interface, the surplus of power can be delivered to the electrolyser: $P_{lt} < 0$. Through electrolysis, hydrogen is produced from the water and then stored in the tank.

Inversely, in a time period where the power P_{ss} of the stochastic source is lower than the power P_{ds} to be transferred to the grid interface, the management and control unit adjusts the fuel cell operation so that the power difference $P_{ds} - P_{ss}$ can be supplied by this module. In this case $P_{lt} > 0$.

IV.5 *Short-Term Access Storage Module*

Even though the hydrogen-based storage module provides long-term storage capability, its response to step changes of power demand is far from instantaneous. Fuel cells can take tens of seconds to adjust to changes in power demand. It is the role of the short-term access storage module to bridge this time interval to provide power quasi-instantaneously as requested. This ensures fast controllability and can prevent the propagation of short-term power fluctuations from the stochastic source to the electricity infrastructure.

One possibility of realizing storage with quasi-instantaneous access for the proposed plant is through a flywheel that stores kinetic energy. For the amount of energy stored through a flywheel with inertia J rotating at the angular velocity ω, the following equation applies:

$$E_{kin} = \frac{1}{2} J\omega^2$$

As indicated in Figure 9, an induction machine is suitable for the purpose of electromechanical energy conversion. In this case, the interface to the DC bus is established via an AC-DC converter.

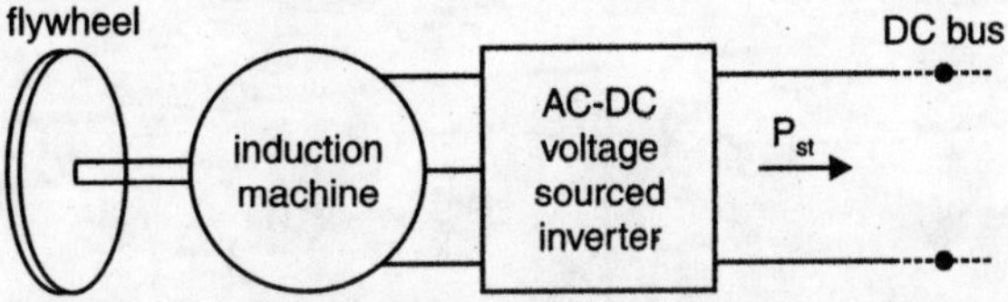

FIGURE 9: Short-term access storage module in form of flywheel kinetic energy storage unit

Interesting alternatives to the flywheel-based storage of kinetic energy are the storage of magnetic energy in SMES systems and the storage of electric energy in super capacitors. As discussed in section III, super capacitors, SMES systems, and flywheels all have fast response times.

V. Application in Urban Centers

Distributed energy resources are also present in urban centers. Their value is mainly recognized in the context of the Uninterruptible Power Supply (UPS). During a period of disturbance or outage of the utility-based power supply, the UPS system can switch to a local backup power supply seamlessly. Such UPS systems are of interest for the supply of power to sensitive loads such as computer, instrumentation and communication systems, medical facilities, and critical-process industries. Popular backup power supply generators are based on diesel or gas engines. The interest in solar energy conversion for space and water heating, daylighting, and electricity generation in urban centers has also been increasing. Rooftops can provide valuable space for the purpose of installation. In Figure 10, the installation of photovoltaic panels for electricity generation is shown. Such installations are particularly useful when combined with measures of energy conversion. Of course, the stochastic availability of these renewable sources is a disadvantage.

FIGURE 10: Roof-mounted photovoltaic energy conversion in urban center

In Figure 11, it is illustrated how SESAM can contribute to the development of sustainable energy systems in the urban environment. Here, the large-scale use of wind energy conversion in addition to solar energy conversion is proposed. The installation of wind energy conversion units on rooftops appears particularly appealing when considering the average wind speed as a function of height. An approximate formula is as follows[7] :

$$\bar{v} = \bar{v}_r \left(\frac{z}{z_r} \right)^{\alpha}$$

where $\bar{v}$ is the average wind speed at evaluation z above the surface; $\bar{v}_r$; is the average wind speed at the reference evaluation level z_r; a typical value of the friction coefficient α is 1/7. The wind power density varies with the cube of the wind speed. Therefore, the average wind power density $\bar{P}$ can be expressed as follows:

$$\bar{P} = \bar{P}_r \left(\frac{z}{z_r} \right)^{3\alpha}$$

where $\bar{P}_r$ is the average wind power density at z_r.

In the Empire State Building[8], the annual average energy consumption is 40 million kWh. This corresponds to an average power consumption of 4600 kW. Obviously, energy consumption is not always as high as in the massive Empire State Building. Investigations have shown that the typical consumption of a modern building is about 230 kWh/m^2.[9] Thus, in a building that has 20 stories, is approximately 80 meters tall and has 40 m by 40 m wide floors, the energy consumption per year is about 7.4 million kWh. This translates into an average power consumption of about 840 kilowatts. The ratings of the SESAM system must exceed the average values as losses are inevitable and electric power consumption varies with time. Furthermore, if it is of interest to supply hydrogen for use in cars or other applications, then the amount of fuel to be produced must be accounted for when rating the overall system.

In Table 1, the average wind speed at different levels of elevation is given. The values were obtained with the formula given above at $\alpha = 1/7$. The reference evaluation is taken as $z_r = 10$ m, and the corresponding reference speeds are given in the same row. A building of 20 stories is about 80 m high. The Empire State Building is 443.2 m high. As the results show, average wind speed and wind power density rise with

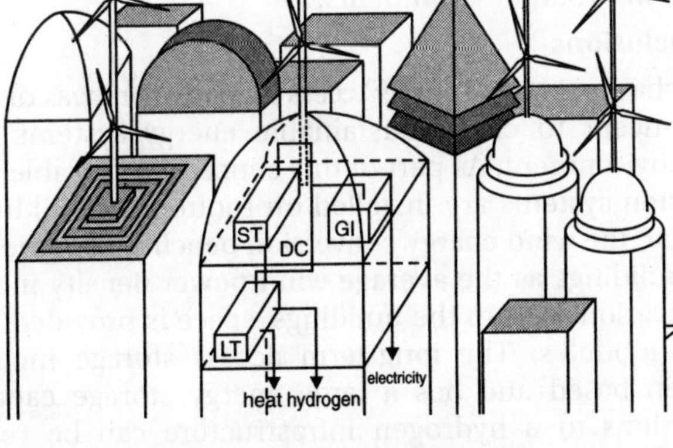

FIGURE 11: SESAM in urban centers; DC: direct current bus; GI: grid interface module; LT: long-term-access storage module; ST: short-term access storage module

evaluation. This speaks in favor of installing wind energy conversion systems on rooftops on a large scale as proposed.

TABLE 1: Wind Speed at Different Heights

elevation in m	wind speed in m/s				
10	4.0	6.0	8.0	10.0	12.0
80	5.4	8.1	10.8	13.5	16.2
160	5.9	8.9	11.9	14.9	17.8
240	6.3	9.4	12.6	15.7	18.9
320	6.6	9.8	13.1	16.4	19.7
400	6.8	10.2	13.6	16.9	20.3
480	7.0	10.4	13.9	17.4	20.9

As indicated in the transparent building in the center of Figure 11, the other modules of the SESAM system can be installed inside buildings. Ideally, such an installation should be combined with energy conservation measures and passive solar heating, cooling and daylighting.

Hallmarks of the concept can be summarized as follows: rooftops are used for the large-scale installation of renewable sources; storage modules are installed within the buildings; electric power output is deterministic and supplied to the building; hydrogen access is provided; heat is reused for improved efficiency. The proposed system can so significantly contribute to the development of modern sustainable energy systems in urban environments.

VI. Conclusions

Stochastic Energy Source Access Management was discussed as a concept to create sustainable energy systems in the urban environment. As part of this concept, renewable energy conversion systems are installed on rooftops of buildings. In particular, the wind energy conversion benefits from the height of tall buildings as the average wind power density increases with elevation. Within the buildings, space is provided for the storage modules. The long-term access storage module is hydrogen based and has a large energy storage capability. Connections to a hydrogen infrastructure can be realized. The short-term access storage module provides less energy storage capability, but the availability of power is quasi-instantaneous. Deterministic power is provided via the grid interface module to the local electricity infrastructure in order to satisfy the demands of electric loads. With its scalability and modular decomposition that facilitates the integration in buildings, high degree of controllability and environmental friendliness, the proposed concept has the potential of strongly contributing to the creation of sustainable energy systems in the urban environment.

Acknowledgments

The authors would like to thank the National Renewable Energy Laboratory (NREL) of the USA for making photographs available.

REFERENCES

1. Strunz, K. and Brock, E.K., Hybrid plant of renewable stochastic source and multi-level storage for emission-free deterministic power generation. Proceedings of the CIGRE/IEEE PES International Symposium of Electric Power Delivery Systems, Montreal, Canada, October 2003.
2. Yu, X. and Strunz, K., Combined long-term and short-term access storage for sustainable energy system. Proceedings of the IEEE PES General Meeting, Denver, USA, June 2004.
3. Energy Information Administration, U.S. Department of Energy: http://www.eia.doe.gov .
4. American Wind Energy Association: www.awea.org.
5. Electricity Storage Association: www.electricitystorage.org.
6. Schoenung, S.M., Characteristics and technologies for long- vs. short-term energy storage. Technical report SAND2001-0765, Sandia National Laboratories, Albuquerque, USA, March 2001.
7. Elliott, D.L., Holladay, C.G., Barchet, W.R., Foote, H.P. and Sandusky, W.F., Wind energy resource atlas of the United States. Technical report DOE/CH 10093-4, National Renewable Energy Laboratory, Golden, USA, October 1986.
8. Empire State Building: www.esbnyc.com.
9. Raman, M., Aspects of energy consumption in tall office building. *The Professional Journal of the Council on Tall Buildings and Urban Habitat*, vol. 1, no. 3, Fall 2001.

9

Policy Strategy and Affordable Housing for Dhaka City, Bangladesh: Need for a Change in View

SABERA SULTANA

payelbuet@yahoo.com

Teaching Assistant, Department of Urban and Regional Planning and Student of Masters of Urban and Regional Planning (MURP), Bangladesh University of Engineering and Technology (BUET), Dhaka.

MD. SHARIFUL ALAM CHOWDHURY

sharifurp97@yahoo.com

Research Assistant, Delta Planners and Builders Ltd., Dhaka; and Student of Masters of Urban and Regional Planning (MURP), Department of Urban and Regional Planning, Bangladesh University of Engineering and Technology (BUET), Dhaka.

ABSTRACT

In the colloquium of the mayors held at the United Nations in New York in August 1994, Housing has been identified as the most severe urban problem.[1] The problem is more severe in developing countries, than the developed countries. The scenario is not different in Dhaka—the capital of Bangladesh. It is become increasingly become difficult for the municipal government of Dhaka, to provide housing to its inhabitants. With no social housing system, thousands of people spent their nights under the open sky. Besides this, another big proportion of Dhaka's population lives in the places which in no standard can be called house, though it provides at least roof over the head (Enayatullah, 1995). So there is an urgent need of a comprehensive housing policy, which would ensure affordable housing for all. A policy along with strategies have been suggested in this paper which would meet the need of affordable housing of the citizens of Dhaka.

Key words: Housing, Housing Infrastructure, Human Settlement, Housing Finance, Low-Income Housing.

Introduction

Housing is one of the basic human rights. In spite of national and international efforts during the past decade there has not been any improvement in the housing condition of the poor and disadvantages.[2] Lack of housing is a common problem in the cities of the developing world. This has major impacts on the urban environment. As all levels of governments are involved in housing, municipal government cannot respond to the problem single handedly.[3]

Problems of human settlement are related to the overall growth of population and its distribution and movement over space. By the year 2000, the world population would be 6.2 billion, 51% of whom would live in the urban areas.[4] One of the most populated area would be South Asia where the population would be 2.2 billion of which 83 million would live in urban areas.[5]

The Problems

General Problem

Bangladesh is one of the South Asian country with one of the highest urbanisation rate (6.2%) in the world.[6] Due to urban pull and rural push factors, thousands of people gathering in the urban areas everyday. Dhaka—the capital city has a population of 6.5 million with a population growth rate of 4.75%.[7] By the year 2000, the population is projected between 7 to 10 million.[8]

Specific Problem

Even today Dhaka is going through severe shortage of Housing. At present Dhaka City Corporation (DCC)[9] has no housing policy. So if a proper policy is not laid down now, pollution and degradation of urban environment seems to be an inevitable outcome.

Aim and Objectives

The aim and objective of this paper is to suggest a housing and human settlement policy with strategies that would eventually ensure a sustainable housing development by the year 2010 the present housing situation in the areas under the jurisdiction of DCC. In the process of developing this policy we hope to add to the body of knowledge. Due to limitation of time and resource the study is though aimed at for a comprehensive housing policy, emphasis has been given on housing for the homeless and housing finance.

Methodology

For the purpose of the study, relevant literature was reviewed to get an overview of the subject matter. The study materials, are related to the housing policies and projects practised in different countries. To put the study in a broader perspective, Internet Browsing was done.

Scope and Limitation of the Study

The scope of the study is limited to only formulating a Sustainable Housing Policy and Strategy for Dhaka City Corporation, for ensuring a sustainable development for Dhaka by the year 2010. However in formulating the policy and strategy no in-depth analysis on economic aspect was made due to data inadequacy.

Geographical Settings of the Locality

Dhaka city is located in-between 90°20´E longitude and 90°35´E longitude and 23°40´N latitude and 24°10´N latitude.[10] The DCC area is bounded by the river Buriganga to the west and south, the river Balu to the east and the Tongi municipality to the north (Fig. 1).[11] The jurisdiction area of the DCC is 344 km^2 with a population of around 6.5 million.[12]

Current Housing Situation

Present Housing Stock

In 1991, the numbers of households of Dhaka was estimated at about 1.3 million.[13] All of these households are accommodated in one form or another. However, the total number of houses produced by government is just 35,000.[14] It is also interesting to note that all of these housing are 'pool housing'[15], thus accommodating government employees during their stay in Dhaka. In other words it has little or no impact on housing system of Dhaka.

The housing system of Dhaka is more or less a product of private initiative. With a few exception, all the residential neighbourhood of Dhaka grew up spontaneously.[16] Studies

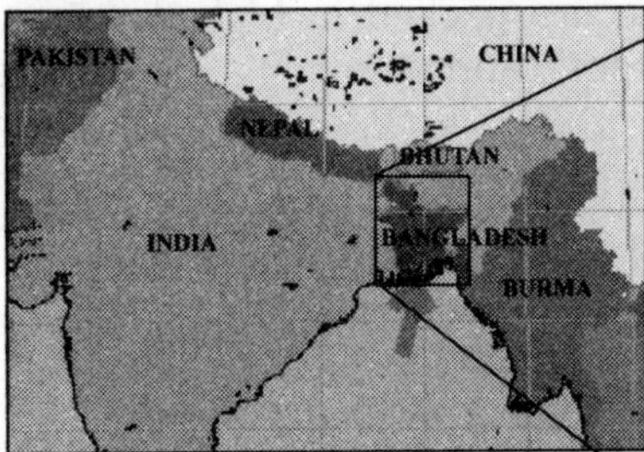

FIG. 1A: Location of Bangladesh
SOURCE: Zunaid K.

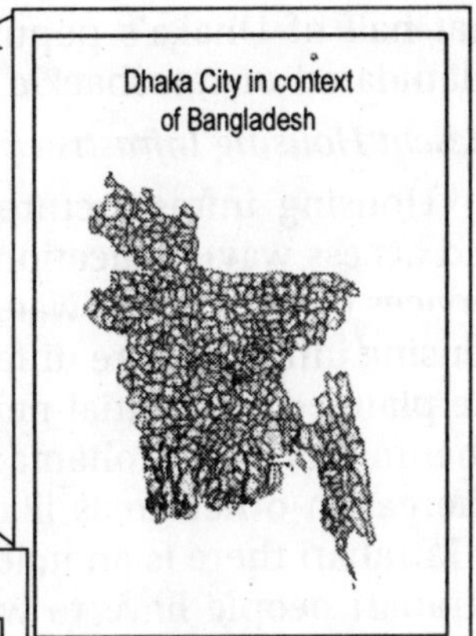

FIG. 1B: Bangladesh with Location of Dhaka
SOURCE: Zunaid K.

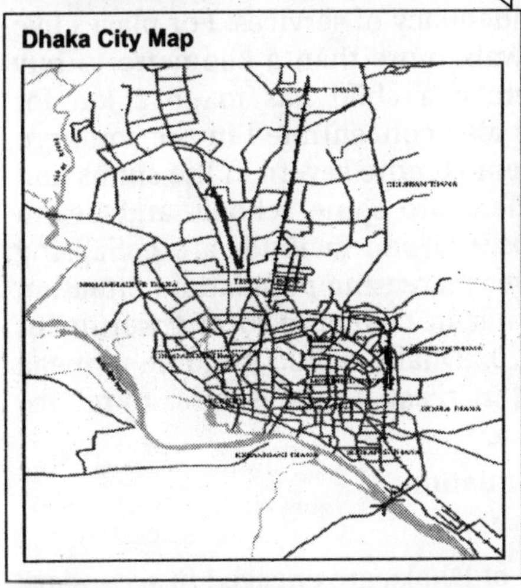

FIG. 1C: Map of Dhaka City Corporation
SOURCE: Enayatullah I, 29

show that only 12% of the population of Dhaka live in proper houses.[17] One of the important aspect of housing system of Dhaka is that 25% of the population is living in the slums and squatters.[18] These slums are spread all over the city. Studies also reveal that an amazing 650,000 (10% of population) are homeless and living in the pavements railway and bus stations.[19]

The another important aspect of housing system of Dhaka is that 2% of the housing stock of higher income group occupy 40% of residential land. Thus the remaining 98% of the land use 60% of residential land.[20] An independent study also reveals that half of Dhaka's population are packed in high density, dilapidated or ramshackle bustees[21] and slums.[22]

Present Housing Infrastructure

Housing infrastructure include transport network (road and access way), education and health institution, and utility services (corner shops, water, gas and electricity supply). These housing infrastructure differ from locality to locality. While in the planned residential neighbourhoods of Gulshan, Banani, Dhanmondi and Mohamadpur these services are sufficient, whereas in other areas like Khilgaon, Kathalbagan, Jhikatala or Jatrabari there is an inadequacy of services. For places like Jatrabari people have to walk more than a kilometre to buy daily necessities. On average a child has to go 2 km for schools. The hospitals are also concentrated in the southern part of the city. The problem is more severe in the slums and squatters, even though there are some schools and health facilities run by the NGOs.[23] Urban facilities are collapsing under the burden of an ever increasing population. Situation is so grave that, the minister in charge of local government said that by the year 2010, Dhaka would become a mega slum at the current rate of increase if no measures to reduce the migration rate of Dhaka.[24]

Present Socio-Economic Situation

Income Source and Income Level

Most of the population of Dhaka are engaged in secondary or tertiary economic activities. A very little proportion of the people are engaged in primary activity (mainly fishing in river and marshy area). However, this is limited only during the monsoon. Most of the income earning people of Dhaka, are engaged in secondary economic activities (industrial labour, small scale industry). A good proportion of the citizenry is engaged in service sector. Though accurate and reliable data are not available, it is estimated that 60% of the work force are in the secondary and 35% of the work force are engaged in tertiary sector. It is interesting to note that almost all labour engaged in Garments sectors—the biggest industrial sector are female.

There is no data available for the income level of citizens of Dhaka city. However, an Asian Development Bank study reveals that more than half of Dhaka's population live below poverty line.[25]

Social Structure

Bangladesh has a very closely knitted society. The society is also conservative. However in Dhaka city the society is more progressive. But whatever the structure it gives much value on owning a land for housing in urban areas. Thus it is creating competition for land and increasing land price which is much higher than the consumer price index (CPI). The increase of land price in recent past varied from 19-41%[26] compare to 2-10% increase in CPI.[27]

Housing Demand

Dhaka is growing very fast. So is the demand of housing. But the supply could not meet the demand. So the rent of housing is growing exponentially. We estimate that, the rent of Housing in Dhaka is almost four times than that of the other cities of the country. Dhaka has a yearly demand of 60,000 unit of housing.[28] With the decent supply of housing unit, the rent is going out of reach of ordinary people. This has led to the creation of slums and squatters.

Housing Supply

Even with the real estate boom, which is going on now, we do not think that, there is any chance of meeting the supply with the demand in the near future. Government, private investors and individuals are in a position to build some 3,000 units in a year.[29] The supply is constrained through the fact that day by day residential areas are skewed up to the hand of a few.[30]

Housing Ownership

Doeble (1987) stated from a United Nations Centre for Human Settlement document that housing market have become integrated to and monopolised by the rich and large corporations due to managerial capacity and finance. Moreover, they are supported by the government. It is unattractive for the big investors for invest for the lower income group while it becomes difficult for the small scale developers to find land for low income settlement.[31] The situation is no different in Dhaka it is not different. Though lots of housing units are constructed now-a-days, it is not possible to own a house in Dhaka due to their high price. To own an average house, it cost nearly eight years salary of a highest paid government employee.[32]

Proposed Policy

Goal and Objectives of the Policy

For a policy to be an attractive tool in delivering government wishes it must have realistic goals and objectives. The strategies and policies should be outlined clear and explicitly to achieve these goals. The general goals suggested in this paper are to:

- Ensure affordable adequate shelter for all; and
- Ensure sustainable environmental development of human settlement.

To achieve the above goals there should be measurable objectives. The objectives, which we think best for meeting, the goals are:

- Enabling legislation, which would ensure the poor to have good housing;
- Improved land management policy;
- Removal of bureaucratic red-tapism in the developing housing sector;
- Increase private sector investment in the housing sector;
- Adopt an integrated approach for housing with the others sector.

Housing Infrastructure Policy

Every component of housing infrastructure has different aspects of their own. Some of these (like road) are also part of other systems (for example road as component of transport system). So there might be a need of separate policy for many of the system components in the housing system. However as they are component of total housing system, there should be integration of the policy with housing policy. As a component of housing system, there should be strategies for each component.

Transport System

The strategy for transport system would include:

- DCC would ensure that sufficient road system is available with every housing locality;
- Though the maintenance of the road under DCC jurisdiction is a responsibility of DCC, DCC would encourage the people to maintain the road better for their own benefit;
- DCC would ensure clear access to the houses, specifying the width of access road through regulation and ensuring its implementation.

Education System

The strategy for education component of housing sector would be that

- DCC would ensure that the areas defined by RAJUK[33] as educational purposes are used for education;
- DCC would set up some school in the low-income area with the collaboration of aid agencies and NGOs.

Health System

The strategy for health component of housing sector would be that

- DCC would encourage private organisation to set up health care institute in the areas where DCC felt that there is lack of medical facility;
- DCC need to introduce basic health care facilities in the slum and low income areas; and
- To ensure adequate sanitation DCC need to strengthen its sanitation department.

Utility Service Sector

The strategy for utility services are as follows:

- DCC would ensure community participation in solid waste management;
- Water supply and sewerage, gas supply and electricity supply in the DCC area are done by separate authorities.[34] They should be brought under the DCC or there should be an umbrella organisation to co-ordinate their activities;

- DCC should ensure that there is some shop in every locality;
- Mixed land use (like Residential use at Top, Commercial use at Bottom) would be encouraged in the lower and middle income neighbourhood.

Role of DCC

Government sector (DCC) has to play a very important role in enabling housing to the poor. However, with the persistent decrease of revenue and scarcity of aid, it is becoming difficult for the government to provide services to her disadvantage groups. Considering this the proposed policy by DCC would be to:

- Devise an integrated programme of good landuse planning, sound transportation strategy and aggressive extension of primary infrastructure in areas suitable for low income population;
- To ensure that low income housing is not converted to middle income housing, legislation for land transfer in low income housing areas would be made tougher;
- To ensure cost recovery from the low income housing areas government would increase tax in commercial plots and higher income residential areas. Every attempt should be made to recover cost from the beneficiary by devising various technique;
- DCC would ensure security of tenure;
- To make investment on Urban land unattractive government should take some fiscal measures which are in practice in Sweden and Singapore. These measures could include taxation, landuse control, credit control or price freezing[35];
- DCC would continue with the existing Slum Improvement Project.

Role of Private Sector

Private sector has a very important role to play for providing housing. The proposed policy for private sector would be to:

- Increase investment in housing, by reducing tax;

- Government would encourage manufacturing and supply of building materials in the housing construction sector;
- Provide housing for middle and higher income groups in collaboration of DCC and private sector investor;
- Encourage private organisation to provide housing to their own employee;
- Increase individuals investment in housing, government would provide loan with low interest;
- Making the loan procedure for housing simpler.

Role of NGO

NGOs could play a very important role in providing housing for the poorest income group. The proposed policy for NGOs are:

- NGOs would be encourage to help the capacity building of urban poor;
- DCC would work with NGOs in Slum Improvement Project;
- Co-operative housing would be encouraged.

Housing Finance

To solve the slum and squatter problem many countries tried through the so-called low cost housing schemes. However, with the exception of Cuba, even with a minimum standard and heavy subsidy, these turned to be expensive for the poor.[36] At present House Building Finance Corporation (HBFC) is the sole agency in Bangladesh specifically housing sector financing. With the declining foreign aid it would be no longer possible for the government to inject more money in the housing sector. So more private investment in housing sector is needed.

To increase private sector participation the suggested policy strategies are:

- DCC act as guarantor against loan for housing for the poor;
- DCC waive tax for housing designated for the poor for a certain period;

- There should be tax increase on vacant plots designated for residential use by RAJUK.

Proposed Strategy

Achieving the goals set down in the policies, there is a need for clearly defined strategies. The authors' view that the policy objectives would be achieved through:

Enabling Legislation

The enable poor with affordable housing we think there need some enabling legislation. The enabling legislation strategy would be:

- The last time building code is modified in 1980. It needed some modification especially on floor area ratio[37] and set back[38] rules which are too high for housing for the poor. There is nothing for sustainable development of housing in Building law. It should be enacted;
- Existing laws do not permit slums. Many times that slums have been destroyed making thousands of people homeless overnight. To stop this happening, destruction of slums would be prohibited until alternatives have not been provided by the DCC. There should be provision in the law that DCC has to try to improve the slum rather than destroy them;
- Much of DCC land is now used by the rich and influential quarter of the society. DCC would regain this land and build housing for the poor.

Private Sector Participation

To increase private sector participation in housing, the following should be taken into account:

- To increase investment in housing, tax should be reduced for five years if an investor invests more than 10 million Taka (Approx. 250,000 US$);
- Existing law require that any investment should show source of the investment. To increase investment in housing, investor in housing sector should be exempted from application of this law. This would injecting more money in housing.

Housing Finance

Strategies for housing sector finance would be as follow:

- DCC would help the poor to get loans for housing;
- Financial institute would be encouraged to provide loan with low interest for housing;
- DCC would provide subsidy to the loan against the houses built for the poor and disadvantages.

Community Participation

To make any system sustainable there should be participation of the user and beneficiaries of the system. To ensure community participation the following is suggested:

- There should be community consultation during every phase of project cycle;
- Any cost recovery measures must be discussed and agreed with the user before being implemented to determine the rate and type of repayment;
- Encourage communities to acquire land for housing;
- DCC would act as guarantor for a loan if a low income community as a whole applied for loan.

Conclusion

Both in HABITAT-I and HABITAT-II held in Vancouver, Canada and Istanbul, Turkey give responsibilities to all level of government to provide housing for all. Though 1987, was declared as the international year of shelter for the homeless, in reality, nothing happened. The Rio Declaration[39] and the Istanbul Declaration[40] urged for a development path without jeopardising our future generations. For the better future of our future generation we need better environment and housing is one of the principal component of the environment. So for the sake of our future, we hope that DCC along with the other government and private organisations and NGOs will work together towards solving the housing problem of the mass low income and homeless people.

NOTES

1. Enayatullah, I. 1995. *A Study of Solid Waste Management for Environmental Improvement of Dhaka City*, 1.
2. Rodwin, L. 1987. Shelter, Settlement and Development, Foreword.

3. Brink, S. 1993. Policy Strategies for Affordable Housing In Cities (Housing Policies and Housing Programme Orientations, Strategies and Evaluation), 58.
4. Towfighi, P.S. 1987. Trends in the growth and spatial distribution of Population in L. Rodwin Shelter, Settlement and Development, 381-84.
5. *Ibid.*, 381-84.
6. Hasan, M. 1996 http://kipcwww.ipc.kanazawa-u.ac.jp:8080/~med2/28/latifas.html
7. *Op. cit.* Enayatullah I., 25.
8. *Ibid.*, 1.
9. DCC is the municipal government of Dhaka City headed by a Mayor.
10 Kazi, Z. 1995. http://www.asel.edu/~kazi/Bangladesh/
11. *Ibid.*
12. Bangladesh Bureau of Statistics (BBS), 1994. *Statistical Pocket Book of Bangladesh,* 1993.
13. *Ibid.*, 1994.
14. Huque, A. 1987. Planners and Pawns in Self-Help System: the Dhaka Case Study in Housing for Homeless, 28.
15. Pool Housing is that type housing in which housing is provided as a part of job facility and resident of the house has to leave the unit when the employee is no more in the organisation or no more lives in that locality where he works for the employer.
16. *Ibid.*, 28.
17. *Op. cit.* Hasan.
18. *Op. cit.* Enayatullah.
19. Hall, N., Mutharia, L. and Azami, S. 1996. *Urban Development Work in Kenya and Bangladesh,* 66.
20. *Op. cit.* Huque, A., 37.
21. Bustees is the local type of squatter settlement, which usually built on public land but the resident pay rent for their shackles to the local hooligans and their influential protector.
22. *Ibid.*, 37.
23. NGO is stand for Non-Government Organisation which work mainly with social and economic development of the poor and disadvantages.
24. *Op. cit.* Hasan, M.
25. *Ibid.*
26. *Op. cit.* Huque, 1987, 38
27. *Op. cit.* Hasan, M.
28. *Ibid.*
29. *Ibid.*

30. Doeble, W. A. 1987. *Land Policy in Shelter, Settlement and Development.*
31. *Ibid.*
32. *Op. cit.* Huque, A., 39.
33. RAJUK—Rajdhani Unnayan Kortipokha (Capital Development Authority) is the organisation responsible for physical planning of the area under jurisdiction of DCC, and its adjoining municipalities of Tongi and Savar.
34. Dhaka WASA for water supply and Sewerage; Titas Gas Distribution for gas supply and DESA for electricity supply.
35. For detail refer to Doeble, W.A., 123.
36. Vestbro, D., *Indian Contradiction about Shelter for Urban Poor in Housing for Homeless,* 50.
37. Floor Area Ratio = Total floor area of the building/Plinth area of the building.
38. Set Back = The area to be kept vacant in the residential plot after construction of house.
39. UNCED 1992. *Earth Summit Agenda. 21—The United Nations Programme of Action from Rio*; United Nations Information Department, New York.
40. Boplats 96, Committee I, 1996. *The Istanbul Declaration.*

BIBLIOGRAPHY

Bangladesh Bureau of Statistics (BBS) 1999. *Statistical Pocket Book of Bangladesh 1999.* Statistics Division, Ministry of Planning, Government of Bangladesh, Dhaka.

Boplats 96, Committee I, 1996. *The Istanbul Declaration*; Boplats 96; Stockholm.

Brink, S. 1993. Policy Strategies for Affordable Housing In *Cities* (Housing Policies and Housing Programme Orientations, Strategies and Evaluation), CIB, Lisbon.

Doeble, W.A. 1987. Land Policy in L. Rodwin (eds.) *Shelter, Settlement and Development,* Allen and Unwin, Winchester.

Enayatullah, I. 1995. A Study of Solid Waste Management for Environmental Improvement of Dhaka City; an unpublished MURP Thesis; BUET, Dhaka.

Hall N., Mutharia, L. and Azami, S. 1996. Urban Development work in Kenya and Bangladesh in Hall, N., Rob, H. and Mitlin, D. (eds.) *The Urban Opportunity—The Work of NGOs in Cities of the South.* Intermediate Technology Publication Ltd., London.

Huque, A. 1987. Planners and Pawns in Self Help System: the Dhaka Case Study\in *Housing for Homeless—Nine articles.* Royal Institute of Technology, Stockholm.

Towfighi, P.S. 1987. Trends in the Growth and Spatial Distribution of Population in L. Rodwin (eds.) *Shelter, Settlement and Development,* Allen and Unwin, Winchester.

UNCED 1992. *Earth Summit Agenda 21- The United Nations Programme of Action from Rio.* United Nations Information Department, New York.

Vestbro, D. 1999. Indian Contradiction about Shelter for Urban Poor in *Housing for Homeless—Nine articles.* Royal Institute of Technology, Stockholm.

INTERNET RESOURCES

1. Hasan, M. 1996; http://kipcwww.ipc.kanazawa-u.ac.jp:8080/~med2/28
2. Kazi, Z. 1995; http://www.asel.edu/~kazi/Bangladesh.

10

Enjoying *Bandhs* and Elephants at Rupees Two: A Story of Urban Poetics, an Essay in Pure Politics

ARNAB CHATTERJEE AND SURBHI TIWARI

ABSTRACT

A ***Bandh*** frequently invoked by political parties from their urban headquarters in Kolkata gives unbridled opportunities to those who hate work and love leisure, love the bedroom rather than the boring office, serve the senses rather than serve others. No wonder that the media together with development and growth minded expert mushrooms condemn this 'culture of *bandh*' in Kolkata in increasingly harsher terms: 'Work', 'work culture', 'responsibility', 'the city's image' etc.,—are the root metaphors that run riot in this discourse. The paper scrutinizes these warm predications. Again, Kolkata—otherwise a cheap city—also engenders euphoric dreams of white elephants at an affordable price. Despite the fact that it did not materialize, the mythopoeics of a grand sale of Chinese goods in May 2001 continues in the wake of fake China bazars held at various transit points in the city. This lust for cheapness haunts and degrades the image of consumption, which is often taken advantage of by unscrupulous traders—thus opine the self-appointed development experts. Hawkers with their cheap knick-knacks flooding the Kolkata streets are removed or fake hawkers by big traders are introduced in their stead. Dreams die, but the dreams of cheap things die-hard. However, what is the effect of this virtual China? What kind of dumping is this—the second one? What kind of mimetic act is cheating? What perversions stir the desire for dumped goods of the associational dustbin? Who are these who enjoy this cheap chirping? What kind of risk and responsibility is left to them in their private moments? Why are they left out by the traditional disciplinary studies? Is it because they are scared of commodity fetishism of this kind? Is this related to the way the history of cricket excludes match fixing lest the reality of cricket matches is brought to revelatory crisis? Or the way film studies don't write an evidential history of the casting couch lest we question the tortuous geography of a few people's progress? How do we grasp the nature and content of the discourse that is so shameless in its deliberate anticipatory exclusion? This, as we will argue, is the moment of pure politics.

Key words: urban poetics, pure politics, politics of dirty hands, bandh, bazaar, idleness, strike, death of work, responsibility, commodities, cheapness, virtuality, risk, perversion.

INTRODUCTION: What is Pure Politics?

This is an essay on urban poetics in the times of development and disguise—like love in the times of malaria. This is also an essay in pure politics. It narrates two uncomfortable experiences stuck onto the underside of urban development narratives: one, narrating how and to what extent the people of Kolkata welcome and enjoy the *Bandh*, which is a voluntary or involuntary general mass closure designating a loss of a day's work for some and that of a working day for the business chambers; two, the other narrating how they fling themselves into a shopping spree in their craze for fake Chinese goods and how, taking advantage of this, local traders have set in motion what may be called an anarchy of adulterated or locally made 'Chinese' goods, much to the chagrin of those who should like to think commodity processes in the city in sane and respectable terms.

Urbanity, to quote Henry James—is "'Well, quite a number of buildings; almost a little industrial colony. But above all it's a thing. The article produced.' 'And what *is* the article produced.' 'I'll tell you next time.'"

Urban poetics consists of those systemic textual vectors that arise out of this urban experience and the cognitive mapping that it suggests. But both the event-texts named above will be inscribed within the realm of 'pure politics' an emerging discourse which in the West has been thinly called 'the politics of dirty hands'; and, to the extent it tries to address the uncomfortable, the secret and the repressed, for understandable reasons denies its absorption in popular political science or political sociology. To do justice to it, then, it is necessary to meditate for a few more minutes on what is pure politics.

Now, to explain what is pure politics let us start with an incident reported with a tremulous and puzzled consideration in a Kolkata newspaper, either *Bartaman* or *Anandabazar Patrika* and conveniently glossed over by the readers. It read: the night Mother Teresa died, some emissaries of the Missionaries of Charity reached a home run by them in order to wake up the inmates with the sad news of the Mother's demise and subsequently absorb them in ritual collective mourning. Now consider what the newspaper report narrates: informants knocked at the door; after some calling, someone from inside the home answered, "who's there?" Those standing outside replied, "Our Mother is no more." Then came the astonishing reply from inside, "So, what are we supposed to do?" [In the original "*Tow, amra ki korbo?*"]

We miss the unreported next link here: The saddened informants might have exploded, "What do you mean by 'what you said?' Just get up and come out." Here our memory fails and we quit the story for good. The fragment could be read in a variety of ways. However what is most relevant to our consideration is that such "untoward" events form the obscene underside of public life. They are less mentioned, less reported and, furthermore—less examined. Why? The answer is not difficult to imagine. A more appropriate question would be: How would we report them? Even if we want them to be included, which is the right and inclusive discourse that might with justice contain them? One simple response to this is to say—all apparently neutral propositions and event syntaxes, descriptions, pedagogies have an uneasy underside which is not covered by disciplinary or sane discursive significations.

For to consign everything to practical political contingencies is to ask for massive quanta of discursive energy competent enough to grasp,—if not evaluate systematically, the underside of 'presented' events. To put it in more embarrassingly brazen terms, pure politics deals with the undergarments of events not subjected to the symbolic dressing of objective ethics. Pure politics shamelessly peeps into your bedrooms, looks inside your bathrooms and recovers narratives of varying degrees and modes of incongruity in agreement with the assumption—wholly justified, in our opinion—that distant, objective, impersonal reflection on value-neutral questions and disagreement in both politics and culture are always already delivered to the intolerant governance of practical political imperatives,—at least here in India.

Now, to subject everything to the practical and eternally and inviolably immediate as well as to the deferred exigencies of party politics, we bring into play here what may be regarded as a pure political *imaginary*. (Pure is 'pure' to the extent an object's form and content cannot be distinguished, and 'imaginary' in its now established usage as "not a set of ideas; rather...what enables, through making sense of, the practices of a society.") All such disciplinary categories as civil society, political society, the family and the State just vanish into thin air before this. (For instance, try explaining the Mother Teresa incident narrated above by these categories.) Pure politics deals with pure experience.

You will be stunned when you come to know that maybe the girl whom you've always loved hates you. Similarly it is likely to be a novel experience to know that the Christian dwellers of a Home should prefer to enjoy undisturbed sleep at night rather than mourn the death of the Mother. Those are the moments when we feel the hand of politics on our back, but nothing—no category—can save us then. They are moments of pure experience. As it happens, we all have had such moments in our lives but rarely felt that those narratives could be included in the textbooks of political science. Those losses were ours and they will remain ours. The politics of dirty hands will cleanse everything, remaining residually and strictly alive on the borderlines of our everyday being, in the fuzzy zone, that is, of our unmastered existence. We might feel exploited but that feeling will persist there only as one that is moral because the apparatus required to structure the feeling has been slowly but evenly de-contextualised: the state socialist project was criticized as being one of the most ruthless regime of techno-scientific, objective, impersonal, instrumental rationality where human beings without a personal touch were simply lost in lovelessness. The grand narrative of only liberal capitalism ought to be alive; the death of the revolutionary grand narrative has thereby been conveniently announced—fine! The theoretician of pure politics will suggest that with the death of grand narratives, we start talking about each other's sexual lives then! No?—Why? Embarrassed?—How? To pure politics the fragment or the micro-local is not a metaphor of place; for it, instead, the fragment is that which you resist from being publicized, that which you want to repress and hide. Then, abandoning grand investigations we need to undertake studies of the micro politics of dirty hands: office politics, the politics within a feminist group, or the intricacies of the rule effectively imposed by the cunning mediocre. How do we read the narrative of manipulation between two singer sisters in the film *Saz*? Why before a one-month (extendable) contract, all laws of sexual harassment fail? Why nobody in Bollywood talk about the casting couch? A Slovenian philosopher exclaims, "Power thus relies on an obscene supplement—that is to say, the obscene nightly law (superego) necessarily accompanies, as its shadowy double, the 'public law'. ...Obscene unwritten rules sustain Power as long as they remain in the shadows; the moment they are publicly recognized, the edifice of Power is thrown into disarray".

Having tried to delineate the domain of pure politics which deals with the experience of politics, it may be said that against this backdrop, the urban narratives of development or their obverse (the so-called 'anti-development' narratives) conceal behind them feelings which do not help in the construction of the two sets of narratives. We document here two instances—both of them are in a sense redundant because neither could be deployed to serve as materials for a broader constructive narrative with a telos. The first instance is here—

1. ENJOYING BANDH: DEATH OF WORK AND THE EMERGENCE OF COUNTER HOLIDAYS; *BANDH* AS A PLEASURE FACTOR IN POLITICAL KOLKATA

Calcutta—now Kolkata—having had been the affective centre of all political movements in West Bengal appropriates the pro-urbanist ideologies of nineteenth century liberalism and has evolved historically, with or without the motivated rigors of its own intentions, perhaps in favour of strikes, processions and *bandhs*, as the city endorsing all these signs of once anarchic, syndicalist and now social democratic resistance; and it is these signs that have gained her the positivity that belongs to the exclusivity of herself and sociale. An urban folk singer in Bengali (Kaji Kamal Naser in his *Made for Each Other* album, New Rhythm Cassettes, 11, Shymananda Road, Kolkata-700025, 1995) has a song written on the pleasures of the *bandh*. The city's self is important because in contemporary Bengali literature the city has often been metaphorically enumerated as sleeplessly haggard because of its sympathetic leftist inheritance, development is thus worked out meticulously in dreams and displaced at the same time. The Kolkata High Court sharply reacting against the phenomenon, observed some time back that there is at least one *bandh* every three months, called by this or that political party. Advantageously instanced by the decision of the Kerala High Court, which ruled *bandhs* as illegal, it has been argued by frustrated supporters of social order in Kolkata, that it would be invoked by political parties, if necessary in cloaked forms. In other words, *bandh* is unstoppable; in Kolkata, it is irresistible.

It has, however, been noticed that, hostile criticism notwithstanding, people in Kolkata have started enjoying the *bandh*. The city media have often voiced their concern that *bandhs* have become instrumental in making people idle by reinforcing idleness; a large chunk of city dwellers, service holders as they are, are reluctant to go out to work; whatever little work-mindedness is still there, it has been alleged, is thus being erased, leading to complete loss of the decaying and nearly destroyed 'work culture' in Kolkata and West Bengal. The media in the vernacular have been branding *bandhs* as *karmanasha* (killer of work) and the parties indulging in the technique as 'irresponsible'. They have also had recourse to a piece of queer argument as to why *bandh* should not be called: quite apart from the fact that it impedes development, they feel, as a weapon of mass protest it is drained of all genuine utility because of massive and indiscriminate overuse, and people—particularly the salaried segments, students, etc., and others—indifferent to those who make a living on their days' earnings, enjoy a *bandh* and look forward to the next one. The media as well as the parties opposing the *bandh* dismiss as no more than a bogus claim the one made by those organizing and supporting the *bandh* with regard to its all pervasive success. People with a genuine commitment to their work don't enjoy having to sit idle within their homes; yet they do not budge out of home simply out of fear. In these circumstances real support cannot be gauged with any degree of certainty—hence it remains elusive. More interestingly, these days political parties—particularly SUCI (Socialist Unity Center of India)—have made it a practice to stage *bandhs* on Fridays or Mondays offering people a three-day holiday of sorts—so much so that even the ruling Left front has these days voiced its disgust over frequent *bandhs* in Kolkata and Bengal!

We need to investigate this queer process which seems to have set in whereby an instrument of political protest has turned into a tool affording pleasure. Can it again become a political weapon? Is it possible to politicize this surfeit of unearned pleasure? A matter difficult to investigate, given the fact that the techniques of governance and resistance have themselves undergone a deeply symbolic transformation. But what are the details when once it is borne in upon us that people in the final analysis are administered by details? To try to address this entanglement by actually discursively engaging these people—who are otherwise called the stakeholders—the citizen individuals, the political parties, the media, etc., we need to have the textuality of utterances made from various subject positions examined against numerous background assumptions—political and commonsense—aiming to foreground a micro-theoretical praxis for a political phenomenology of the *bandh* in Kolkata itself.

For instance, to refer to a pilot study we conducted, the questions we asked ourselves were: how do the segments of the Kolkata population for whom a *bandh* is no more than a windfall gain look at a general mass strike or a *bandh* in the city? How do they actually enjoy it without a political commitment on their part? Why do they not feel for those who are being deprived of a day's living, as the media accuse them of doing? In what other ways could they have felt or reacted?

From the interviews, we have gathered a complex semiotics of reading utterances as texts revealing the nature of this politics turned pleasure factor: That enjoyment is a political factor and that the obscene underside of Law eroticises the notion of obstruction and its limit by its own "quota of affect" no more strike us as new; the one who enjoys a *bandh* and welcomes another one is perhaps a true political pervert. But the political having been reduced to what affords 'pleasure', it would then be interesting to go for a new notion of the political. Is it the counter holiday which breaks with the National or State holidays enlisted and defined by the calendar? In the middle ages—named by some symbolic anthropologists as "time out" and reiterated by Foucault—there used to be the festival of collective role-reversal where the rich used to adopt the role of the poor, the fool used to lead the congregation at the church and *vice versa*: "it was a counter holiday in relation to Sunday, Christian or Easter, one that escaped from the habitual circuit of ordinary festivals." Has the *bandh* in Kolkata set such a time in? Why not?

Secondly, the subject structure of political parties as strategic interventionist actors together with the institutions and organizations in Kolkata as other crucial stakeholders in this debate were explored: What do the *bandh* specialists say about this phenomenon? The left still boastfully claims it to be their weapon; the moderates trace it to the days of Gandhi. A sample review (of relevant literature) tells us that classical discussions on strikes have nothing to tell about the *bandh* which is very different from the fourfold classification that Roland-Holst prepared on Kautsky's suggestions: solidarity strikes, anarchist general strikes, the economic mass strikes, political or social mass strike etc.—it's none of them. The

1889's ultimatum for a general strike in London didn't gain the approval of Engels himself. The aim was to paralyze the daily life of London. Engels wrote "...it was creating millions of hungry mouths for no reason but because they had some tens of thousands they could not feed." However, this argument today would be classified by the *bandh* protagonists as reactionary. It is evident that the *bandh* is a kind of sympathetic mass strike in solidarity, though essential services are excluded. Again, the CPI objected to the immunity granted to the essential services when the ESMO bill was passed in Parliament in August 1957. How do these things stand today in the wake of the *bandhs* and the recent legal row over uncontrolled processions and rallies? How would Sorel's strike as myth be invoked by CPI(M) ideologues today? Interviews reveal: there is doubletalk on all these points; party ideologues haven't heard of Sorel.

Thirdly, in the trade and industrial circles in Kolkata, it has been a commonplace to accuse the *bandh* culture as destructive of the city's, and consequently the state's, work culture. A preliminary exploration in the raging discourse of the death of work through the sieve of various notions of work, now being mourned, and the notions of responsibility offers interesting theoretical possibilities. For instance, work in the modern sense is a paid activity in the *public sphere* as Andre Gorz argues by branding it as the *monetarization* of work, separated from the daily tasks "indispensable for the maintenance and reproduction of our individual lives"; but the realm of labor performed under necessity does not belong to the realm of freedom. Marx says, "...in fact, the true realm of freedom actually begins only where labor which is determined by necessity and mundane considerations ceases; thus in the very nature of things it lies beyond the sphere of actual material production...beyond it begins the development of human energy which is an end in itself, the true realm of freedom...". If this be so, what kind of freedom do the innumerable Kolkatans who have vanished into their own homes to carry life world-tasks enjoy? Is it not the better kind —the true realm of freedom? What do their wives say? Foucault reminds us that Freud was correct when he wrote that a mad person is he who could neither work nor love; and with the romance of the industrially developed state setting in, it was obvious that the mad, the sick and the old people who could neither work nor love were confined and excluded along with the unemployed. Do the psychologists in Kolkata need to activate the psycho-trendy *Work therapy* for everyone of those who have been noticed to escape the monetary work for a day's (counter) holiday?

Fourthly, what do the media representatives think when they say the parties have been irresponsible in calling a bandh? What do the youths and the employees think of responsibility when they are told that their enjoying the *bandh* is a lapse into irresponsibility? In contractual terms, how is responsibility defined or inscribed? How do people react when they are put in their place as tacit legal beings? What do lawyers say? How does common sense envisage the matter when responsibility fades into—not oblivion but obligations?

Only one half of the answers to the many questions that have been posed above are in order. It is easy to talk glibly about responsibility, or responsibility to the 'other', but we are in a fix when we want to consider it as a discursive question (or consider it with the cogency a discursive practice demands). What is the techno-utilitarian apparatus of this responsibility? In a complex framework of *rights* and *'non-rights'*, *claims*, *duties* and *privileges*; negative, positive and neutral *freedom*, rarely do we know what form that social responsibility, dissociated from the economic rationality innate in the impact studies of mass closure in terms of income effects and consumption effects, will assume.

To present a brief sketch and attempt a beginning, we can adopt and transform some ideas of Neil W. Chamberlain who, borrowing from Hohfeld, has tried to address this question of responsibility in a concrete discursive context. Firstly, we might want to re-state the morpheme *responsibility* in the sense of loose duties. That is, in a legal relationship there are expectancies of conduct different from those in non-legal ones. Responsibilities that are inscribed in customs bear social or conventional sanctions with them, while legal ones are prized with enforceable sanctions backed by the constraints of legitimate coercion. In a legal relationship it is a duty which is a correlative of right. (Throw in here also the fact that different job-responsibilities may be seen here as enumerated kinds of duties without the normative gloss borne by the latter.) If A has a *privilege*, B has a *negative obligation* or a *no-right* not to "prevent the other's initiative if s/he chooses to exercises it". If A possesses *legal power*, B must have a *legal liability*; A's *legal immunity* will impose on B a correlative *legal* disability; *rights, privileges, power, and immunities*—all according to Hohfeld are rights which set up enforceable expectancies of particular kinds of responses; the correlative relationships he denominated as *duties, no rights, liabilities* and *disabilities*. Following Chamberlain four correlative obligations as against four types of Hohfeldian *rights* may be delineated here. For (i) *right*—there is the obligation of *specific performance*, for (ii) *privilege*—the obligation of *non-intervention*; for (iii) *power*—the obligation of *submission*; for (iv) *immunities*—the obligation of *non-deprivation*. "In this framework of reciprocal rights and obligations, what is the nature of responsibility? In this legal system the possession of a right carries with it an authority, an authority to compel specific performance from another whose specific obligation was the correlative of the right. The latter person has a responsibility to comply." But as visible from above, responsibilities emerge within the complex context of liability, disability, etc., etc. The *specific performance* issue could be broached only when it occurs within the authoritative claims of a particular kind of right and not elsewhere. Chamberlain argues elsewhere in order to distinguish between obligation and responsibilities that a "right for one person is defined by the conduct (obligation) he can expect from others, and authority is defined by the conduct (responsibility) he can command from others". Therefore responsibilities in this framework is a response to authority while obligations are responses to rights. If we are willing to dispense with the confusion that is generated here, we could just insert a modifier.

Responsibilities as loose duties are a matter of interpretation; they cannot be claimed as duties; they are contextual, contractual, contingent and a matter of arbitrary adjudication, nevertheless they have specific meanings and applications attached to them. Duties are broad narratives of compulsion. The prolific but cheap use of "irresponsibility" in exalted urban circles deployed in order to argue against *bandh* evades these questions in order to make a quick point. This is most unfortunate.

While opportunistically the question of responsibility is raised there, in an age of fading social securities and social responsibilities, how risk becomes a paradigmatic relata used to mark the moment when I'm taught to live alone and acknowledge the erasure of responsibilities, the second story is offered below.

2. ENJOYING ELEPHANTS AT RS. 2 OR FROM CHINA *FEAR* TO CHINA *FAIR*: THE REAL STORY OF HOW THE PRODUCERS AND THE PUBLIC NEGOTIATED THE RUMOR OF CHEAPNESS IN KOLKATA

This section should have begun with an analytical explanation of a picture published on 26 May, 2001, in *The Telegraph*, a daily published from Kolkata showing disgusted buyers walking out of the China fair "that never was".

Instead let's begin with a linguistic narration. The interesting event took place in Kolkata, the supposed cultural capital of India, in May 2001; rumors were rife that unbelievably cheap Chinese goods would be made available at the Netaji Indoor Stadium. This information reached the public through randomly distributed pamphlets, news clippings in daily newspapers, and through all-pervading electronic mails. But the rumour was given a concrete form by a few traders who actually feed on such rumors. There were price lists cataloguing consumer items for which there is a large demand at throwaway prices: 14″ color television sets which actually costs in the Indian market Rs. 6,500 each, would allegedly be available for just Rs. 3,000; a motorcycle, which costs at least Rs. 32,000 here, would be available at an unbelievable Rs. 11,000; a fridge which costs at least Rs. 10,000, would be available at the great China fair at Rs. 1,400 each and so on and so forth. Interestingly, even before the real 'sale' of these coveted articles took place, what actually sold according to news reports, were these price lists, particularly at Patna, Guwahati and Cuttack. Consequently, on 25th May, the fateful day for the mammoth sales, a large crowd gathered at the gates of the stadium, which were (un)expectedly closed. The authorities refused to allow anybody to enter, because, as they clarified, no such sale was scheduled. They instead blamed the people for having been that gullible. However, the ever-swelling crowd, demanding that the doors be opened, refused to lend ears to what they heard now. To avoid a possible gate-crash, at last the gates were thrown open for 'public' verification. People rushed in and were witness to an empty stadium but still would not believe that they had been fooled by the perpetrators of the fraud. They rather believed that the government had played them false by selling the cheap goods to wholesalers who would charge a lot more now if they chose to buy them. They left the arena cursing the government, calling the traders names, heaping abuses on the parents of the respectable ministers.

Following this, the Kolkata Police initiated a probe to find how the whisper campaign had actually begun and how the whole big 'tamasha' took place. As a result of this investigation two companies—a Bangalore based company dealing in electronic goods and a Mumbai based company, by name *Shangrita Electronics and Automobiles*—were charged with fraudulent practices. A retrospective survey by the media brought to light queer results: it was revealed that when the rumor was doing its rounds in Kolkata, genuine dealers of Chinese goods had as a result of confusion, been seriously disturbed. They had reported that there was a steady decline in their sales resulting from the ambiguous prospect of cheaper goods. Later, talking to news personnel, the city police commissioner Sujoy Chakravorty said, "If somebody tells you that you can buy elephants at Rupees Two and you believe it, who is responsible?" This remark underscores the element of irony in the incident. However, where the show ends, the story begins.

Following the gala event, or non-event, an increased sale of goods supposedly imported from China was noticed. Local *China bazars* began to be organised in nearly all local transit points throughout the city where locally made goods were sold as those imported from China; and fake China fairs in the wake of the failed grand China show at the Netaji Indoor Stadium continued to draw consumers who were not apparently daunted by the pallid beauty of a defeated rumor. And yes, even after two years, this mysterious craze for consumption remains alive. (Near Hazra crossing in Kolkata the last China Bazar could still be visited for buying any good at Rs. 60.)

Some have tried to explain the incident as owing to the falsification of information and bad media effect leading to the embarrassment of thousands. In the same breath they have asked why such things don't take place in the developed North. Some others have thought it on the whole desirable that such rumors have begun to spread in India, which is symptomatic, they claim, of the country's growing induction into the processes of globalization. As they perceive it, normally at other times there are rumors about adultery, black money, god drinking real milk, etc., and, of course more electrifying rumors about the members of a religious community being killed or raped by the members of the hostile community (in India it is Hindus vs. Muslims) leading to dangerous riots and organized pogroms. The rumor about *commodities* to be sold and the huge rush that followed are, as in this case, signs of increasing material sensibility and visibility of Indian citizens and point to emergence of a positive consciousness pertaining to consumption hitherto absent from our society. These theorists do not keep at a discount the fact that what these people believed to be true was not, or could not be, factually true; the prices for all they care might have been the content of a classical rumor. But that hardly matters. What, instead, they lend importance to is that the people did believe that such impossible prices *could be true,* which in itself is a thematic subtext in favour of globalization conceived as the gift or *daan*[1] of globalization. At last common men have got globalization correct, at last it has started to work in favour of them!

These are the interpretations that have been doing the rounds and we have no quarrel with them; they are pretty plausible. In fact globalization will spawn rumors about its own self, though in all likelihood they will differ in kind and quality. Through such rumors globalization perhaps advertises itself and will continue to do so in future. However, the point that we want to make here is different altogether: True, the rumor of cheap commodities may be a product of globalization.

However, does it not by default also give credence to the fact that Chinese commodities upon which our eyes are riveted are cheap only by virtue of cheap labor in China shut in innumerable sweat shops? This invokes a debate which has by now become classical.

As we pursue the matter, from our vantage point let us give it a different twist: consider the fake China Bazars in Kolkata selling fake Chinese goods. This involves a theoretical departure: when commodities are not real, in the case of counterfeit Chinese goods, sweat shops are virtual; they are not practically real. Here we keep in mind what happened at the Netaji Indoor Stadium, and also what followed. How the China fair actually served to dispel the fear of imported Chinese goods among local producers and then led soon to the setting up of a model of local China Bazars held at nearly all trade transit points and how through the sale of fake, forged Chinese goods, local businessmen here in Kolkata came to negotiate this fear and shifted the success in trade in their own favour invokes a kind of mythopoeics. We have our own sweat shops, there are cheap goods made locally which are then sold as genuine Chinese goods in no need of anti-dumping laws, trade restrictions and police intervention. The anti-dumping laws are really redundant in this sphere. Our local 'con tradesmen' pass off the goods they manufacture as Chinese goods. So who's afraid of dumping any more? This creative economic action, we suggest, can be studied as a literary act—the way one copies the image of a bird through painting or words, one forges a Chinese label, inscribes a Chinese script on the objects and gets over the Chinese bugbear. We find this a literary feat to dispel an economic fear, created and produced by the businessmen themselves. The urban poetics of cheating is still to be written, but the poetics of the 'will to be cheated' is ready at hand!

Similarly we would argue that even in the case of counterfeit Chinese goods, the Chinese imaginary is always already present. It is a phenomenon of virtual commodities with a Chinese signature. Let us elaborate upon our thesis by explaining a few categories linked to this: What is virtuality? Why, as we claim, do the sweatshops become virtual here? In the sales organized by the Kolkata businessmen, the factual

China is absent but the virtual China is present. Those who throng these exhibitions in search of Chinese articles have the dubious satisfaction of buying cheap, and this they derive from the rumor that once caught hold of the Kolkata market. The goods were Chinese—no matter! *China is there in their minds.* It is present by its absence: This is what we call virtual. Julia Kristeva in one of her novels, *Possessions,* gives a narrative of virtuality, "Gloria was lying in a pool of blood with her head cut off. The ivory satin evening dress, the rounded arms, the long manicured hands, the cartier watch,.... The sun tanned legs, the shoes matching the dress—no doubt about it, that was Gloria. There was nothing missing except the head. "My sexual organ," as she laughingly used to call it, referring to the cerebral pleasure she got out of her work as a translator and the equally intense pain she suffered from her headaches. Some times she'd amend the description and called her head "the tool of her trade". And now here she was, bereft of her organ or tool, and so made almost anonymous. But only almost. For, head or no head, Gloria Harrison was easily recognizable. This is virtuality: Gloria is not recognizable, but still recognized. We can say the same in regard to the mushroom growth of China Bazars whose commodities resemble the 'original' Chinese goods. Therefore even if they are not Chinese in reality, they are recognized as such because they are imaged on the order of the Chinese. A virtual China is present here, and with this virtual China at their disposal, those who deal in local goods negotiate the fear of cheap Chinese goods. What is more, it becomes a tool in their trade.

Now to address a more philosophical question as to whether we are, in this case, essentialising the idea of Chinese by claiming truths in favour of a real Chinese in contrast to a fake Chinese article, we should like to reconsider Jean Paul Sartre's advocacy of Cartier-Bresson's photographs (available in his book *Colonialism and Neocolonialism*) which, according to him, were less than or not quite Chinese. Sartre, introducing Cartier-Bresson's album of photographs, is said to have declared the "death" of the picturesque: Other photographers "seek out a Chinese who looks more Chinese than the others, in the end they find one. They make him adopt a typically

Chinese pose and surround him with chinoseries. What have they captured on film? One Chinaman? No...the idea of what is Chinese". But then what *difference* does Bresson *make*? His photographs, Sartre argues, find those Chinese who are "not quite Chinese". No doubt this construction makes for an excellent post-coloniai theatre, but is this appropriation of Sartre justiciable? No, Let's see why.

Please note that while the picturesque brings to focus someone who is more Chinese than others, Bresson endeavours to portray someone who is less Chinese or not quite Chinese; that is to say, there is an element of 'excess' in the first and 'lack' in the second but both are paradoxically foregrounded on some subject called 'Chinese' and an elemental system called 'China'. Or else how could one explain away the fact that, well, something is more or less than *Chinese.* But then what is this measuring standard ideally called *Chinese* judged by which you decide something to be an 'excess' or a 'lack'. This is where Sartre's troubles begin and those who have read Sartre's *Psychology of Imagination* and linked it with a bit of Lacan will agree—that all these boil down to the regime of the image. Let us regard here Sartre's analysis of the portrait of Charles VIII who is 'at one and the same time absent and also present'. This would testify to the fact that the *less than Chinese* notion is already present in the *more than* Chinese images. This would be consonant with the recent suggestions made by Ashis Nandy that a history of the poor can be written by concentrating on the lives of the superrich and similarly a history of knowledge can be written simply by trying to write a history of errors. It follows that—Bresson's *less than Chinese* photographs reconstruct more emphatically than any others—the *more than Chinese* notion.

But isn't there a constitutive deception involved here? Who will take the responsibility of faking Chinese goods and selling them to people as real? What has it to do with the new economic order? For this, let us take to the other register available in the narrative of the Grand China Fair. The Police Commissioner of Kolkata (anti-cheating section) accused the people of believing the unbelievable. He put forward the philosophical question of responsibility. We would like to put forward here the question of risk. This will link our story to the globalized world where social securities are withdrawn, salaries go down, jobs vanish and fake things are sold in the name of the real. Ulrich Beck in his now famous book *World Risk Society* comments on this world in dangerously secular terms "as the bipolar world fades away, we are moving from a world of enemies to one of dangers and risks". Let us add here that to move into the world of risks suggests that we move out of the world of responsibility; in that good old world somebody would take the responsibility of the other. Here now risk means to be responsible to one's own self, to one's own desires and needs—nobody is there to satisfy them. Beck argues that the new risk regime predicts an absolutely new future symbolized by the emergence of private insurance. However, the greatest symbol of calculation and alternative security which does not cover nuclear disasters or climate changes. It would also not cover anything which does not have any risk. It would also refuse to cover everything which bears too less or too much risk. Do we expect the blind consumers who thronged the stadium to be covered by such an insurance? If not then it is no use subjecting them to the grand sermons of responsibility. They should be left to themselves in a volatile market society to bear the risk for themselves. To satisfy desires through an economic shortcut—one takes risk without becoming irresponsible. Beck, concluding for us, says, "...one thing is clear how one acts in the situation" (of the risk trap) "is no longer something that can be decided by experts". Let us then in the matter of the *bandh* too stop preaching the gospel of responsibility to the irresponsible people who have made it a habit to convert a day of *bandh* to another (counter) holiday and look forward to the next in the series.

Finally, one historical question remains to be examined: the claims of novelty attributed to the moments generated by the grand narrative of globalization. Contextually put, consider the mad drive for the great China fair. Is it something capricious without historical antecedents? By no means. In fact the early days of mass consumption in Europe began with the promise of cheap goods. There is nothing wrong in this expectation or nothing new. John Carrol in his book "Skeptical Sociology" recalls the novelist Emile Zola who, according to him, has provided us with the perspective. Carrol writes, "In his richly sociological novel *Au Bouhevr des Dames,* written in 1882 he described the great department store. The new emporiums were eclipsing all the tradition shops in their neighborhoods. Zola attributed their success to the factor that they exploited the "bargain" [by] "seducing women into buying things they did not need *by making them so cheap that the customer imagined every time she bought that she was bringing off a brilliant economic coup*" [Italics mine]. When producers sell fake Chinese goods they do take advantage of the already established rumor about the cheapness of Chinese goods. But people, by buying or trying all the time to buy still cheaper goods and by never giving up exhibit their desire to go in for an economic coup everyday. They must go on buying cheap goods. That is how the public negotiates the rumor; the virtual China fair has provoked the dream of cheapness which, like Will O 'The Wisp,' keeps ever eluding. Communism is the final stage of this longing for cheap things, which however turned to be very costly. And now the resurrected 'cost' of things have become a nightmare.

Lastly, as the word dumping suggests, it is at one level the desire for the dustbin. Isn't there something sick and perverted about the abnormal wish to go for dumped goods—fake or real? Here is Carrol again, "To know a society means above all to know its irrationality. Sociologists do well to take as their exemplar the haughty madame in Louis Malle's brothel, in his film *Murmur of the Heart,* who claimed that she could tell a man's perversion at a thirty-second glance."

As for our producers of Chinese goods and their consumers alike—if the Madame were here, bet it—it would have taken her an hour.

AFTERWORD

Then the man who enjoys a *bandh* is a true political pervert; the person who has a desire to consume dumped goods is also as much a pervert. The first is a pleasure which is abandoned rather than politicized, condemned rather than criticized. For, as we have seen, the moment we launched a critique, the media sociologists and the growth-development-cum-'city's good name' experts were easily identified to have been operating with a keen singular notion of work, idleness, holidays etc., demanding that everybody agree with them without engaging in a minimal discursive process to test those validity claims of the arguments they put forward. This has been conveniently and constantly done by the media and the pop sociologists and economists here in India which is also, at the same time, a fascist-capitalist funny gesture since it tends to ignore larger theoretical issues. To sum up in a few words, 'closure as pleasure' cannot be appropriated by those narratives according to which the loss of a working day is equivalent to the mourning that follows the moment someone loses one of their parents; neither is it part of the usual resistance critique which fuels the anti development narratives. "I've vanished into my home with my girlfriend or boyfriend, wife or husband; I hate work, do whatever you want to out of doors." The second part narrated how people are enjoying and increasingly desire elephants at rupees two. And that too at their own risk. Risk means that the responsibility is mine. Risk means being uncovered by the politics of insurance. In other words risk is the vanishing point of utterance. And the two examples elaborated above and commented on stage a queer theatre. Responsibility is invoked in the first instance to argue why *bandh* should be dumped; in the second, it is evident that in an age of diminishing responsibilities and expectations where all are encouraged to become selfishly rational—private pleasure maximisers, responsibility is a doubtful and disputed neo liberal gesture, perhaps interpretable only within the semiotics of 'private' insurance. Briefly, all our secret economic coups were failed encounters with the moral boundaries of the market.

In other words, these are words—these are worlds—these are ears which can only be arbitrarily pierced. But these ears are long and inevitably cast a long shadow; the question is, are they those of the elephant bought at rupees two? And lest we forget, let us rehearse for the last time the discourse of pure politics which deals with the narrative of experiencing the political narrates experiences and not answers.

NOTE

1. In fact this is one of the major arguments of Bhaskar Mukhopadhyaya's incisive paper 'Rumor of Globalization: Globalizing Counter-works and the location of commodity'. Manuscript.

11

Development and River Water Resources

ADEBAYO J. ADELOYE

a.j.adeloye@hw.ac.uk

School of the Built Environment, Heriot-Watt University, Edinburgh, EH14 4AS, United Kingdom.

ABSTRACT

Rivers adjoining sites of human settlement have, since time immemorial, been utilized as sources of meeting domestic and agricultural water needs. Rivers have also been used since the earliest times as sinks for the disposal of waste material and effluents. The ever increasing pressures placed on river water by these demands, accentuated in recent times by population increases and climatic change, call for better strategies for managing river water if it is to continue to adequately meet the demands. This paper discusses the very many uses of river water, consumptive and non-consumptive, and details some of the analytical tools for assessing river water resource with a view to ascertaining its quantitative adequacy for the various human needs such as water supply, irrigation, agriculture and power generation. Pollution of the available resources is also a major factor limiting water resources availability. Procedures for monitoring, controlling and preferably reducing river water pollution are outlined. The paper then reviews contemporaneously advocated paradigms for coping with the rapidly vanishing freshwater supply-demand "headroom". These paradigms include source control of urban runoff, conjunctive management of water resources facilities, demand management and integrated water resources management. In essence, it is argued that the importance of rivers as water supply sources for humankind cannot be emphasized enough. However, coping with rising demands, pollution and climate change impact requires better management and more conscientious use and conservation of combined water resources.

1. INTRODUCTION

Rivers have been the backbone for most human settlements for generations. Indeed, the development of many major cities in the world has been close to rivers, which have served the need of the communities for drinking, irrigation, agriculture and the assimilation of their wastes. Rivers can also be a source of human misery, particularly during floods when they overflow their banks and cause damage to anything in their course. However, this paper will only concentrate on the beneficial effects of rivers, and takes the view that by proper management, the negative effects of rivers can be minimized or eliminated. In discussing the benefits of rivers to humankind, particular attention will be given to the technical and engineering aspects of river water development. The paper will end with a brief outline of contemporary issues affecting further development of river sources.

2. RIVERS AS SOURCES OF WATER SUPPLY

Although water in rivers constitutes only 0.0001% of the total amount of water available on the earth's surface (Maidment, 1993), rivers are still very strategic for human development. River water is vital for human existence. It is used in various domestic activities, in agriculture, irrigation and in industry. All of these uses are regarded as consumptive uses because the return flow from such activities is often less than the original abstraction. However, unlike the water in groundwater aquifers, river water is also valuable for non-consumptive uses such as hydroelectric power generation, navigation, and wastewater treatment plants' effluent dilution. Besides, for most countries as illustrated by the African examples in Figure 1, the surface water resources far outstrip the easily accessible (*i.e.* shallow water table) groundwater resources.

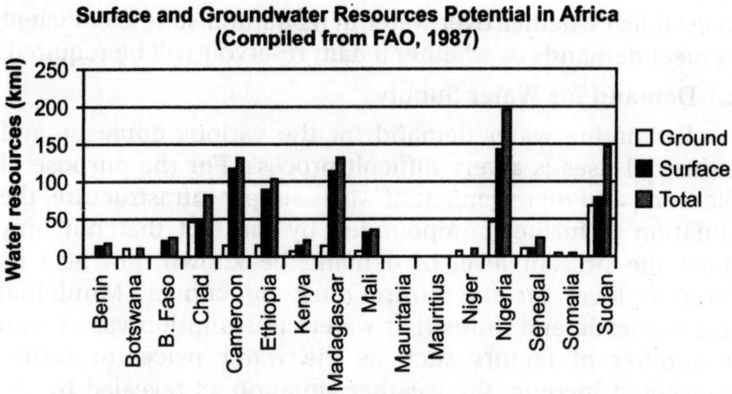

FIGURE 1: Surface and shallow groundwater resources potential of some African countries

While river water serves the above consumptive and non-consumptive purposes, its availability for the various uses is highly variable, both temporally and spatially. As a consequence, it is often not possible to rely on river water in its natural occurrence to meet these needs without one form of human intervention or another. Human intervention in the form of dams has been used since historical times to regulate river water, thereby storing the excess water during periods of high rainfall and runoff for later release during periods of low rainfall and runoff. The combination of water in rivers, dam reservoirs and other natural lakes increases the contribution of surface water sources to world's water to 0.014% (Chow *et al.*,. 1988).

As will be expected, the main factor determining whether or not river water conservation by dams and reservoirs will be required for meeting water supply needs is the demand level. Demand is used in a purely economic sense here and represents what consumers actually desire. It is different from the notion of water demand used in less developed regions where, due to limitations posed by available water resources and/or supply infrastructure, the amount of water actually supplied is well below that desired. In sections 2.1 and 2.2, respectively, demands for water supply and irrigation are examined, paying particular attention to models for their estimation. Section 2.3 details the river data analyses required to establish whether river water in its natural state is sufficient to meet demands or whether a dam reservoir will be required.

2.1 Demand for Water Supply

Estimating water demand for the various domestic and industrial uses is a very difficult process. For the purpose of planning and management of water supply infrastructure, the situation is further compounded by the fact that not only must the present level of demand be known, but also its forecast level for the future must be known. Municipal (*i.e.* domestic and industrial) water consumption varies with a number of factors such as the water price (or tariff), household income, the weather situation as revealed by the temperature, and the general standard of living. Leakage from distribution networks and consumer taps is also an important factor since this can mean that the total amount of water put into supply is much higher than the demand. Leakage rates vary from one water supply area to another depending on a number of factors not least of which are the age and integrity of the supply network and the management experience of the water undertaker. However, in recent times most water undertakers have realized that reducing leakage rates can partially meet increasing demands and delay investment in the development of new resources.

McMahon (1993) discusses a number of models for forecasting future levels of domestic and industrial water demand, using the above factors as independent variables. The discussion by McMahon (1993) distinguishes between static forecasts, in which time is not a parameter, and dynamic forecasts in which time is a parameter. The use of dynamic models is recommended for short-term forecasts or in situations where current water use is influenced by past water use. Static models are recommended for long-term forecasts. Example of either class of models is (McMahon, 1993):

$$Q = a_0 + a_1P + a_2D + a_3Y + a_4W + u \text{ (Static model)} \quad (1)$$

$$Q_t = c_0 + c_1P + c_2D + c_3Y + c_4W + c_5Q_{t-1} + u \text{ (Dynamic model)} \quad (2)$$

where Q is the monthly water consumption of the average household;

P is the water price charged to the average household;
D is the difference between what the typical consumer actually pays for water and what would be paid if all the water were purchased at the marginal rate;
Y is the personal income per household;
W is the evapotranspiration less the rainfall
U is the random error term
t is the time; and
$a_{i},\ _{i = 0,\ 1,...,4}$ and $c_{j,\ j=0,1,...,5}$ are empirical coefficients obtainable by least squares regression techniques.

Equations (1) and (2) can be applied if the independent variables can be quantified, but often some if not most are impossible to quantify. Another common approach for forecasting future demand levels is by (linearly) extrapolating past trends. However, the danger of such an approach is that past trends may accurately indicate the future trend, particularly where societies have reached a level of saturation regarding living standards. This is clearly demonstrated by the United Kingdom (UK) example illustrated in Figure 2. Indeed, where changes in the economy mean a shift in emphasis from heavy industry to the less water intensive service industry, as happened in the UK during the 1980s, future water demand can be much less than that of the past.

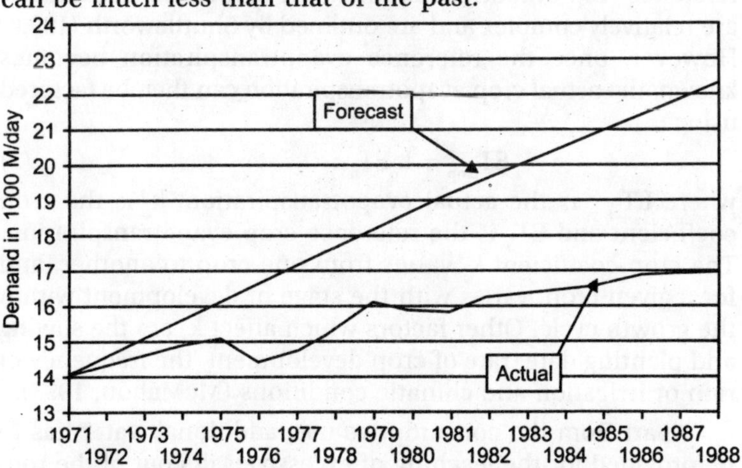

FIGURE 2: Example of possible error in forecasting future demand in England and Wales using the past trend (*Source*: Gray, 1994)

2.2 Irrigation Water Demand

Since irrigation water diversions account for over 80% of the total water withdrawals in some parts of the developing world (Oyebande, 2001), any serious attempt addressing water scarcity must focus on this sector. Irrigation water demand, also termed the consumptive use, depends on the type of crops grown, the area under cultivation and the efficiency of the water conveyance and water application facilities. The consumptive use is often approximated by the actual evapotranspiration, which is in turn factored from the reference crop evapotranspiration. The reference crop evapotranspiration is a theoretical concept, which assumes that water for crop growth is non-limiting. It is defined as (Doorenbos and Pruitt, 1977): "the rate of evapotranspiration from an extensive surface of 8 to 15 cm tall, green grass cover, actively growing, completely shading the ground and not short of water".

The reference crop evapotranspiration can be estimated using the Penman-Monteith equation as recommended by the United Nations Food and Agricultural Organization, FAO (Doorenbos and Pruitt, 1977). The Penman-Monteith equation uses weather measurements—wind speed, solar radiation, humidity, temperature, sunshine hours—to estimate the reference crop evapotranspiration. The associated calculations are relatively complex and are outlined by Shuttleworth (1993). However, once the reference evapotranspiration becomes known, the actual crop evapotranspiration can then be factored using:

$$ET_{crop} = k_c ET_o \tag{3}$$

where ET_{crop} is the actual evapotranspiration, k_c is the crop coefficient and ET_o is the reference crop evapotranspiration. The crop coefficient k_c varies from one crop to another, and for a given crop, varies with the stage of development within the growth cycle. Other factors which affect k_c are the sowing and planting date, rate of crop development, the frequency of rain or irrigation and climatic conditions (McMahon, 1993).

Apart from the consumptive use, additional water has to be provided for the leaching of excessive salts out of the root zone of crops, and to compensate for the water lost during conveyance and application. In general, only about 40%

of the water released at head works actually goes into consumptive use (McMahon, 1993). In addition, the leaching requirements vary with the type of irrigation system, the salinity of the irrigation water and of the root zone, and the soil texture. Doorenbos and Pruitt (1977) provide practical guidance on making allowances for leaching requirements and losses in water conveyance and application, during irrigation planning. If all these factors are taken into account, then the total monthly irrigation water requirement can be obtained using (McMahon, 1993):

$$V_{irr} = C\frac{f}{\eta_p}\sum_{i=1}^{cr}\left(\frac{A(ET)}{1-R}\right)_i \tag{4}$$

where V_{irr} = total irrigation requirement (m^3/month)

η_p = the project irrigation efficiency (fraction)

f = flexibility factor, typically 1.2

A = area under a given crop (ha)

ET = irrigation requirement for a given crop (see Equation 3) (mm/month)

LR = leaching requirement (fraction)

i = crop type counter

cr = number of crop types

C = conversion factor = 10

As would be expected, a successful irrigation needs more than the availability of water resources. It also requires good seeds and soils, fertilizers, effective control of insects and pests, and effective institutional management structure for the scheme. Discussion of the precise impacts which some of these factors have played in irrigation is not the purview of this paper but is available elsewhere (see Alam, 1991). However, if these factors are favourable, then water resources availability becomes the factor limiting the yield of agricultural crops as proposed by Doorenbos and Kassam (1979):

$$1-\left(\frac{Y}{Y_m}\right) = f\left[1-\frac{ET_{crop}}{ET_0}\right] \tag{5}$$

where Y is the actual crop yield, Y_m is the maximum attainable crop yield (*i.e.* when water is not in short supply), f is a yield response factor and all the other terms are as defined previously. Equation (2) is known as the crop water production function and has been successfully used in a number of studies investigating the effect of water deficit on crop yields (*e.g.* Oluwasemire *et al.*, 2002). Furthermore, all the seemingly complex technical tasks involved in irrigation development can now be carried out using SIMIS (scheme irrigation management information system), the user-friendly decision support systems developed by the FAO for the wholesale planning, water application scheduling, operation and maintenance of irrigation systems. Essential details of SIMIS are described by Mateos *et al.* (2002).

2.3 Meeting Water Demands: Analysis of River Flow Data

With the demands known, it is then necessary to determine whether or not a dam with reservoir storage will be required. This will require analysing the record of river flow data at the potential abstraction site. To be reliable, the available record must be relatively long, usually at least twenty years of continuous flow measurements (Adeloye, 1990). This is a problem because good quality data sets of even half that length are often a rarity. For direct abstraction from rivers, daily flows are required because abstraction decisions are made on a daily basis. If the decision is made to build a dam, then monthly data will be adequate for obtaining the relevant information.

One rule of the thumb commonly used is that when the demand is less than 5% of the average daily flow (Twort *et al.*, 1974), there is no need for a reservoir. In such a situation, the required water can be obtained by directly abstracting from the river, subject to constraints imposed by environmental considerations. In many countries, specifying a minimum residual flow in the river below which abstraction is not permitted caters for environmental needs. The determination of the minimum residual flow to be maintained at the abstraction site is a difficult exercise involving considerations of downstream riparian requirements, the need of migratory fish, and the impact of low flows on river ecology and habitats. However, once determined, it is important that the limit is rigorously enforced. Twort *et al.* (1974) give examples of residual flows for some UK rivers in which it is apparent that the residual flow, expressed as a ratio of the average daily flow, can vary widely.

2.3.1 *Meeting water demands from a river: Estimating the unregulated yields of rivers*

The water that can be abstracted from a river after making allowance for the residual flow is known as the net yield. One way of obtaining this is to examine the daily flow record for the minimum and then to deduct the specified residual flow. However, rather than using the minimum flow on record, the daily flow having some specified p% probability of exceedance is used. In the UK and other countries, p is generally taken to be 98% but it could be any value.

To determine the net yield with a p% probability exceedance for a direct abstraction scheme, the starting point is the construction of the 1-day low flow frequency curve. In some rivers, there may occur large variations in the daily flows within any given week particularly where there are large industrial users who do not operate during the weekends. In such situations, Twort *et al.* (1974) recommend using the total weekly flows instead of daily flows in the flow frequency analysis. A flow frequency curve relates the flow magnitude of a given duration, here 1-day, to its probability of exceedance. A flow frequency curve can be developed using the following steps:

1. Extract the minimum daily flow in each year of the record and denote this by Qi, i =1, 2,...,n;
2. Sort the extracted minimum flows in ascending order of magnitude. Assign ranks to the sorted flows, giving rank 1 to the lowest and rank n to the highest, where n is the total number of years of record;
3. Assign probability to the ranked events using an appropriate plotting position formula such as that proposed by Cunnane (1978):

$$P(q > Q_r) = 1 - \frac{r - 0.4}{n + 0.2}$$

where r is the rank of event of magnitude Q_r;

4. Plot Q_r (ordinate) against P (abscissa) on an appropriate probability paper.

Often, the normal probability paper is used; however, better fit may be obtained by using the log-transformation of Q_r rather than Q_r itself. If the data follow the normal or log-normal distribution, then they should indicate a straight line when plotted on the normal probability paper in step 4 above. The theoretical straight line can then be superimposed based on the normal (or log-normal) probability distribution function (see Figures 3 and 4 as examples). This theoretical straight line is the flow frequency curve from where flows corresponding to any desired probability of exceedance can be read off.

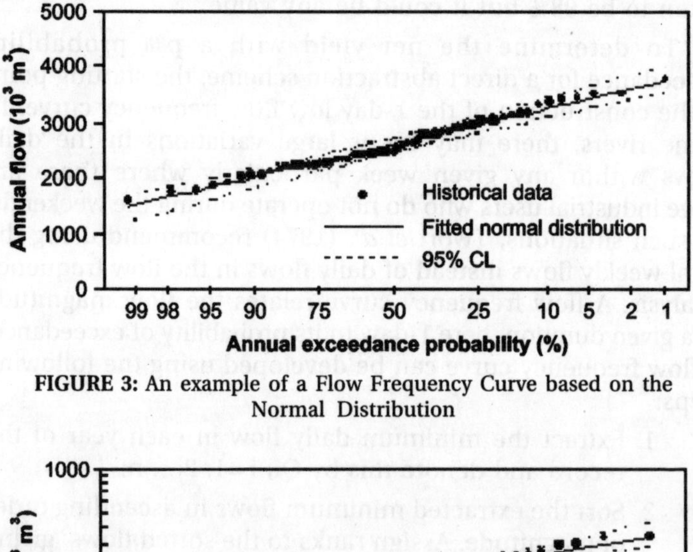

FIGURE 3: An example of a Flow Frequency Curve based on the Normal Distribution

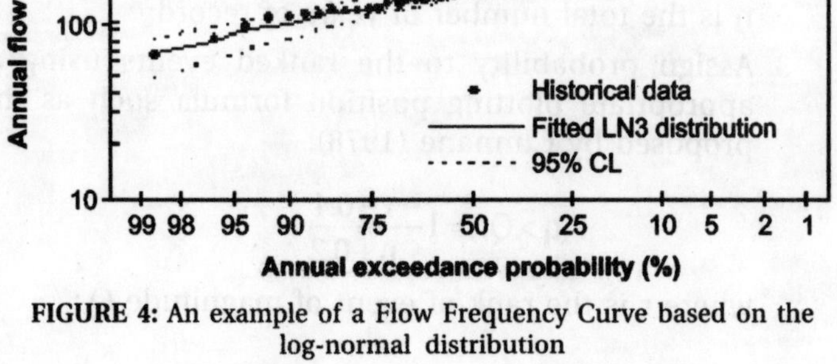

FIGURE 4: An example of a Flow Frequency Curve based on the log-normal distribution

Then the net p% yield at the abstraction site, taking into account the residual flow, becomes:

$$t_p = Q_{1\text{-day, p\%}} - Q_{res} \tag{6}$$

where tp is the net river yield, $Q_{1\text{-day,p\%}}$ is the 1-day flow with a p% probability of exceedance and Q_{res} is the prescribed residual flow at the abstraction site.

2.3.2 *Meeting water demands with a dam: Estimating the storage capacity of dams*

Dams form major components of most water supply systems in many countries. Table 1 is a list of some of the major dams in various parts of the world, together with the primary purposes for the schemes. It is evident that a sizable number of the dams are used for water supply purposes, although those in developing countries appear to store water mostly for irrigation rather than industrial/domestic water consumption purposes.

As far as meeting consumptive water demand is concerned, the storage provided in dams can be required to meet within-year needs, over-year needs or a combination of both. In over-year systems, the demand (as ratio of the mean annual runoff) is so large, typically > 0.75, that should the reservoir become empty, it will take several years before the system can refill. This is to say that an over-year system will have a critical drawdown period of several years. On the other hand, within-year reservoirs are much smaller systems, which empty and spill at least once in a given year. In either of the cases, the problem facing the planner is to determine the storage size for meeting the estimated demand.

The first systematic methodology for determining the capacity required in a dam for meeting a given demand was published by Rippl (1883). The mass curve method, as the approach by Rippl is widely known, estimates the capacity as the maximum difference between the accumulated demand and inflow during a critical low flow sequence in the historic runoff record at the reservoir site. An example of the mass curve is shown in Figure 5, which also illustrates the concept of the critical period.

Since the mass curve designs for the worst historic drought, there is the implicit assumption in the technique that a more

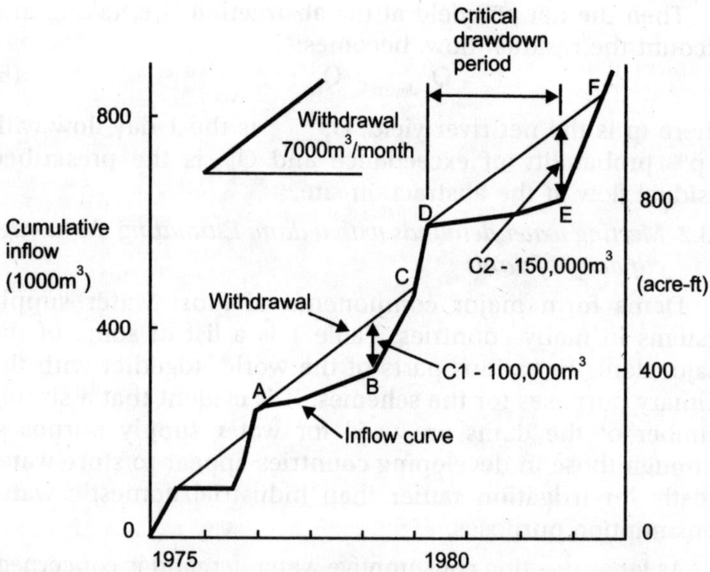

FIGURE 5: Mass curve for estimating critical period and reservoir storage capacity (Adapted from McMahon, 1993)

severe drought will not occur during future operation of the reservoir. This is unlikely, implying that a reservoir designed in this way carries with it the risk of being unable to meet the demand in the future. Failure to also accommodate evaporation losses when using the mass curve produces a similar undersizing effect, as these losses will inevitably occur, eating into the useful yield of the reservoir.

Consequently, other methods have evolved which have attempted to attach a notion of reliability to capacity estimates. The reliability is a measure of performance of the reservoir in meeting the demand and is commonly expressed as the proportion of time a reservoir is able to meet the demand (Adeloye *et al.*, 2001). McMahon and Mein (1986) document some of these newer methods of reservoir sizing. Among them are those quick methods, which give estimates of the storage under some conditions. For example, when the annual inflows at the site follow some known probability distribution hypothesis and where seasonal effects of demand are insignificant, the over-year reservoir capacity for a given reliability can be obtained using:

$$K_a = \frac{Z_p^2}{4(1-D)} C_v \sigma, D < 1 \tag{7}$$

where K_a is the reservoir capacity, Z_p is the reduced variate for p% probability for the assumed distribution hypothesis (a measure of the reliability), D is the demand as ratio of the mean annual runoff, C_v is the coefficient of variation of annual runoff (*i.e.* standard deviation divided by the mean), and s is the standard deviation of annual runoff. Equation (7) was specifically developed for the normal and gamma distribution hypotheses (McMahon and Mein, 1986) and their respective reduced variates can be obtained using:

$$Z_{p,n} = \frac{p^{0.135} - (1-p)^{0.135}}{0.1975} \tag{8}$$

$$Z_{p,g} = \frac{2}{\gamma}\left(1 + \frac{2Zp,n}{6} - \frac{\gamma^2}{36}\right)^3 - \frac{2}{\gamma} \tag{9}$$

where $Z_{p,n}$ and $Z_{p,g}$ are the normal and gamma reduced variates respectively, p is the probability of non-exceedance and g is the skew coefficient of the gamma distribution function. In general, g = $2C_v$. As remarked previously, equation (7) only estimates the over-year storage capacity principally because it uses statistics based on annual flow; where there are significant within-year storage requirements therefore, equation (7) will underestimate the total storage requirement. Adeloye *et al.* (2003) have analysed data for 15 international rivers to develop adjustments for within-year capacity requirements during reservoir planning (see Figure 6).

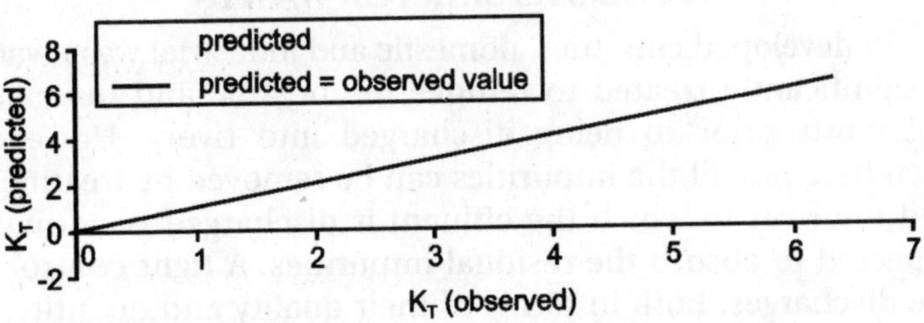

FIGURE 6: Performance of predictive regression models for total (*i.e.* within-year + over-year) reservoir capacity, KT (*Source*: Adeloye *et al.*, 2003)

Equation (7) also needs to be adjusted for evaporation losses. McMahon and Mein (1986) provide an approximate scheme for adjusting the reservoir capacity estimates for evaporation losses. Montaseri and Adeloye (2004) also develop a simple graphical rule shown in Figure 7 for evaporation correction based on data from the Urmia region of northwest Iran. Although not as generic as the correction scheme presented in McMahon and Mein (1986), the rule in Figure 7 is more complete because it was developed using a technique which considers both within-year and over-year storage requirements, and also relates the evaporation loss to the reservoir reliability. Another advantage of Figure 7 is that one does not need to know the evaporation rate (mm) to use it, thus making it applicable in regions where evaporation measurements are scarce.

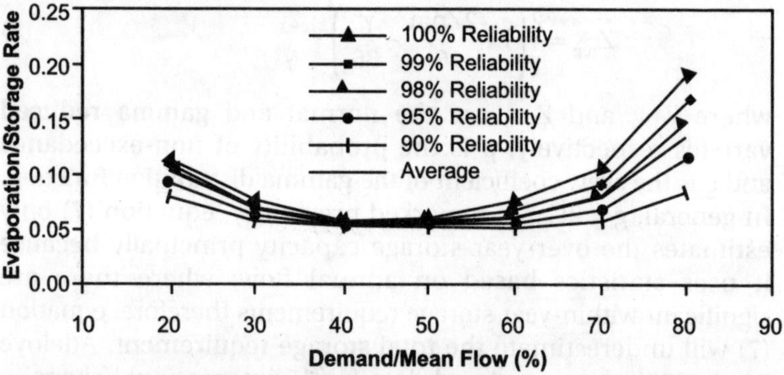

FIGURE 7: Rule for evaporation loss correction based on data from Urmia Region, Iran (*Source*: Montaseri & Adeloye, 2004)

3. RIVERS AS SINK FOR WASTES

In developed countries, domestic and industrial wastewater is significantly treated to remove the organic and inorganic pollutants prior to being discharged into rivers. However, even here not all the impurities can be removed by treatment and the river to which the effluent is discharged is normally expected to absorb the residual impurities. A tight control of the discharges, both in terms of their quality and quantity, is necessary if the quality of the receiving water is to be maintained. On the other hand, the return of the wastewater into river systems is a major component of the total river discharge, particularly during the low flow periods. Indeed, in the absence of such return flows, some rivers have been known to be completely dry.

TABLE 1: Catalogue of some large dams in the World (reproduced from Takeuchi *et al.*, 1998)

Dam (river; country)	Capacity (km^3)	Inundated area at full capacity (km^2)	Purpose(s)
1. Bratsk (Angara; Russia)	169.0	5470	H, N, S
2. High Aswan (Nile; Egypt)	162.0	6500	I, H, C
3. Kariba (Zambezi; Zambia)	160.0	5100	H
4. Akosombo (Volta; Ghana)	148.0	8480	H
5. Daniel Johnson (St Lawrence; Canada)	142.0	2000	H
6. Guri (Orinoko; Venezuela)	135.0	4250	H
7. Krasnoyarsk (Lena; Russia)	73.3	2000	H
8. WAC Bennet (Mackenzie; Canada)	70.3	1650	H
9. Zeya (Amur; Russia)	68.4	2420	H, N, C
10. Cahora Bassa (Zambezi; Mozambique)	63.0	2580	I, H, C
11. Kuibyshev (Volga; Russia)	58.0	6150	H, N, I, S
12. Rybinsk (Volga; Russia)	25.4	4550	H, N, S
Total of 2575 Japanese reservoirs in 1994	18.7	1250	

H: Hydropower; I: Irrigation; C: Flood control; N: Navigation; S: Water supply

In less developed countries where there are no formal sanitation systems and/or legal instruments for water pollution control, it is not uncommon for rivers to be used for defecating, rubbish dumping, and waste assimilation. This problem is most serious where large cities are founded on river corridors. The resulting modification of the carrying capacity of such rivers particularly by the rubbish dumping is the most common cause of serious flooding in such cities. Furthermore, since such rivers are also often abstracted for drinking, sometimes also at the point of pollution and with little or no treatment, it is not surprising that water borne diseases are also very rampant in such communities.

When discharged into rivers, the waste first undergoes dilution followed by, where appropriate, bio-degradation. The main pollutants in the effluent discharge are the organic substances as characterised by the biochemical oxygen demand (BOD), ammonia, organic micro-pollutants and a host of other microbial and inorganic impurities. The main effect of the BOD and other oxygen demanding substances in the water environment is to affect the oxygen balance, which in turn affects the size and diversity of the flora and fauna communities within the river environment, as illustrated in Figure 8. Oxygen is very essential for the survival of all living organisms in water; yet, its amount that can be dissolved in the water and hence available for the use of aquatic animals at a given temperature is limited. This limiting value of the dissolved oxygen concentration is termed the saturated concentration, and can be estimated using (Huber, 1993):

$$C_s = \exp\left[c_o + \frac{c_1}{T} + \frac{c_2}{T^2} + \frac{c_3}{T^3} + \frac{c_4}{T^4} + \mathrm{Sal}\left(c_5 + \frac{c_6}{T} + \frac{c_7}{T^2}\right)\right] \qquad (10)$$

where C_s is the saturation dissolved oxygen concentration (mg/l), T is the temperature of the water in kelvins (K= °C+273.15), Sal is the salinity (related to chloride concentration in g/l: in general, Sal = 1.80655Chl, where Chl is the chloride concentration) and $c_{i,\ i=0,1\ldots,7}$ are coefficients (see Table 2). Huber (1993) also presented an equation for correcting C_s for the effect of altitude, which can be written in metric form as:

$$C_s(E) = C_s(0)(1 - 0.000115E) \qquad (11)$$

where E is the elevation (m) above sea level (E = 0.0).

The difference between the C_s and the actual dissolved oxygen concentration in the river at a given time is known as the *dissolved oxygen deficit*. This depression of the dissolved oxygen caused by the BOD decay is partly compensated for by the introduction of oxygen through atmospheric re-aeration. However, in the immediate vicinity of the discharge, the consumption of the oxygen exceeds its replenishment; this trend is reversed at some distance further downstream when a net recovery in the dissolved oxygen concentration occurs.

TABLE 2: Coefficients in Equation (13) for Saturated Dissolved Oxygen Concentration (Huber, 1993)

Coefficient	Value
c_o	-139.34411
c_1	1.575701×10^5
c_2	-6.642308×10^7
c_3	1.243800×10^{10}
c_4	-8.621949×10^{11}
c_5	-0.017674
c_6	10.754
c_7	2140.7

This characteristic of the dissolved oxygen profile is often referred to as the sag (see Figure 8).

The nadir of the dissolved oxygen profile is the critical oxygen concentration and was first studied by Streeter and Phelps (1925) who showed that under steady-state conditions, the *critical dissolved oxygen concentration* is given by:

$$DO_c = C_s - \frac{K_1 L_0}{K_2} e^{-K_1 t_0} \tag{12}$$

where DO_c is the critical dissolved oxygen concentration, K_1 is the BOD decay rate constant (day^{-1}), K_2 is the atmospheric re-aeration rate constant (day^{-1}), L_0 is the initial ultimate BOD concentration for the well-mixed river and waste discharge (mg/l), C_s is the saturation dissolved oxygen concentration [equation (10)] measured at the temperature of the well-mixed river and waste discharge, and t_c is *the critical time* (days), where t_c can be obtained using:

$$t_c = \frac{1}{(K_2 - K_1)} \log_e \left\{ \frac{K_2}{K_1} \left[1 - \frac{(C_s - DO_0)(K_2 - K_1)}{L_0 K_1} \right] \right\} \tag{13}$$

where DO_o is the initial dissolved oxygen concentration in the well-mixed river and waste at the point of discharge.

The *Streeter-Phelps* model, as equations (12) and (13) are commonly called, has several practical limitations principally due to its neglect of other dissolved oxygen sinks (*e.g.*

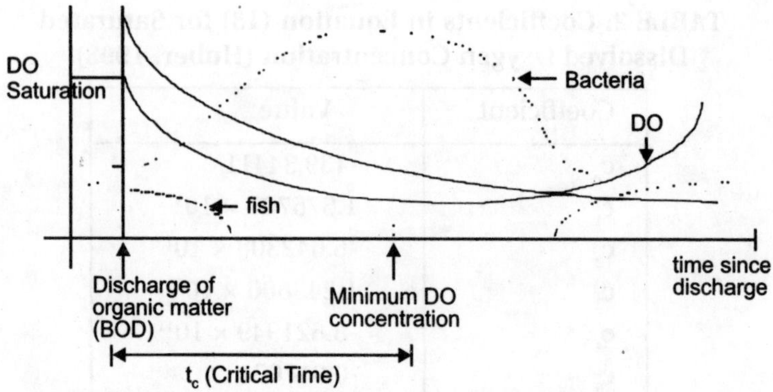

FIGURE 8: Schematic illustration of downstream effects of BOD discharge on dissolved oxygen concentration, fish and bacterial population in a river

nitrification, respiration) and sources (*e.g.* photosynthesis), both of which make it to tend to under-predict the dissolved oxygen profile. Nonetheless, it is widely used in waste load allocation, during which levels of BOD discharge from wastewater treatment works for achieving target critical dissolved oxygen concentrations, usually > 5mg/l, are determined.

The waste allocation analysis is a trial and error procedure involving first selecting a trial effluent BOD concentration and then computing DO_c. This is then compared with the target critical concentration and if there is a difference, the assumed BOD load is modified appropriately and a new DO_c obtained. The process is repeated until the DO_c obtained equals the target.

The approach of fixing effluent BOD load to achieve a target dissolved oxygen concentration belongs to a broader class of water pollution control strategy known variously as *river quality objective approach, environmental quality objective approach* or *in-stream quality objective approach.* It is a much more holistic approach in that, by focusing on the river rather than just the effluent discharge, it integrates the pollution effects from both point and diffuse sources. River quality objective approach also means that river quality improvement activities are concentrated in river stretches that matter: there is no point spending huge sums of money trying to clean up a river which serves no useful purpose. The main disadvantage of the river quality objective approach is that it is very difficult to enforce and, as revealed by the example of the Streeter-Phelps model described previously, requires significant scientific knowledge for its implementation.

The second commonly used approach for controlling river pollution from effluent discharges involves fixed emission standards. Fixed emission standards stipulate maximum concentrations of some water quality parameters in effluent discharges. Most of these standards use BOD and suspended solids (SS), although increasingly, other quality parameters such as nitrates, phosphates and bacterial counts are now being added. An example is the UK Royal Commission Fixed emission standards, where the BOD is pegged at 20 mg/l and the SS is restricted to 30 mg/l. Although resulting from studies in the UK, these standards are also widely used in other countries. This is because the fixed emission standards approach only looks at the effluent and by so doing is much simpler to implement than the river quality objective approach. Unlike the river quality objective approach, however, it does not protect river water quality from the impacts of diffuse sources of pollution.

Whatever the approach adopted, the policy must be enforced if the desired objective is to be achieved. The enforcement of water pollution control policies in most countries rests with an appropriate environmental agency such as the Environmental Protection Agency (EPA) in the USA and the Environment Agency (EA) in the UK. Furthermore, it should be stressed that increasingly in the UK, most of the environmental policies are being formulated as Directives from the EU (see Haigh, 1987); these Directives are then incorporated into the national legislation to become law.

4. RIVERS AS SOURCE OF ENERGY

The production of electricity by a hydraulic turbine using the energy of water flowing from a higher to a lower elevation has been traditionally hailed as a renewable energy alternative to the indiscriminate burning of fossil fuels. The gross hydropower potential of the world amounts to some 2300×10^9 W but only a fifth of this is installed (Kundzewicz *et al.*, 1998). This large discrepancy between potential and installed capacity has to do with the sustained opposition by environmentalists to dam construction, a major feature of most hydroelectric projects. However, it should be remarked that this opposition is not limited to hydropower projects alone; it targets all forms of water conservation structures whatever their purpose. The main criticisms leveled against dams include:

- the enforced relocation of people natural to the river valley;
- destruction/inundation of fertile land;
- destruction of vital natural habitats in river valleys due to modifications of natural flow and channel characteristics;
- degradation of the in-stream water quality downstream of dams; and
- reduction of the self-purification capability of river channels.

However, despite all of these criticisms, reliance on hydro-projects is still common particularly in developing countries where projects have ranged in size from those with installed capacity of a few MW to large schemes with installed capacity of tens of thousands of MW.

Hydropower generation does not constitute a consumptive water demand; consequently, the water used to drive the turbine is still available in practically undiminished amounts for other uses such as irrigation, effluent dilution and other in-stream requirements. However, the usefulness of the returned water may be somewhat limited due to its slightly elevated temperature caused by the exchanged heat, as the water passes through the turbines. Such marginally elevated temperatures might reduce the ability of the river to assimilate wastes by increasing the rate of reaction and by reducing the level of dissolved oxygen in the river.

The relevant consideration for most hydro-electricity projects is the determination of the energy production potential. In this regard, two types of energy are distinguished: the *primary (or firm) energy*—which is that generated during the critical low flow period and hence guaranteed for most of the time; and the *secondary energy*—which is the energy in excess of the primary energy. The power generated by a turbine can be estimated using:

$$P = 0.001rgQHe \qquad (14)$$

where P = electrical power, kW
Q = flow, m^3/s
H = net available head, m (see Figure 9)
e = overall efficiency = $e_t e_g$
e_t = turbine efficiency and
e_g = generator efficiency
r = density of water (1000 kg/m^3)
g = acceleration of gravity (9.81 m/s^2)

Just like water supply projects based on rivers, a hydro-project may or may not involve the construction of a dam reservoir. Where no reservoir is involved, the hydro-project is termed a run-of-river scheme. For such a scheme, the available head is fixed by the topography of the river channel bed relative to the turbine entrance; variations occur in the power production (equation 14) principally because of variations in the daily flow at the diversion site. The determination of the flow for the computation of the firm power using equation (14) is based on the flow duration curve analysis.

A flow duration curve is the curve relating the flow (on the y-axis) against the percentage of time (days) the flow is exceeded (on the x-axis). The flow duration curve is generally constructed using the daily flow record at the site (See McMahon, 1993), and because the logarithm of such daily flows often follow a normal distribution, the scale on the x-axis can be represented with the normal probability exceedances. A flow duration curve is constructed using the entire flow record and so the events are not independent which makes the interpretation of the flow exceedances rather difficult. This is in contrast to the flow frequency curve introduced in section 2.3.1 where, by including only one event per year, independence of events is assured and the resulting low flow exceedances constitute valid statistical events.

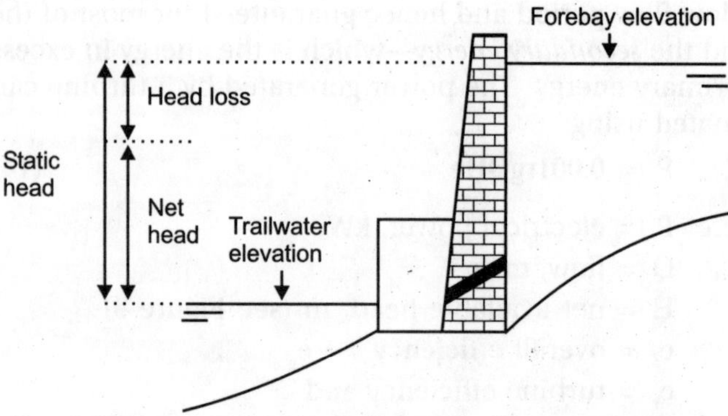

FIGURE 9: Schematic definition of net head for a reservoired Hydro project (Adapted from McMahon, 1993)

Examples of flow duration curves are shown in Figure 10. These are for two example rivers, one with significant baseflow contribution (River 1) and the other with little in the way of baseflow (River 2). This lack of baseflow contribution by groundwater is causing River 2 to cease to flow for approximately 93% of the time whereas River 1 is constantly flowing. For the computation of the firm yield, the flow exceeded 100% of the time, *i.e.* the lowest daily flow in the historic record, is often used. This will represent the power that can be guaranteed 100% of the time, if the historic flow scenario repeats itself exactly in the future.

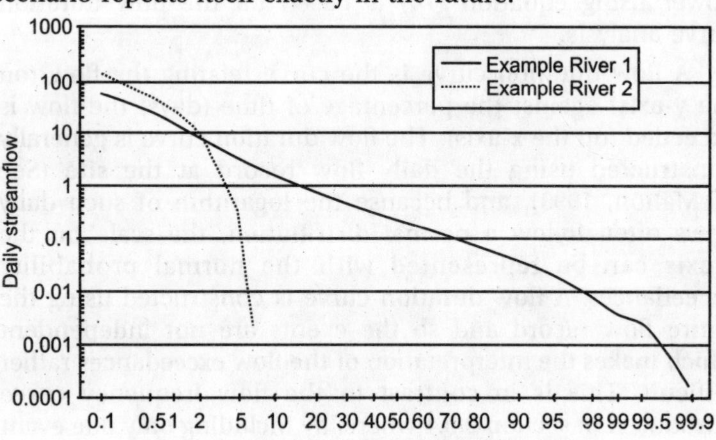

FIGURE 10: Examples of daily Flow Duration Curves

Sometimes, the power that can be guaranteed for 95% of the time is required; this can be obtained by using the flow exceeded 95% of the time; this Q95 flow can easily be read from the flow duration curve. In general, the secondary power is defined as that which can be guaranteed at least 50% of the time (Mays and Tung, 1992) and is based on the Q50 or the median flow magnitude.

The construction of a dam reservoir for hydroelectric power generation modifies both the available flow and head when compared with a run-of-river scheme. During the critical drawdown period in the reservoir, the available head will continuously fall and with this, the power output. The release or outflow from the reservoir may also vary during the critical drawdown period. Since all these three variables—storage, head, outflow—affect the energy production, then the computation of the firm power for a reservoir system should involve a sequential simulation of the reservoir to determine the variation of the storage with time. The sequential routing uses the reservoir mass balance equation, which can be expressed as:

$$S_t = S_{t-1} + I_t - Q_t - Lt; \quad 0 \leq S_t \leq K_a \tag{15}$$

where S_t = the storage at the end of t

S_{t-1} = storage at the beginning of t

I_t = inflow during t

Q_t = release during t

L_t = losses (evaporation, seepage, etc.) during t

K_a = active storage capacity

The routing starts by assuming a value for the K_a and for simplicity, the losses L_t can be assumed to be negligible. Adeloye *et al.* (2001) present more complete algorithms for explicitly including volumetric evaporation losses in reservoir mass balance equations. Applying equation (15) over the data record will produce the time series of the storage (S_t) and releases (Q_t). From this, the critical drawdown period can be isolated. The storage (S_t) over the identified critical drawdown period can be converted to head (H_t) using the storage-head relationship at the reservoir height. Applying the release (Q_t)

and head (H_t) in the power equation (14) will produce the power-time diagram. Integrating this will give the firm energy for the selected reservoir capacity K_a. The process can be repeated for other assumed storage capacities and ultimately, a plot of the firm energy against reservoir capacity K_a will be obtained. From here, the required capacity for any desired firm energy can be obtained.

To obtain the secondary energy for the chosen reservoir capacity, another routing for the known reservoir capacity will have to be undertaken. After the routing, the power-time diagram for the entire record rather than just over the critical drawdown period is obtained. Integrating the power-time diagram over the entire simulation period gives the total energy; the difference between this total energy and the firm energy is the secondary energy.

5. RIVERS AND GROUNDWATER

Although this piece is about river water resources and its role in human development, the discussion will be incomplete without a brief mention of groundwater particularly in relation to how this strategic resource is affected by river systems. In terms of quantity on a global scale, groundwater is almost 70 times the total amount of water in surface systems (rivers, lakes, reservoirs, etc.) of the world (Bouwer, 1978). Groundwater aquifers and rivers are hydraulicallylinked. This intrinsic link is what makes the conjunctive use of waters from both sources a more attractive proposition than using them independent of each other. In locations with distinct water-surplus and water-deficit seasons, water from rivers are best utilised during the wet seasons, leaving the groundwater reservoirs to replenish for later use during water-scarce seasons. Rivers are also a constant source of natural recharge for groundwater aquifers. Adequate recharge not only replenishes water taken out of the aquifer, thus elevating water table and reducing pumping costs associated with groundwater extraction, it also helps to prevent pollution such as saltwater intrusion in coastal aquifers. On the other, the occurrence of perennial streams, such as river 1 in Figure 10, results from the constant supply of baseflow by water table aquifers; without such, most rivers will be intermittent or ephemeral, only flowing during periods of sustained rainfall.

6. CONTEMPORARY ISSUES IN RIVER WATER DEVELOPMENT

The increasing world's population and the attendant need to provide adequate water for the various consumptive uses identified in this report is continuing to place further pressures on river water resources. Pollution from domestic and industrial effluents, agriculture and urban runoff among others further limits the usefulness of the dwindling freshwater stocks. For reservoired water resources systems, much of the stored water is simply lost to evaporation, particularly in arid and semi-arid regions of the world. According to Shiklomanov (1997), the evaporation losses from surface water reservoirs is so large (particularly in the tropical regions) that they exceed the total municipal and industrial uses of water in the world. So, quite apart from the established opposition from environmentalists, attempting to meet increasing water demands by further dam construction is not a sustainable proposition.

The precarious situation of the world's river water resources is further compounded by predictions of climate change and its impacts on watershed runoff. To date, a countless number of studies have attempted to quantify these impacts (see Kaczmarek *et al.*, 1996), but there are widespread uncertainties. Impacts studies use climate change scenarios derived from General Circulation Models' (GCM) simulation experiments and are couched in terms of percentage (or absolute) changes in climatic attributes—temperature, rainfall, humidity, solar radiation, etc.—in the future relative to some baseline conditions. These changes can then be used to force a rainfall-runoff model of the watershed to derive resulting changes in runoff. As a result of these numerous stages involved in a typical impact study, there are wide variations in impact estimates. Estimates have also varied from one analysis to another, depending on the particular GCM from which scenarios were derived, the method of downscaling the GCM's predictions at global scale to the watershed scale, the rainfall-runoff model and whether or not watershed feedback has been incorporated into the analysis. As a result, Lettenmaier *et al.* (1996) have warned that impacts estimates should not be taken as anything more than the sensitivity testing of the consequences of alternative climate scenarios.

Whether or not they are sensitivity studies, some of the findings of climate impact studies and other evidence of the dwindling river water resources call for a radical rethinking of the way these resources are managed. If climate change also affects the quality of the water, as is being predicted, then this will further exacerbate the problem. Climate change may also cause the actual demand to increase, which even for a static population can mean a significant increase in the total water requirement. Already, in some countries, demand management strategies are being pursued as a way of reducing the growing gap between water demand and supply. In demand management, various instruments—charges, metering, etc.—are used to encourage consumers to reduce unnecessary water use. Water undertakers are also pursuing active leakage detection strategies with a view to cutting leakage to the minimum level feasible economically. All of these options will require the cooperation of the stakeholders to be successful.

Water can be used more than once, as illustrated previously in the case of hydroelectric power generation whose water can become useful further downstream in the river. However, water recycling is much more than this and can include the use of wastewater effluents in irrigation, aquifer recharge, and potable water systems. In these latter applications, quality concerns have to be addressed. Indeed, where effluent is to be directly recycled in potable water systems or for recharging aquifers through injection wells, then the effluent must have been distilled literally.

Controlling urban runoff at source also offers a potential for increasing water availability (Urbonas and Roesner, 1993). Traditionally, urban runoff is normally collected in network of pipes and channels, which rapidly discharge to nearby streams and eventually to the sea. However, apart from losing the runoff to the sea, this traditional approach also often results in flooding and can have negative impacts on river water quality. Besides, by collecting the runoff as quickly as possible, there is little time for infiltration and subsequent recharge of aquifers. In source control, or sustainable urban drainage management, the water can be detained at source and put into beneficial uses such as in infiltration basins, lawn watering and other uses that do not require high quality water. Rainwater harvesting at the household level contributes to the objectives of source control and need not be a practice limited to water scarce areas or poor communities alone.

Finally, much can be achieved in terms of meeting rising water demand levels by proper integrated management of existing resources of rivers, reservoirs and groundwater aquifers. Much has been said in an earlier part about the intrinsic link between rivers and aquifers; by using these resources conjunctively, the overall yield of a water resources system can be significantly increased. Changing reservoir operational and release practices can also help to ameliorate the vulnerability of water shortages. For example, as found by numerous investigators (Hirsch *et al.*, 1977; Palmer *et al.*, 1982; Montaseri and Adeloye, 2002), the yield of a group of reservoirs operated as a conjunctive, integrated system can be at least 6% higher than the sum of the individual yields if they are operated as stand-alone systems.

7. CONCLUSION

Rivers are obviously important for human existence. They serve in providing a significant proportion of the water demanded by humans for various activities including domestic, industrial and irrigation water supply. All of these are consumptive uses but river water also serves non-consumptive uses such as hydro-electric power generation and effluent dilution for pollution control. However, the continued performance of these functions in a satisfactory and sustainable manner is being threatened by rising demands, more incidence of pollution and impacts of climate change among others. These threats call for more radical thinking about how the world's river water resources are managed. By and large, more use will have to be made of "grey" or recycled water for meeting some needs particularly those that have no direct implication for public health. Demand management, whereby consumers are encouraged to use less water principally through reduction of wastage, also offers a promise as does the improved management and coordination of water resources systems. All of this will become more attractive in the future as the more traditional options of meeting increased demand—*e.g.* more reservoirs, mining of groundwater aquifers, more river abstractions, etc.—become less and less favoured due to environmental and other considerations.

REFERENCES

Adeloye, A.J. (1990). Streamflow data and surface-water resource assessment—a quantitative demonstration of need for adequate investment in data collection in developing countries. *J. Water Supply Res. Tec.* (Aqua), 39(4), 225-36.

Adeloye, A.J., Montaseri, M. and Garmann, C. (2001). Curing the misbehaviour of reservoir capacity statistics by controlling shortfall during failures using the modified sequent peak algorithm. *Water Resour. Res.* 37(1), 73-82.

Adeloye, A.J., Lallemand, F. and McMahon, T.A. (2003). Regression models for within-year capacity adjustment in reservoir planning. *Hydrol. Sci. J.*, 48(4), 539-52.

Alam, M. (1991). Problems and potential of irrigated agriculture in sub-Saharan Africa. *J. Irr. Drain. Egnrg.*, ASCE, 117(2), 155-72.

Bouwer, H. (1978). *Groundwater hydrology.* McGraw-Hill Book Co., New York.

Chow, Ven T., Maidment, D.R. and Mays, L.W. (1988). *Applied hydrology,* McGraw-Hill, New York.

Cunnane, C. (1978). Unbiased plotting positions—A review. *J. Hydrol.*, 37(3/4), 205-22.

Doorenbos, J. and Pruitt, W.O. (1977). Crop water requirements. Irrigation and Drainage Paper, 24, FAO, Rome.

FAO (1987). Irrigation and water resources potential for Africa. FAO Publication No. AGL/MISC/11/87, Rome, Italy.

Gray, N.F. (1994). *Drinking water quality.* J. Wiley, Chichester, England.

Haigh, N. (1987). EEC environmental policy & Britain. 2nd Edition, Longman, Harlow, England.

Hirsch, R.M., Cohon, J.L. and ReVelle, C. (1977). Gains from joint operations of multiple reservoir systems. Water Resour. Res., 13(2), 239-45.

Huber, W.C. (1993). Contaminant transport in surface water. Chapter 14 in *Handbook of Hydrology* (ed. D.R. Maidment), McGraw-Hill, Inc., New York.

Kaczmarek, Z., Arnell, N.W. and Stakhiv, E.Z. (1996). *Water resources management.* Chapter 10 in Intergovernmental Panel on Climate Change Second Assessment Report, Cambridge University Press.

Kundzewicz, Z.W., Hjorth, P. and Takeuchi, K. (1998). Multipurpose reservoirs *versus* alternatives Energy. Section 3.2.2 in *Sustainable Reservoir Development and Management* (eds. Takeuchi, K. *et al.*), IAHS Publication No. 251.

Lettenmaier, D.P., McCabe, G. and Stakhiv, E.Z. (1996). *Global climate change: effect on hydrologic cycle.* Chapter 29 in Water Resources Handbook (ed. L.W. Mays), McGraw-Hill, New York.

Mateos, L., Lopez-Cortijo, I. and Sagardoy, J.A. (2002). SIMIS: the FAO decision support system for irrigation scheme management. *Agric. Wat. Managt.*, 56, 193-206.

McMahon, T.A. (1993). Hydrologic design for water use. Chapter 27 in *Handbook of Hydrology* (ed. D.R. Maidment), McGraw-Hill, Inc., New York.

McMahon, T.A. and Mein, R.G. (1986). *River and reservoir yield.* Water Resources Publications, Littleton, CO.

Maidment, D.R. (1993). *Hydrologic cycle.* Chapter 1 in Handbook of Hydrology (ed. D.R. Maidment), McGraw-Hill, Inc., New York.

Mays, L. and Tung, Y.K. (1992). *Hydrosystems engineering and management.* McGraw-Hill, Inc. New York.

Montaseri, M. and Adeloye, A.J. (2002). Effects of integrated planning on capacity-yield-performance functions. *J. Wat. Resour. Plan. Managt.*, ASCE, November issue.

Montaseri, M. and Adeloye, A.J. (2004). A graphical rule for evaporation loss correction in reservoir capacity-yield-performance planning in Urmia Region, Iran. *Water Resourc. Managt.*, 18, 55-74.

Oluwasemire, K.O., Sigter, C.J., Owonubi, J.J. and Sagtap, S.S. (2002). Seasonal water use and water productivity of millet-based cropping patterns in the Nigerian Sudan savanna near Kano. *Agric. Wat. Managt.*, 56, 207-27.

Oyebande, L. (2001). Water problems in Africa—How can the sciences help? *Hydrol. Sci.* J. 46(6), 947-62.

Palmer, R.N., Smith, J., Cohon, J. and ReVelle, C. (1982). Reservoir management in the Potomac river basin. *J. Water Resour. Plng. Mgmt.*, ASCE, 108(1), 47-66.

Rippl, W. (1883). *Capacity of storage reservoirs for water supply. Minutes Proc. Inst. Civ. Eng.*, 71, 270-78.

Shiklomanov, I.A. (ed.) (1997). *Assessment of water resources and water availability in the world.* WMO, Geneva, Switzerland.

Shuttkeworth, W.J. (1993). *Evaporation.* Chapter 4 in Handbook of Hydrology (ed. D.R. Maidment), McGraw-Hill, Inc., New York.

Stedinger, J.R., Vogel, R.M. and Foufoula-Georgiou, E. (1993). *Frequency analysis of extreme events.* Chapter 18 in Handbook of Hydrology (ed. D.R. Maidment), McGraw-Hill, Inc., New York.

Streeter, H.W. and Phelps, E.B. (1925). A study of the pollution and natural purification of the Ohio River. *US Public Health Bull.* No. 146.

Takeuchi, K. and Simonovic, S.P. (1998). *Land efficiency discussion of large reservoirs.* Section 1.3.2 in Sustainable Reservoir Development and Management (eds. Takeuchi, K. *et al.*), IAHS Publication No. 251.

Twort, A.C. and Law, F.M. (1974). *Water supply*. Edward Arnold, London.

Urbonas, B.R. and Roesner, L.A. (1993). Hydrologic design for urban drainage and flood control. Chapter 28 in Handbook of Hydrology (ed. D.R. Maidment), McGraw-Hill, Inc., New York.

Contributors

Prasenjit Maiti [1971-] *<pmaiti@vsnl.com>* was recently associated with the Kolkata Environmental Improvement Project [as Member, Resettlement Implementation Working Group] <http://www.kolkatamunicipalcorporation.com/keip.html> funded by the Asian Development Bank and implemented by the Kolkata Municipal Corporation in association with the Government of West Bengal. Dr Maiti worked as Research Associate at the Council for Development Studies [Calcutta] on a UNIFEM project and was consultant to Shelter Promotion Council [India] where he worked on an urban development project funded by the Ministry of Science and Technology, Government of India [2003]. Maiti was on secondment as a Doctoral Fellow at the Institute of Federalism, University of Fribourg, Switzerland [1999] while employed as a Lecturer in Political Science, University of Burdwan, India [1995-2002]. He was promoted to Senior Lectureship after his Ph.D. [University of Burdwan, 2001] was awarded. Maiti taught Tourism Administration at Burdwan University and served as a resource person at distant education and teachers' training programmes sponsored by the University Grants Commission [New Delhi]. He also served as an academic counsellor to the Netaji Subhas Open University [Kolkata]. Maiti's maiden publication based on his doctoral research [*Problems of Governance in India since Independence: The Bengal Success Story* (New Delhi: Vedams, 2002)] developed from a German Research Council project on "Governance in India" [1997-98] coordinated by the Department of Political Science, South Asia Institute, University of Heidelberg, Germany. He was invited to the International Conference on Federalism 2002 organized by the Swiss Government at the University of St Gallen. Maiti served as reviewer [2001] for *Policing: An International Journal of Police Strategies & Management* [College of

Education, Division of Criminal Justice, University of Cincinnati, USA]. He is also referee for *Environment & Development Economics* [University of York, Heslington, York, UK] published by the Cambridge University Press and *Crime Prevention & Community Safety: An International Journal* [Perpetuity Press, Leicester, UK]. Maiti is Life Member of the Indian Political Science Association, West Bengal Political Science Association, Council for Political Studies [Kolkata] and the Indian Institute of Public Administration [New Delhi].

Raghu Bir Bista rbbista@wlink.com.np is Assistant Lecturer at the Department of Economics in the Patan Multiple Campus, Nepal. His research areas include History of Economics, Macro Economic Indicators of Nepal, Bio-diversity and its valuation, Foundation of Nepalese Economy, Fiscal Policy and Monetary Policy, Public Debt and Foreign Aid, Regionalism and Globalization, Structural Adjustment Programme and Economic reform, Poverty and Poverty Alleviation Programme, Planning of Nepal, Bottlenecks of Nepalese Development & Future Perspective. He worked on research assignments for Action Aid, GTZ and DFID in areas such as study the Impact of Foreign Direct Investment on Poverty and Inequality, the Assessment of Policy Impact on the Poverty and Employment. Bista edited the Nepal Year Book Series [1998, 1999, 2000 & 2001] for IIDS. He researched on the 'Assessment Study of Production Credit for Rural Women Programme' (PCRW) in Lalitpur, [1999] for Centre for Integrated Development Studies.

Md. Shariful Alam Chowdhury [1977-] sharifurp97@yahoo.com is a Research Assistant working with the Delta Planners and Builders Ltd. He is also a Masters of Urban and Regional Planning student at the Department of Urban and Regional Planning of the Bangladesh University of Engineering and Technology (BUET) in Dhaka. Chowdhury earlier worked as a Junior Urban Planner with the Digital Architects Ltd.

Andrew Kirby <andrew.kirby@asu.edu> is Professor of Social and Behavioral Sciences at Arizona State University in Phoenix. He received his PhD in Geography from

Newcastle University and has been a faculty member at the University of Reading, England, the University of Colorado, and the University of Arizona. He has held visiting appointments at the Institute for Urban and Regional Development at the University of California, Berkeley, and at the Center for Advanced Studies at Stanford University. He has also been a faculty associate at the National Center for Atmospheric Research in Boulder, and recently a Residential Scholar in the ASU Center for Urban Inquiry. His research on urban change and development has appeared in journals such as *Urban Geography, Urban Studies, Urban Affairs Quarterly*, and the *Journal of Social Issues.* His most recent books were *Pentagon and the Cities* (Sage, 1992) and *Power/Resistance* (Indiana University Press, 1993), and he has also published edited collections *Globalization and its Outcomes* (2004), *The Spaces of Hate* (2003), *Geographies of Power* (2002), *Geopolitical Traditions* (2000) and *The Urban Growth Machine* (1999). He is currently working with two multidisciplinary teams, one on a National Science Foundation supported project dealing with neighborhood change in Phoenix, the other a critical examination of the human dimensions of homeland security post September 11. A board member for a number of international journals, he has been Editor for the Elsevier journal *Cities: An International Journal of Urban Policy and Planning* since 1995.

Vinit Mukhija [1967-] vmukhija@ucla.edu is an Assistant Professor at the Department of Urban Planning, School of Public Policy and Social Research of the University of California, Los Angeles (UCLA). Dr Mukhija is an architect-planner and his main area of expertise is housing and the built environment. He is particularly interested in analyzing the role of various institutional actors and property rights in urban development, and his focus is on comparative approaches in policy and planning. He has consulted for the Fannie Mae Foundation and the World Bank. The California Policy Research Center, the United Nations Development Programme (UNDP) and the Lincoln Institute of Land Policy have funded his research. He teaches courses on Land Use Planning, Design and Development, Urban

Revitalization, and Housing in Developing Countries. Mukhija completed his doctoral dissertation at the Massachusetts Institute of Technology (MIT). The research was on an unconventional programme of housing in Mumbai, India and was published by Ashgate (United Kingdom) Squatters as Developers? Slum Redevelopment in Mumbai in 2003. He has also published papers in several academic journals, including Housing Studies, World Development, Cities, Habitat International, and International Development and Planning Review.

Michael Murray [1967-] michael.j.murray@MAY.IE did his PhD in Sociology from NUI [Maynooth] in 2004 on 'Waste Management in Ireland: A case study on the impact of Transnationalisation on Governance'. He was offered Doctoral Fellowships from the National Institute for Regional and Spatial Analysis (NIRSA) and the Irish Research Council for the Humanities and Social Sciences. He teaches three hours per week as part of the CCIS Programme based at NUI Maynooth. The title of the course is 'Sociology of Northern Ireland'. He is at present Post Doctoral Research Fellow at NIRSA, NUI Maynooth and engaged in a research project entitled 'E-Consultation: evaluating appropriate technologies and processes for citizens' participation in public policy'. This project is funded by the EU Programme for Peace and Reconciliation'. His publications include Honor Fagan, Denis O'Hearn, Gerard McCann and Michael Murray (2001), *Waste Management Strategy: A Cross Border Perspective* [NIRSA Working Papers Series funded by the Centre for Cross Border Studies, Armagh]. His research interests include Political Sociology, Governance, The Sociology of Power, Sociology of Global/Transnational Processes, International Relations, Sociology of Northern Ireland, Sociology of the Environment and Epistemology & the Social Sciences

G. Honor Fagan honor.fagan@may.ie is a Senior Lecturer in Sociology at the National University of Ireland, Maynooth and Research Associate at the National Institute for Regional and Spatial Analysis. She was born in the Republic of Ireland and her doctorate was awarded from Miami University, Oxford, Ohio, in 1991. She lectured in the United

States, Northern Ireland, South Africa and the United Kingdom before taking up her current position in the Republic of Ireland. She has published on political identities, empowerment, conflict resolution and environmental politics. Her current research interests are around placing Ireland in a globalisation framework ('Globalisation and Culture, Placing Ireland', The Annals of the American Academy of Political and Social Science, May 2002). Her research on environmental sustainable development in Ireland has most notably been published in leading journals ('Grounding Waste: Towards a Sociology of Waste Networks' in Irish Journal of Sociology, 2003; 'Waste Management and its Contestation in the Republic of Ireland' in Capitalism, Nature, Socialism, March 2004). She has done field research on urban early school leavers for her book Cultural Politics and Irish Early School Leavers; Constructing Political Identities (1995) and on women in South African Townships which culminated in a chapter in the best seller Critical Development Theory: Contributions to a New Paradigm edited by R. Munck and D. O'Hearn (Zed Press, 1999). She is currently engaged in field research on an EU funded research project on e-democracy in Ireland and is also researching for a book titled Globalisation and Culture: Re(Locating) Politics.

Diane Payne [1966-] works at the Department of Sociology and is also the Assistant Director (Graduate Programme) of the Institute for the Study of Social Change (ISSC) at University College Dublin (UCD). Prior to being offered academic tenure at UCD, Dr Payne managed the Masters in Social Sciences Degree Programme (Applied Social Research) in the Department of Sociology at the University of Dublin (Trinity College). Dr Payne spent several years as a doctoral research fellow at the Inter-university Centre for Social Science Theory and Methodology (ICS) at the University of Groningen in the Netherlands (1992-1997). Following this, she worked as a researcher at the University of Cambridge in England and co-authored with the then Leverhulme Research Professor Robert Bennett, a book and several papers on local and regional economic development in the United Kingdom (1997-98). She is currently involved in a number of different research programmes. She leads the Irish team, as part of an international group of researchers, collaborating on the cross-national research project *Patterns of Urban/Regional Innovation. A Comparative Study of Eight European Countries.* She is also a major partner in the UCD-based Irish team, which leads the European Commission funded Fifth Framework project *Organising for EU Enlargement* and which involves international collaboration with universities in Greece, Finland, Slovenia, Hungary and Estonia. She has recently co-edited a book entitled "Irish Social and Political Attitudes", forthcoming later in 2004 and which presents the first research findings, based on the analysis of the large-scale ISPAS data set. In 2001, she was co-funded by the Centre for Cross-Border Studies in Armagh and co-authored a major report in 2001, entitled *Creating Living Institutions, Cross border and regional co-operation after the Good Friday Agreement.* At about this time, she also collaborated with Dutch colleagues on a project examining national wage agreements and organised a research workshop at UCD entitled *Negotiating Wage Agreements: Social Partnership in Ireland and the Netherlands* and presents an updated version of her research material in this field at the IREC conference, at Utrecht University in August 2004. Dr Payne has published various articles in international, peer-reviewed journals and she is a referee and/or book reviewer for several leading academic journals including American Sociological Review, Papers in Regional Science and Regional and Federal Studies. Dr Payne studied Economics and Sociology for her primary degree and then completed a Masters Degree in European Social Policy Analysis (1st class honours) at Maynooth University, National University of Ireland. Whilst studying for her doctoral degree at the ICS in the Netherlands, she received an ICS doctoral scholarship and was also awarded an EU Jean Marie Fellowship. In 2000, she received the UCD President's Research Award for her study of social partnership and wage bargaining in Ireland. Dr Payne is a member of various international sociological and political science associations. She is also the Irish representative for the Steering Committee of the European Science Foundation (ESF) programme *Quantitative Methods in the Social Sciences (QMSS)* and chairs the ESF Topic Team *Analysing social networks*, as part of the QMSS programme.

Peter Stafford is Research Fellow in the Governance Research Programme based in the Institute for the Study of Social Change, University College Dublin. In addition, he is Research Fellow of Dublin European Institute, UCD. He holds a Doctorate in Government from the University of Manchester, UK and a Master of Arts (Economics) in Economic and Social Studies also from the University of Manchester. In his rôle as researcher with Dublin European Institute, Dr Stafford is currently working on an EU Fifth Framework funded project entitled Organising for European Union Enlargement, examining regional policy in the Republic of Ireland. His current research with the Institute for the Study of Social Change is a Study of the Development of the Voluntary and Community sectors in Irish cities, and their relationships with local government, especially during periods of urban renewal projects. He has recently been involved in an eight-country research project examining innovative forms of urban and regional co-operation in eight European cities. Working with Dr Diane Payne of the Sociology Department, UCD, Dr Stafford examined the politics and co-operation in Irish urban regeneration projects. It is from this research project that his present research agenda has developed.

Prior to his work in Ireland, Dr Stafford was a researcher and archivist in England, working for various private sector institutions included landed estates and a short secondment to the Archives of the Houses of Parliament, London. In addition to his research programme, Dr Stafford tutors in modern history in the Department of History, UCD.

Labode Popoola [1960-] labopopoola@skannet.com is presently a Senior Lecturer (Forest Economics) and Head of Forest Economics and Management Unit, Department of Forest Resources Management, University of Ibadan, where he also leads a research team of young academics in diverse areas of Renewable Natural Resources Management. Dr Popoola has carried out research extensively in the areas of marketing and utilization of non-timber forest products; agroforestry economics, environmental impact assessment and urban forestry giving rise to over fifty-five scientific publications in various academic and scientific journals. He has also edited manuscripts for journals within and outside Nigeria. He is the Managing Editor of the Journal of Tropical Forest Resources, a member of the Editorial Boards of both the Nigerian Journal of Forestry, a publication of Forestry Association of Nigeria and the Ibadan Journal of Agriculture, a publication of the Faculty of Agriculture and Forestry, University of Ibadan, Nigeria. Dr Popoola is a life member of Forestry Association of Nigeria. He was the Business Manager of the Association (1997-2002) and National Secretary (2002-date). He has been a Council member of the Association for seven years. Between 2001 and 2003, Dr Popoola was the Vice-Dean of the Postgraduate School, University of Ibadan. He was an executive member of the Regional Agroforestry Training and Education Group (RAFT) for the Humid Lowland of West Africa (1999-2001) and received an award for invaluable service from the World Agroforestry Centre for invaluable service. He is the National Contact Person for the African Forest Research Network (AFORNET) for Nigeria. Dr Popoola has at various times consulted for the International (now World) Centre for Agroforestry Research (ICRAF) Nairobi, African Development Bank (ADB), World Bank, Food and Agriculture Organization (FAO), Federal and State governments and several Private Sector Organizations in Nigeria. Dr Popoola holds a 1990 Doctor of Philosophy Degree in Forest Economics from the University of Ibadan, Nigeria.

Kai Strunz strunz@ee.washington.edu is Assistant Professor of Energy systems at the University of Washington, Seattle, USA. Dr Strunz graduated with the Dipl.-Ing. degree, the German equivalent to the Master degree, in electrical and electronic engineering from the University of Saarland in Saarbrücken, Germany, in 1996. He received the Dr.-Ing. degree from the same university in 2001. From 1995 to 1997, Dr Strunz pursued research at Brunel University in London, where he worked in collaboration with the National

Grid Company in the fields of power system stabilization, electromechanical transients and power system modeling. In 1997, he joined the R&D division of Electricité de France (EDF) in the Paris area. At EDF, his main research work was concerned with the development of efficient numerical methods for digital simulation of electromagnetic transients. In the framework of a collaborative research project, he worked as a visiting scholar at the University of British Columbia in Vancouver from January 1998 to August 1998. Since April 2002, Dr Strunz is assistant professor of electrical engineering at the University of Washington.

Kia Lashgari is a senior undergraduate student in the Department of Electrical Engineering at the University of Washington, Seattle. His research interests include simulation of energy systems, power electronics, and renewable energy. In 2003 and 2004, he was awarded the undergraduate assistantship of the Electric Energy Industrial Consortium (EEIC) at the University of Washington. In 2004, he won a first prize for his contribution in the annual poster contest of the EEIC. He is a student member of the Institute of Electrical and Electronics Engineers (IEEE) and the activities coordinator for IEEE branch at the University of Washington. Also, he is a member of the Professional Ski Instructors of America (PSIA).

Sabera Sultana *payelbuet@yahoo.com* is working as a Teaching Assistant in the Department of Urban and Regional Planning of the Bangladesh University of Engineering and Technology in Dhaka. She earlier worked as a Research Assistant at the United International University.

Arnab Chatterjee is presently Research Fellow at the Centre for studies in Social Sciences, Kolkata.

An ex-RTP scholar at the Centre for Studies in Social Sciences in 1998, he is also a former lecturer in Social Philosophy at Jaya Prakash Institute of Social Change and Vidyasagar School of Social Work, West Bengal. Also an independent Project consultant, he was most recently associated with the CHILD IN NEED INSTITUTE (CINI), Pailan, 24 Pgs (South)—a corporate N.G.O as a Programme Officer in charge of the project "Sustainable Development of Health & Nutrition of women, children & adolescents" funded by Interchurch Coordination Organisation (ICCO), The Netherlands. He is more well-known and is regarded with unease for his badly unorthodox, against the mainstream and uncomfortable but theoretically robust interventionist review essays and articles on the editorial pages of The Statesman, Ajkal and once upon a time—Anandabazar Patrika. His research interests are topics related to public debate & reasoning: Personal attacks, abusive speech in politics, boredom and bureaucracy in dry cleaning, semio-stylistics of ragging in Indian colleges to 'the sense of shame and civility in pornography'.

His book Gynocolonies or pure politics? Essays in the cultural and political phenomenology of excess is forthcoming.

Surbhi Tiwari is an Independent Research Associate and a writer. She is just about to begin her post graduate study strongly opting for an MA in Human Rights. Born in Kolkata she went to Mauritius to pursue her pre-graduate studies where after she joined Loreto College, Kolkata with Political Science (Hons.). Her interests are human and animal rights, religion, fiction and law.

Adebayo J. Adeloye, CEng, MCIWEM a.j.adeloye@hw.ac.uk is the Director of the Water Resources Engineering Management graduate programme at Heriot-Watt University in Edinburgh, Scotland. Dr Adeloye graduated with a First Class, First Position BSc (Hons) degree in Engineering from Ife University (Nigeria), and also holds the MSc and PhD degrees from the University of Newcastle upon Tyne, England. He is a chartered engineer, a chartered water and environmental manager and holds a corporate membership of the Chartered Institution of Water and Environmental Management. Dr Adeloye has over 26 years of water and environmental engineering experience, involving consulting, research and training and has worked on projects internationally. Dr Adeloye's research in water resources has been widely published in leading international scientific journals including Water Resources Research, Journal of Hydrology and the Hydrological Sciences Journal. Dr Adeloye has through his work received numerous awards and recognition, most notable of which is the prestigious Fellowship of the Royal Commission for the Exhibition of 1851. Dr Adeloye was until recently a Partner of Messrs Osot Associates Consulting Engineers, Nigeria, where he was responsible for the design of various water supply and environmental projects.